W.H. Dozier III

Decide to Dominate

You Hold the Rights to Nothing Less

Bob,

Good Bless,

D. [signature] #42

"Keep learning until the destiny you seek and the person you become occupy the same space at the same time. This is how winning is done."

Ayub Fleming

Decide to Dominate

You Hold the Rights to Nothing Less

2018 Decide to Dominate Series

W.H. Dozier III

Published by
CMC Publishing, a division of AHF Media Inc.

Written & edited by: Ayub H. Fleming & W.H. Dozier III

Cover Design by: Dfusion Designs

Table of Contents

*The opportunity to **Decide to Dominate** is your birthright as a human being and accompanies you as a perfect masterpiece of the Creator. We wrote this book to deliver a message of hope and inspiration to those who yearn to transcend. Regardless of where you find yourself in life, you were designed and built to overcome life's challenges and empowered to run on a road we call "perpetual success." In your vocation, whether you are just starting, an entrepreneur or becoming one, rising as a manager or c-level executive, you can dominate your industry, master your potential; develop tangible and intangible wealth for the greater purpose of service to mankind.*

***You Hold the Rights to Nothing Less** as you develop into the giant killer you are called to be. Having a purpose justifies your significance in life and gives you a focus, in which, to pursue your destiny. As part of creation, you can accept the identity of a kingdom or domain with unshakeable principles. This domain we speak of is one of purpose and conscience, expressed in the individual mandate to become all that you were meant to be in its fullest. It's your right and your responsibility to profit in life as an example to your family and your circle of influence, bringing honor and glory to the One who created you. We hope you accept our invitation to do so and enjoy the book on the way.*

W.H. Dozier III, Founder of UTake Dominion

Ayub Fleming, Author

Introduction

"Chase your dreams until someone is chasing you. If no one wants to be you, then you have built your house amid conformity among the masses. The air is only clear and vision greater at higher elevations where few have left footprints to follow."

Ayub Fleming

The philosophy and practical lessons in this book will work for the rising c-level executive, middle-level manager, an individual entrepreneur, or anyone wanting to exert greater self-mastery over their lives and vocation. Most of us will not become a Chief Executive Officer (CEO) of a multi-billion or even a multi-million dollar enterprise. As you read about a few of these high-powered individuals, keep in mind that although it may not be in your future, you are empowered as the CEO of your life and your life's endeavors. In part, what that means is that you, other than your Creator, are your greatest asset!

Domination is intentionally and relentlessly pursuing action that leads to both small and great victories. It's not about being right all the time or being perfect; it is about discovering the will, as well as, the strategic game plan, and your life's mission; it's an adherence to a personal code of excellence.

I use the specific word "excellence" because it is something you own. Your progression toward success is personal and must be intentional because the fulfillment of one's purpose is at the heart of every true successive journey. We cannot succeed or dominate apart from our created mission. Dominance personally and professionally requires a consistent philosophy of self-assessment and improvement that establishes a guiding post leading to overall self-development. It's a process that paves the way for progressive motion and vertical movement toward an excellent mark.

Sports and entrepreneurs were constants when I was growing up. I loved going to the basketball courts with my dad and watching him play in the "pick up" games. As a youngster, I wanted to be out there with him. Instead, like most kids, I created my own game on the side and stayed out of the way.

At home, my father loved watching anything sports related on television, and so it was natural to grow up admiring athletes of all kinds. On both sides of the family, there have been and are many creative entrepreneurs. I gravitated toward being creative, so learning from others and experiencing their creativity was inspiring.

To share some of our family histories, I had an ancestor named Paul Cuffee who was a Quaker born in 1759. He became a well-known entrepreneur, patriot, and abolitionist. Cuffee went on to build a shipping empire that was used in the British effort to resettle freed slaves from America to Nova Scotia and Sierra Leone. To our knowledge, Cuffee was America's first African American Ship Captain; exactly 200 years after his death, he was honored by the Governor and other politicians of the state of Massachusetts. January 17th, the date of his birth, is now known as "Paul Cuffee Day" in that state.

My mother's oldest brother, John Reid (aka Uncle Jr.) designed, created and implemented the Student Diversity Program, an educational program for struggling or at-risk students, while employed at Cal State Fullerton University (CSUF). It is a program that was heavily influenced by George Boole's Boolean Logic. This British Mathematician believed that you could develop a process, given you had all the relevant information, which would yield results which were always certain.

This remarkable program, which started as a thesis project while Uncle Jr. attended the university as a 47-year-old student, was initially introduced to CSUF's Men's Basketball team. Due to the program's profound success, it was quickly expanded to include all student-athletes and any "at risk" students on campus. As the program expanded, so did its results. After 20 years, the program had changed the lives of countless students on CSUF's campus and beyond. It would reach the campuses of other universities, as well as, primary and secondary schools throughout Southern California. At CSUF, it created millions of dollars for the university, and until recently it was managed by some of Uncle Jr.'s mentees. It's a program that deserves high praise. Ironically, the message I delivered about 25 years ago while speaking to the students enrolled in the Student Diversity Program (SDP) was titled "Perpetual Success," a theme I continue to wholeheartedly embrace today.

My father's family owned a small company that held an interesting patented design for years in the late 60's. Almost half a century ago, our cousin and his older brother invented a tuning and recording programming system for televisions that eventually would prove to be a building block for a DVR-like process. Unfortunately, without the initial investment of $60,000 (equivalent to 600k today) to develop a miniature version of the design they were not able to bring the product to market. It would be further enhanced by other creators.

I hate to say it, but I am a bit of a history buff. A few of my favorite historical figures are Thomas Edison, George Washington Carver, and Henry Ford. All were inventor-entrepreneurs. These men undoubtedly left their remarkable footprints on the earth. Thomas Edison was one of those entrepreneurs and inventors who manifested excellent ideas. He reshaped the way humanity lived and continues to live today. After starting several companies and merging with others, he would eventually become one of the founding members of General Electric (GE). In 1892, Edison Electric merged with Thomson-Houston Electric Company, and GE was officially born.

It would be almost a century later that another man would be at the helm of this entrepreneurial endeavor. GE, now quite a mature corporation, had a corporate leader who would prove to be one the most celebrated modern-day CEOs in American history. His name is Jack Welch (aka Neutron Jack), and after a century of operating under the name General Electric, this behemoth of a company now had a market value of $14 billion. With Mr. Welch at the top position, the company accelerated from $ 14 billion to an impressive $410 billion market value on his last day. Not a bad day's work.

.

How does the vision of one person have such a profound effect on such a large organization? Vision is a prerequisite for leadership, but the greatest of leaders often have a strong non-negotiable vision that is displayed constantly throughout their spirited pursuit. It's a simple but effective method that many can adopt, implement with passion, and a persistent attitude that cuts through anything in its way. It is the way they operate every day.

Many leaders gauge risks, but the greatest seem to speak of it differently. Risk? What risk? In their mind, the risk is having a strong desired vision and not taking the precise action to fulfill it. **A healthy approach to risk is that failure doesn't exist; only learning until goals are reached, and the target is precisely hit.** It's part of becoming more educated in the environment you're operating in. The best leaders refuse to be outworked by anybody around them. Neutron Jack was unyielding in his pursuit and decided that if the company wasn't dominating in a market at the number one or two positions that business was eliminated.

The destination is domination or nothing.

Welch's managers needed to lead with a similar mindset if his vision was going to be executed. My uncle, a 25-plus year veteran at GE, testified to the fact that when Welsh took the helm the culture within the company changed immediately and quite dramatically. Uncle Charles Reid aka Uncle Charlos (nickname given to him by my son) was one of those area managers that fit the ideal profile that Neutron Jack needed. He worked his way up through the company by hard-work and always staying in "the know."

His insatiable appetite for knowledge and his fearless approach to getting things done eventually landed him a position as the top purchasing manager in Tidewater, VA with more promotions on the way. Even as a youngster, he was no stranger to hard-work and began working a 40-hour week at the age of 11. He had the aspiration of getting a college degree, but due to deceased parents and no means, he opted or was forced into the workforce after just three semesters at Norfolk State University.

Uncle Charlos spent just under three decades at GE and instead of accepting another promotion; he decided he was ready to take early retirement at the young age of 48. Jack Welch's leadership style, which provided a hefty increase in market value, paved the way for my uncle to make a bold move to retire. It's a move that still today has people perplexed as to how he could have accomplished such a thing at a young age and without a college degree.

When you decide to dominate, it is most certainly about making bold moves, regardless of where you find yourself in life. Remember, whether you are a corporate leader, homemaker, currently without employment, or have no real vision for your life; you are still the leader and CEO of your life. You must find the strength to make bold moves at the appropriate times proving that you desire to move toward a position and place of dominance.

George Washington Carver, another favorite historical entrepreneurial inventor, was another of those fearless at making bold moves. He had the strength to do it during a time when African Americans were former slaves seen as second-class citizens. He made comments in that time that today would be considered ludicrous by some, if not most.

"When I was young, 'I said to God, God, tell me the mystery of the universe.' But God answered, 'That knowledge is for me alone.' So, I said,' God, tell me the mystery of the peanut.' Then God said, 'Well George, that's more nearly your size.' And he told me."

George Washington Carver, American Botanist, and Inventor

Thomas Edison and Henry Ford once offered Carver an opportunity to work with them which came with a six-figure income. Carver declined the offer and instead remained focused on his mission to aid both Caucasian and African-American farmers who were struggling with their farms in the south. This was a remarkable mission given that he was a man born into slavery.

In 1920, Carver was initially given ten minutes to speak before Congress at the United Peanuts Association of America. The committee was so captivated by his delivery that his allotted time to speak was no longer an issue. Explaining the many products derived from the peanut including milk, mock beef, and chicken, Carver stated: "If you go to the first chapter of Genesis, we can interpret very clearly, I think, what God intended when he said, **"Behold, I have given you every herb that bears seed. To you, it shall be meat." Genesis 1 v 29**

"This is what He means about it. It shall be meat. There is everything there to strengthen and nourish and keep the body alive and healthy." After nearly two hours, the chairman asked: "Dr. Carver, how did you learn all of these things?" Carver answered; "From an old book."

An old book? Is it possible that this old book also is known as God's Handbook or the Good Book could also equip us with the knowledge necessary to make effective bold moves and dominate? In my life, I would say yes. What I've found is that whether a business owner or employee of an organization; it's not the money generated that provides the ultimate prize, but it's the fulfillment of mission and purpose that yields the most satisfying return. This purpose undoubtedly involves serving others as its highest mission.

On Carver's Tomb it reads:

"He could have added fortune to fame but caring for neither he found happiness and honor in being helpful to the world."

A captain like Paul Cuffee, Henry Ford, founder of the Ford Motor Company, was a captain of a different sort. As Captain of Industry Henry Ford, another great mind strongly believed in serving people. He established a business that positively affected the lives of his employees, his customers, and other employers that witnessed the way he treated his employees. Mr. Ford was especially known for the wages he paid. Ford was destined for greatness when as a teenager; he became known for dismantling and reassembling timepieces and eventually worked as an engineer at Edison Lighting Company (owned by Thomas Edison). Edison would eventually give Ford his blessing to design his second automobile. Early in the 1900s, Ford took up interest in building and driving racing cars as well. Until this day, it's the Ford GT that wins my heart as being my dream sports car.

My father is an automobile lover and although I didn't share his dream of being a race car driver; like Ford, my father's love for cars was passed to his grandchildren and me. Ford's entrepreneurial endeavor and dominance initiated an economic and social impact across the globe that the Ford family continues today. I had the pleasure of meeting and working for William Clay Ford, the Chairman of the Detroit Lions. He was a humble and gentle man, who, before passing away in 2014, was the last surviving grandchild of Captain Henry Ford.

Sometimes it's hard to fathom how some of these large multinational conglomerate corporations started with just a thought or an idea, but this is an undisputed fact. Large companies like Ford, GE, Nike; or newcomers like Verizon,

Amazon, and Under Armour are simple examples of an idea whose time has come. Regardless of where we find ourselves, we are heavily influenced by the entrepreneurial experience.

I hit a point where I was done with just meandering through life and instead wanted to thrive. Early one morning when I first heard these words, "Decide to Dominate," my initial thought and reaction were "I am, I am dominating." I fully believed that I was until just a few minutes later when I began to see parts of my life unfolding before my eyes. Then I also began to realize this was not just a message for the world around me, but a directive for my life. You see, literally ten days after I awoke from my bed on August 20th, I received a phone call that would begin reshaping my methodologies.

No, I had not hit rock bottom circumstantially. When I realized that I was not dominating but was being dominated by life's constant storms of mediocrity, yielding both compromising results and outright failure, I experienced a "fight or flight" moment.

We don't need someone's permission to succeed in life, but it's going to be one heck of a fight to rise to the top of any worthy climb! I wasn't one to run from a fight but what I didn't understand at first, was the fight needed to begin with me. Yes, there are circumstances in life that the "fight or flight" decision must be made, but regardless, the most vital and most important fight and battle needed to start within me!

Coming face to face with your inadequacies, insecurities, fears, doubts, and thoughts of being inferior is not easy. It's a hard reality that allows you to stop relying on false narratives and begin to live a life based on principled truth and the fulfillment of purpose. I've always been the one who inspired others; it's part of my DNA and purpose. At that moment, I needed to begin to focus on what was happening to me and allow the changes that needed to occur! Allowing is to give access, so we must give access to hear new directions for our lives to change. This means, of course, that changing is a choice and that's the good news. However, for some of us that have less patience than most, the not so good news is that this process is not instantaneous. TIME, it will take time. For us, that's a lifetime of evolving to and through higher levels.

"Change can be good and at times inevitably needed, but the lack of evolving as a person or a professional is a platform for regression, not progression."

W.H. Dozier III, Founder, UTake Dominion

Some fear change, but there is plenty of good that can come from changing and evolving. Have you ever heard the saying that when we correct a wise person, they become wiser? It's because they learned from a previous mistake and was given a new methodology to yield a better result. This is a basic truth that many understand, but few implement. Change in the method will bring about change in results; it's a simple equation. If we assume the result is positive, then change certainly is good in that case. We should not run from, hide, or fear change, but embrace the idea of changing for the better! No need to see potential failure as an obstacle; similar to Edison's line of thinking, Henry Ford said:

"Failure is simply the opportunity to begin again, this time more intelligently. Obstacles are those frightful things you see when you take your eyes off your goal."

Henry Ford, Founder Ford Motor Company

Past glory? My hope is that this book will light the fires to consume your past and illuminate a path to your next worthy fight and climb. It will prepare you for the next great victory; reminding you that you were born to dominate and accomplish greater things. In the arduous struggles and tests of life; will you take the opportunity to wallow in mediocrity, a mid-level of accomplishment or will you separate yourself from the pack and Decide to Dominate?

We know that mediocrity constantly knocks seeking access to various parts of our lives. To achieve the highest levels of excellence, it must be diligently sought after! It will be a pursuit with zero intentions of going backward, putting mediocrity completely to rest. It's not that you won't have challenges; you will. It's that you have decided that mediocrity and adversity will be overcome. Like most people, I've had many opportunities to quit, lose my footing, make excuses, or not find traction toward things that I wanted most in life.

I have also had success at the highest levels. I think it's a common theme to approach life through the lenses of both failure and success. There have been tough obstacles that I had to fight through and contend with, things that seemed determined to work against me. There were also moments in my life that seemed to resonate as my truth and worked in my favor to overcome. Having tasted and experienced successes in the past, this book acts as a present assessment of our endeavors and as a reminder of our birthright. That said, there is only one choice to make, and that's to set the mark to dominate.

"At some point in life's endeavors, we must realize excellence and the pursuit of it, leave no room for the acceptance of mediocrity or compromise of any kind."

W.H. Dozier III, Founder, UTake Dominion

It's not that easy a decision to make for any of us, especially during the times when the odds are seemingly stacked against us. So successful living doesn't look the same to everyone; it must be based on what you decided to do with what you have. It's not what you had to face in life as much as it is what you decided to do with the challenge. Again, that challenge magnified for me early that morning as I awakened, and I heard those words, "Decide to Dominate." This book offers a real-time examination of how to respond to the challenges of the present and the future. We will dominate by consistently identifying with and committing to purpose to reach our fullest potential. Our purpose is synonymous with connecting what we do with who we are, what we desire the most, and are equipped to do.

One's purpose is synonymous with one's significance; we all seek to discover why or even how we are significant. **Our significance is encased in the reason why we exist at such a time as this. I believe unlocking that case not only exposes the essence of our significance, but its connection to**

dominating throughout our endeavors and provides the path for guaranteed success. The pursuit of purpose is different for everyone and I challenge you to make it a life study.

"Probability is expectation founded upon partial knowledge. A perfect acquaintance with all the circumstances affecting the occurrence of an event would change expectation into certainty and leave neither room nor demand for a theory of probabilities."

George Boole, English Mathematician

This quote by George Boole, in simpler terms, states that when you have a predictable system in place, and constant effort is applied, the results should be equally predictable and not random. In other words, it's plausible and possible that there are scenarios that have a guaranteed positive outcome. That is one of the dominant goals of this book and later programs that we are developing to give you access to systems and information that almost guarantee success.

I believe that by picking up this book, you also have an internal compass that always points north. No matter the victories, challenges, or setbacks you are striving to continue witnessing the manifestation of the best version of yourself.

Circumstances will come into your life that will reveal your strength and your weaknesses; that's life and understanding both is vital to overall development. The act of dominating is the free will exercise of intention, influence, and at times force in response to circumstances until you achieve mastery or control over it. It is the state of being in control of your performance, responses, and expression. We rarely have total control of the outcomes we get in life, but there are a few things that we cannot influence.

The trajectory of our lives is derived from our thought life and then followed by our actions. Next is our response to positive and negative situations in our life and the attitude in which we approach each challenge. I have always said and will repeat it in this book that "You own the effort, not the results." I may not be able to control specific outcomes, but I own and am solely responsible for the effort that influences the outcomes. The effort is in my control and is in direct response to how determined I am to achieve success; however, remember that crisis quite often reveals a person's will to attain the highest levels of achievement.

Dominion is the state of being dominant. According to the Old Book or God's Handbook for Success, dominion is connected to our birthright or who we are and taking ownership of the life and the gifts that we were given. Your talent is something you were born with, and you have responsibility for utilizing it; however, it's a skill acquired over time that is necessary to achieve mastery with your natural talents. Talent is a matter of expression; skill is a matter of acquisition and to what level you can execute that talent. That is why talent alone does not create a championship result. The most talented are not always crowned as the greatest, but those who hone their skills and work the hardest are. Hard-work is at the core of every successful endeavor.

Maturity is the state of accepting the condition of your life and your response to the conditions of your life for which you may or may not have control. Dominion is always related to the position. You may not be the CEO of the business in which you find yourself working, but you are the CEO of your brand, the life, and purpose you have been given. Own the strategy and effort; when you add purposeful effort, you will begin to dominate.

Domination is connected to authority which is the natural state of influence through trust and not forces. Real trust is based on the ability of you and someone else to make a promise and see it through. To walk in dominion that is your birthright means you must trust in the ability of the one who gave it to you. In this case, dominion is a spiritual principle. I believe God created you with certain intentions for your life, as well as, inalienable rights that belong to you. If you can settle this in your mind, then you can trust that the one who gave it to you can execute that intention if you walk in line with those principles. I don't have to force a great life that is already given to me by the intention of someone that I can trust to bring it to pass.

Authority is related to positioning and the ability to enforce. We must first influence ourselves and not allow an emotional state to determine our response to crisis or stress. Then we influence others positively through our position, as well as, through our character. To use our ability to influence others through clever persuasion, intimidation, or force is not conducive to our longevity and quest for perpetual success.

Persuasion is the strongest influence; however, force is the weakest long-term persuasive strategy. People will eventually push back against force. Most of the time influence is not going to be in your favor unless it is an intentional influence. When you get the right people around you, influence is working in your favor. People of like mind and spirit work together to achieve similar successes in life. The same can be said in the negative. Like weeds, if you leave your life unattended or unmanaged for a short period, before long, weeds show up, grow up, and mess up.

Some influences should not be tolerated in our lives. The process of sanctification or separation is one of the terminations of certain things, ideologies, and unmotivated people in your life. Life, as well as, a business must be directed and managed precisely to achieve the greatest outcomes. I have a friend who says that nothing, absolutely nothing worthy is done without leadership. There are few things in life that get better without directed and focused effort. That is not to say that everything can't be taken to an extreme leading to devastating results. The point is that we as human beings need structure to feel that we have the base that we need to step out or step up. Like the martial arts, you must master the basics to move on, allow your personality and ability to shine and progresses pass the style itself. Tradition can only be replaced by expression after it has been mastered which gives way to self-mastery and domination. Bruce Lee was a great example of this principle in the way he lived and what he taught.

I can remember a great example of the power of persuasion when I played professional football, and the Players Union agreed to strike. Although close to 100% walked out on strike, the initial vote indicated that 93% of the players agreed to demand change during a strike. There were a few who did not want to strike because they were making a lot of money. They did not want to prolong the strike and not get paid as the National Football League (NFL) made a move to bring in other athletes to play. When that 7% of the players started to cross back over the line, that small trickle convinced most of the other players to end the strike and sit down to negotiate. A few convinced the masses to defect without a shot being fired; due to the missed games and the income per game; we received 25% less income for the season. There was very little acquired through the strike itself. Becoming consciously aware of the people in your life who are influencing you and why is not something that you can leave to chance. Rather, it is another powerful tool to keep you sharp and headed in the right direction.

Carefully selecting who you have on your team and why that selection is made is the difference between what's possible and what's achieved. Choosing those with similar goals, desired outcomes, passion and experience is in part the ticket to reach for the incredible. Having individuals with different gifts and even different perspectives is good if you're collectively committed to the same goals and most importantly share the same values.

Think about the power of influence if you picked a team of people including family members or friends of a certain caliber, outlook, and training who could influence you and your endeavors on a regular basis. This is the group that keeps you inspired and helps prepare you to achieve your life's goals with the potential of pushing you further and beyond. What I am telling you is that influence should not be left to chance. It should be carefully chosen by a designed plan to dominate, hit successful points at the highest levels, remain on a solid trajectory, and set it at a perpetuated pace.

Career politicians when running for office must choose a team to help them win and guide them to achieve the goal. They do it as well as or better than anyone else. If you're in business, your employees are that team. If you're a mid-level manager, you have a team that should grow and develops over time to achieve certain company goals. If you're an employee, become a relevant part of that team with the opportunity to assert influence that creates value for your employer. Work hard and lay a foundation for potential raises, promotions, or ownership participation. These types of opportunities become available based on the value you provided. It's your service to the company that has purposefully put you in that position; so be influential by striving to serve the most.

Understanding who you are, even from a spiritual sense, is a critical path to understanding dominion and the purpose for strength to influence things positively. Our identity is so connected to self-definition that this is something we all need to work on. Our own identity is a combination of what we accept others are saying about us and what we intentionally or unintentionally think about ourselves.

We must decide on who we are, how we feel about ourselves and the concept we have of ourselves to determine the image and expression of our lives. We are most profoundly what we think, feel, and see about ourselves. We can achieve no higher without real intervention.

This self-branding will affect every relationship, every business venture or endeavor you will ever enter and leave. Every job you have ever taken is a business venture that will be affected by whether you see yourself as dominant or one that is being dominated. Think of it this way; when you enter a job, you are investing your skills, talents, and gifts to the success of that company. You are exchanging the essence of who you are for something of value which in most cases is a fee or equity. In everything, there is an investment and a return. It's not always comfortable to think of everything and everyone as an investment. Dominant people think of life investments regarding purpose and return on investment (ROI).

I want to challenge you to see everything in your life as an expression of who you are. That brand assessment will inevitably mean that some of the conditions, relationships, and circumstances are either not a fair representation of you or maybe a true indicator of what you need to change. It may be that you are attracting the wrong people and circumstances; making the wrong decisions on bad information due to an inflated or deflated ego, or just making decisions out of a lack of information. In athletics, you can't just play the game; you must be serious about your preparation for game day, as well as, how you perform throughout the contest. In the end, winning and losing have definite measurements of performance.

I would be remiss if I did not talk about my alliance with God as the key to my successes. It's a buffer between me and life-changing mistakes secured by following His principles for developing and shaping character, as well as, making decisions. Trust me I have made my share of mistakes. Most of them were either from lack of experience or because I consciously or unconsciously strayed from the practice of His Handbook for Success.

It's late in the season now, and it won't matter the successes or failures of the past. We are all in the playoffs now, and it's either win or go home. As a paraphrase to the quote said at the beginning of the introduction, "Let's chase our goals and dominate until we build the life that others want to emulate because of our character and example." There is no life greater than the life that is celebrated because of the legacy and hope that it leaves behind for others and the perpetual rewards that lay ahead. Be counted among the "greats!"

Chapter 1

Decide to Dominate

"Audacious-habitual thinking is the bridge to audacious living; it unlocks and opens the door to the previously unknown where we discover the personal right and privilege of deciding to dominate."

W.H. Dozier III, Founder, UTake Dominion

How would you answer the question of whether you are dominant on the issues of your vocation or personal matters? How about in your approach to a healthy lifestyle or the management of the other areas of your life? At some point in our lives, we become the sum-total of our decisions. The question then is what does the sum of those decisions become? In other words, our choices are the front end of an equation that ultimately determines the results. So, realizing we can decide and have the power to create results that are certain is crucial and liberating. We all want extraordinary results but let's be honest; sometimes we are not attaining what we want because our perception, strategy, and actions are not in concert with our true desires. As Dr. Eric Thomas would say, *"Everyone wants to be a beast until they have to do what beasts do."*

Accomplished individuals who are champions in their lives and crafts always stop to ask questions to understand the "why." They have an insatiable thirst for understanding their purpose, gaining experience and knowledge, and compiling an exceptional list of achievements. They are tirelessly committed to asking the right questions, getting the appropriate answers, and making the proper choices. These individuals from various walks of life, fields, and industries want in some way to be in control. They want to at least feel that hard work and doing the right thing will produce reliable results.

You or anyone can join this formative group that takes life head-on and learns from their wins, mistakes, and losses in life; only to further gain insight and carve new paths for the future. At moments of defeat or in the midst of a failing venture, it's a tough pill to swallow. Yes, it is difficult to process and accept, but champions rise above it all. So, winning isn't avoiding the test; it's learning from all the answers, even the wrong answers, and getting it right; providing answers that empower us to make decisions.

Achieving greatness is not an exclusive opportunity for a select few; it's a conscious choice to unleash the beast inside that knows you were created for something great. When you come face to face with anything threatening your goals or vision for successful living, you accept the challenge because it's not in comfort that you change, but in the fight. I have never met a person with a measure of success who liked not knowing where they were or where they stood in a situation. I also have yet to meet anyone who enjoys losing. You may not always see the reason "why" regarding the results, but it is imperative to find out for future strategy. I believe we are all dominant in some areas of life and have limited success in other areas. However, it's human nature to desire to be good at everything we do, and so we strive for perfection when at best only excellence is obtainable.

When I was drafted into the NFL in 1987, I attended the World Series during our football season that same year. While there something extraordinary happened. A seed was planted in my mind during one of those evening games while the fans were waving Homer Hankies throughout the Metrodome. While the Minnesota Twins battled hard against the St. Louis Cardinals, in my mind and imagination, I randomly thought, "I can do that. I can play this game." At the time, this was merely an imaginary thought, yet a powerful perception. There wasn't any plan or process that I was considering to play professional baseball, but the desire was brewing.

I did have a Minneapolis reporter later ask me about playing baseball during the series, but I was completely oblivious to the idea of playing the sport again. It had been over four years since I'd played the game while in high school. That small seed in the form of thought and imagination took over two more years to take root and grow into a decision. Years later part of my dream to compete as a professional baseball player was realized. **Decisions we make with a high level of confidence will lead to powerful outcomes.** Who knew that I would have the opportunity to train and play with members from both of those World Series teams; players like Kirby Puckett, Gary Gaetti, Frank Viola, Vince Coleman and Pennsylvania native, Tom Herr. These were athletes that proved to be dominant champions in their craft.

Over 20 years later, having a leadership position with Verizon's Global Strategic Services team; I would have the opportunity to observe and interact with another dominant group of champions. These individuals were CEOs, entrepreneurs, and top corporate executives from numerous companies. We could label this group as "athletes in the office."

This group was prepared, highly skilled, and motivated to perform at their best while managing large enterprises. Regardless of the size and scope of what we are assigned to manage, large or small; we manage it as best as we can. **Most of us will not become a CEO of a multi-billion-dollar enterprise. We also may not be among our organization's elite group of decision-makers but realizing we are the CEO and the sole decision-maker of our life's endeavors is imperative.** Other than the Creator, you must see yourself and all the attributes you've been given as your greatest assets.

On one occasion, as one of the representatives of Verizon, I walked into the new MetLife Stadium to take part in showcasing the $100 million investment that both the New York NFL franchises had made in the technology within the stadium. As strong technology partners, Verizon and Cisco equipped MetLife Stadium with the capability of providing one of the most technologically advanced and memorable experiences in the sports and entertainment industry. Cisco's partnership with AT&T at Cowboy Stadium would have similar technologies. Intense competition was brewing, and our team was tasked with the initiative of equipping venues, especially Verizon sponsored venues, with the same advanced technology across the country, as well as, a few international "hot spots."

As the competition with AT&T intensified, I gained valuable experience, and there were a solid number of important lessons learned. It was an opportunity I had discovered during a conversation with Troy Cromwell aka "Chief" about his newly awarded position as Group President of Verizon Global Strategic Services. His division was projected to exceed $4 billion in revenue annually. During one of our conversations, Chief mentioned one of the eight verticals he was responsible for was Media & Entertainment (M&E), and something inside of me said, "That's it; that's where I need to go." I decided that very moment to express my desire and intentions to move into the M&E vertical. This move was an opportunity to make a less calculated but a bold career move.

Within a few weeks, I transferred. Ironically, just a few weeks after transferring and officially joining the M&E vertical, the entire vertical was dismantled, and my bold decision looked more like a short-lived, awful career retreat. Well, looks can be deceiving. In this case, I needed to regroup and decide how to best overcome this sizeable obstacle. Cisco Systems was still vying for a partnership with a Verizon business unit focused on venue technology deployments. After I made a few calls and shared my thoughts with Cisco executives from its Sports & Entertainment Group; they invited Chief and me out to San Jose, CA to discuss why a partnership made sense. It was an easy "yes" for us, and Verizon's Global Strategic Services' Sports & Entertainment (S&E) was born. We quickly ramped up the new vertical with projected revenues of just under $1 billion. This experience would be significant for my professional growth as I was promoted to lead this initiative.

Dominating in your vocation, at times, includes making bold moves as mentioned in the introduction. Dominance and boldness or bold moves work together but are not accompanied by a perfect set of circumstances; that part of the process is quite the opposite. Some have learned that our desires, vision, and level of commitment will always be tested and tried. Regardless, passing the test is an important part of evolving and becoming dominant.

The next week after returning from San Jose, CA, Chief brought in Tom Lair (now the President & CEO of Unified Connections) to assist us in building out what would become an incredible Verizon cross-functional team for our S&E initiative. To our knowledge, this was the first of its kind for the $100 billion company. With the vast resources of this conglomerate and numerous relevant business units having independent goals and objectives, Tom's hand in building out our collaborative team was imperative. Through his internal networking, he was nothing short of prolific in our team's development. Eventually, 15 different Verizon business units signed up for this collaborative. We were poised to compete with AT&T's stadium technology initiative and provide entertainment fans with a new innovative experience across the globe. Verizon's goal was to become the most dominant partner in the NFL. Its focus and relationship with the NFL began to evolve, come to the forefront, and take precedence over other like partnerships. Today, the company is sitting on a $2 billion live-streaming partnership deal with the NFL.

"It is change, continuing change, inevitable change that is the dominant factor in society today. No sensible decision can be made any longer without taking into account not only the world as it is, but the world as it will be."

Isaac Asimov, Professor, and Writer

I believe that people who want to achieve significant things in life have a natural desire to dominate within themselves which is projected into the world as competition. The difference is some only have desires for material possession but are without desire and a plan to acquire them. Desires without a plan and execution only lead to unfulfilled dreams and delusion.

Truly successful people have a purpose in mind and desire a full expression of life that includes family, great relationships, and material gain; but they also ask the question, how do I do it? Less accomplished people desire the same things but stumble to get pass impediments to their success. We must always ask questions in an empowering manner on our way to becoming students of the answers and solutions, which feed the decision-making and strategic planning process. Focus on the solutions, not the problem or the obstacles in the way. Impediments should be expected as part of the process.

The beginning of domination is coming into a deeper understanding of what you desire, why you desire it, and finally deciding to obtain it. Not wanting it only, but truly deciding to pursue it. If it does not exist, then create it. If you don't know how to get it, find someone who does dominate and ask them what has worked for them. Volunteer, do whatever you need to, but glean what you can from them.

Several years ago (before my stint with Verizon), I had the opportunity to work for and glean daily from a sharp entrepreneur who is a top executive known across the globe. I observed three important traits that were commonly seen every day while working with him. His love for people was witnessed, his strong work ethic was undeniable, and his uncanny attention to detail was simply mind-boggling. He was the President of Woodward Camp, a uniquely positioned global brand. As a true visionary, he positioned the company for incredible growth, while becoming a pillar in the Action Sports Industry. The company's global brand equity was no accident, but purely by design, accompanied by a ton of hard work.

Before ESPN developed the X Games in 1995, Woodward Camp had been a facility where young and not so young athletes could perfect their craft with disciplines in BMX and Skateboarding. It was a destination that became known for having the largest skate park in the world. Disney's interest in partnering with Woodward peeked in the early 2000s, and a proposed site for the camp and training facility was next to Disney's Wide World of Sports in Orlando, Florida.

The partnership was full of excitement and promise, but due to a $32 Million capital expenditure to build the facility alone; the cost was too steep for the ROI.

Woodward would go on to attain various types of partnerships with companies like PlayStation, Target, IMG, Red Bull, and Playworld Systems (a leading worldwide manufacturer of playground equipment). Witnessing the growth of this brand was nothing short of amazing; especially, when it landed a reality television show with Fuel TV in 2008. The show became one of the network's top programs and was often listed as the Fuel TV's #1 watched program. Throughout my time with the president, I enjoyed many occasions where I observed, listened, and learned. Eventually, I had the opportunity to implement winning strategies while learning to manage and lead with my style.

What an amazing time of both personal and professional growth it was for me. Eventually, this unique company was bought and absorbed by Powdr Corp as part of its branding strategy. The Woodward Camp executive was Gary Ream, aka "Uncle Gary," and that's exactly how my kids would address him, particularly, when they would see him on television. Today he is the former President of Woodward Camp. As a seasoned executive, he is now creating wins for the International Olympic Committee as the Chairman of the 2020 Tokyo Skateboarding Commission, bringing two skateboarding disciplines to the Olympics.

We all desire to win. Much like others, winning comes naturally to me, and it also requires hard work and dedication. Thinking about winning and the spoils of it are where I live mentally; so, not dominating is not natural for me. I suspect that is it not natural for you either. Our natural state is to dominate, so it's vital for us to have a positive and creative effect on our environment, to control and direct our present and future. For me, anything contrary to that brings out the fight in me refusing to accept that I can't. I don't easily accept my failures, as I believe no one should, but I have learned to learn from them regardless of the magnitude of those failures.

After being introduced to John Chambers, Chairman and CEO of Cisco at the time, we were walking to an event, and he asked me a question that was simple, but it caught me completely by surprise. He asked me what message I wanted him to deliver to Ivan. Ivan Seidenberg was then the Chairman & CEO of Verizon. I knew that Chambers was a sharp and dynamic leader, but I didn't realize his level of commitment to his team of employees and partners. He saw his staff and corporate partners genuinely as family members. I was not prepared for that opportunity and therefore failed to deliver a real impacting message. From that failure, I learned a hard lesson.

It became fairly obvious that I needed to take another step toward a more exhaustive approach to my professional preparedness. Before this moment, I believed that I needed to act like a CEO, a visionary, and leader of a business unit. On the other side of this experience, I realized I needed to become the CEO of my endeavors. I needed to understand in great detail where things were currently and what needed to happen next! Now we can't be prepared for every scenario possible, but I needed to work as though it was possible with the idea of being prepared for whatever comes my way.

I learned something else when I first met Chambers, and that was the real passion he had for his alma mater. He was a graduate of West Virginia University (WVU), and it was the first thing he said to me when we shook hands. Why is that important? Well, for those of you that are not aware, the football contention between Penn State and WVU was as bitter as it gets. Before 1984, Penn State was the winner 25 consecutive times. You can better understand the rivalry that exists between the two football teams. I was on that team that fought hard to gain a come-from-behind victory but lost to WVU in 1984.

As I mentioned, Chambers was a dynamic leader. He had no qualms about shaking things up by reinventing Cisco. Chambers was an aggressive innovator who adopted Jack Welch's philosophy of only competing in markets in which the company could become #1 or #2. After over 20 years as the CEO of Cisco, the company's sales revenue grew from $1.2 billion to close to $50 billion. What was most impressive was that Chambers would personally follow the conditions of all employees that were fighting a serious illness in the company. That included their spouses or children. It's safe to say that with all the wealth he accumulated and helped others to attain, it's secondary to how he leads the charge to build close relationships with Cisco staff members having serious health issues.

He would get personally involved in their health challenges! Is this an example of dominating? I would say so; his entrepreneurial vision proved that you could lead a business, even one that becomes a multi-billion-dollar corporation and passionately serves those who are most needy in the organization. **Having a servant's heart is the ideal prerequisite for promotions and leads to places and positions of dominance.** I'm guessing that like John Chambers and countless others; you are no different because you are reading this book to discover how you too will dominate in your vocation and personal life. **A CEO consistently positions their company for growth; as the CEO of our endeavors and life, we must remain in a position to grow personally which leads to personal dominance!**

We hear so much about the top 1% or the rich as if they are gifted beyond the masses, and none of their material success has to do with focus, hard-work, and making principled choices. We all must learn how to make choices that have a direct and lasting effect on the condition and quality of life for the positive. When I grew up the societal expectations were different from today. Although my parents carried an entrepreneurial spirit, they were more persuaded by the general process of establishing a professional life. My parents, much like many other parents expected you to go to college, learn a skill, go into the military and work a respectable 9 to 5. We looked forward to meeting the person of our dreams, having a family, paying off our mortgage and growing old with family and friends. Somewhere along the way, it appears we have lost some of our precious values in our culture, that I fear if we don't reverse some of what is going on in society, being free in America to chase your dreams will be replaced by something else. What does it mean to dominate?

Domination: the exercise of control or influence over someone or something, or the state of being in control:

I don't want to focus only on control as it is defined but rather control as it relates to influence and its underlying power. Control typically is power as it relates to position and ability to enforce rules and decisions. It can be dictatorial and demeaning over time though this type of control has built great organizations but not without having internal struggles and limiting potential growth. Influence instead is power as it relates to persuasion. Great sales forces have been built on the power of persuasion because it is rapport and service more than demand that closes the sale. Again, this is not to say that influence is not the first cousin of manipulation and can be used in the wrong way. Persuasion, service, caring, authenticity, empathy, and developing soft skills, in the long run, are better than strength through position.

In your vocation and personal life, even when you are not in a position of strength, you still have the unused power of influence? I like the word influence because I believe that things can change regardless of the condition. To stay on the path of progress toward the success, you must see yourself as holding the power of influence to invoke change. There are many great books describing how those who are succeeding think and behave. There are also a ton of examples of why people continually fail. If you then become a scholar of success or failure and act consistently on one side or the other, then you experience what you have studied, focused on, and committed to in your action; either success or failure. Let us be clear, people are either studying success or failure every day, and they become habitual in either building a success story or otherwise.

What is the genesis of this desire to affect your life? I believe that God created us in His image; therefore, we can reflect Him within our natural limitations and at fitting times exceed those limits. Continually connecting with God is the guiding principle of my life. Therefore, I cannot separate myself from what I believe, and so I share in my journey from that perspective. I believe we were created with the innate desire to succeed and dominate in our environment.

The discussion of humanity having dominion over the earth is connected to having a birthright from the Creator because of our identity in Him, as well as, His purpose for us. We have a natural desire to create, subdue and to dominate. That is not to say that our desires are always His desires; nothing could be further from the truth. The point I am making is that the desire for domination in all parts of life rather than one area, such as business, comes from our identity and it is increased in establishing an alliance with our Creator or by living a spiritually empowered life.

In your life you, on your own, may desire and seek the beauty in life; but when you relate with God, beauty is the most natural state of life and so is the desire to make all things that way. The more we relate to Him, the more we become a reflection of His nature. In other words, we have the potential to be God's reflection on the earth. **One of those mirrors holds the reflection of domination.**

Even the person who rejects their ego finds that this is an eternal struggle because we all desire to be known as individuals and to have a full expression of our lives; not because we have too, but it is the most natural mental state. I am defining the ego as the central part of a person who has a sense of self, survival instinct, and needs to express himself as an individual. In the right context that is a good thing; out of control, the need to survive is stronger than the desire for others to survive. Our connection with the world becomes a narcissistic expression of service to ourselves and consumption of others rather than service. Even the Creator is there merely to answer our prayers and prosper us.

No matter how much we try to lose ourselves to something larger, our desires to create, own and control that desire is still there. So, we desire to dominate because it is God's intention for mankind to reflect His image in the earth. It is our natural state to desire to dominate. Until we come in line with our created intention and fully commit to action with all our faculties and resources, Providence does not move and will not move until we act fully and consistently in faith. We desire to dominate because we were created and born with that intention, purpose, and significance.

Domination

I want to address for a moment what I call the active side of domination. If we were to break this down into its smallest parts, then the first part would be for any individual realizing at any age or after some event or circumstance that they can have a profound effect on their lives. You don't have to stay a victim. No matter where you come from you can be different from others, and the past or present circumstances don't define your future. Dominion can be exercised, taken, or expressed in any circumstance because it's our birthright to excel; we were created that way. We were created to reason, think, grow, and act upon our needs and desires. If you believe that circumstances can be overcome, then you can look for solutions rather than accept being a victim.

We can't change the environment in which we were raised, but we can overcome shortcomings or build upon the lessons of our youth. Dominance is about using authorities we have been given to accomplish our responsibilities; only you can decide to do so. You must cultivate the belief that you can excel. If you don't have great natural talent, you can overcome that too through dedication and hard work. Natural talent leaves breadcrumbs that lead us to what we were designed to become and the potential we have to be our best. However, the decision to put in the work and hone the skills is one that no one else can make for you. Talent alone never breeds long-term success. GE was great because they and others chose a model only to compete where they could be number one or two. That is leaning on your talents, strengths, and determination to dominate the market, and your personal life.

This process of writing the book allowed me to think back and hone in on where this subconscious desire to dominate became part of me. I was, and still am at times, completely unaware of this thought process and how it affects me until I am faced with a situation where I am challenged. Then the fight in the dog comes out. I mean full on pay per view. Domination is the state of victory, not the fleeting victory of a single game but the consistent intent and expression of winning over and over again. It is about doing the right things for the right reasons and producing outcomes based on affirmative actions taken that create consistent results. I can tell you this; winning and losing is an easy condition to adopt.

I was born far from perfect. I had physical limitations that would suggest to the average person that I could not have any level of success in athletics. I suppose that if I looked at it from some other perspective, then I might have chosen to settle for limitations that someone else placed on me and would have accepted them. In life you are always being tested, it's a part of the quest. In track, a great sprinter is always being tested by their competition; but, so is it in business as well. The real test though is in your mind and what perceptions or limitations you place not only on your potential but on how much pain you are willing to endure for that potential. You must endure a certain amount of pain and the sacrifice of many things to find out how far you can go. Discovering your limits and moving beyond those limits is a path you must travel.

As a toddler, I wore a corrective bar between my feet with the shoes attached to change how my feet and ankles were growing. It was the fierceness that I sensed from my parents that would not allow anyone to place limitations on me or say that I was different. As a child, my father's passion was my only reference point that I could not accept the limitations of my physical body as my limits. I had to find a way because he believed. His determination is not a casual statement of him not feeling sorry for me but strength that I adopted from him, like a heavyweight prizefighter. He was not just like that toward me that was his attitude toward life. I flat out was not going to quit or allow anyone to tell me what I could or could not do. My father was fierce not just standing against something that opposed him, but he wanted to overcome it, knock it down, and destroy it. At the age of 30, it only took my father one visit to the doctor to stop smoking, drinking alcohol, and design a regimen to lose 25 plus pounds in less than 30 days. If you saw him today, he is as fit as any 75 years old. Although the truth is told, after he threw away all his cigarettes those many years ago to officially stop smoking, he did sneak off for his last puff of a "sweet" smelling cigar. How do I know? Well, during a recent conversation I had with him, he confessed, and I then recalled us being at the airport when this happened. We continued the discussion with both of us carrying smiles on our faces.

I want to make this point because I think it is important to say that the first element of building a champion attitude was my parents. They were steadfast in their beliefs and expressed them profoundly in the way they chose to live. I never sensed from them any wavering in who they thought I was and what I could achieve, especially when I followed them choosing hard-work and character as my path. The hard-work and strong character was something my parents learned and did as young teenagers. My grandfather on my mother's side of the family was accidentally killed when a bulldozer fell on top of him. My mother was 15 years old when this devastating accident occurred, and just a year later my maternal grandmother was diagnosed with a fatal disease. It would be my mother that had to help run her family's house as a teenager. My father was 17 at the time, and he would often assist the family both by giving his time and money. Two and a half years later my mother was off to college, paying her way by working on campus, obtaining student loans, and scholarships while continuing to help run the house that included her aunt and her seven younger siblings. Understanding the example of all they endured and had to overcome is why I believe hard-work, a refusal to quit, and real character is the very foundation of my success.

With clenched fist and hands white from the blood leaving them; I grabbed hold of opportunities and refused to let go until I prevailed. I learned that my limitations did not define me, and the sheer will to win would guide me. There was never an identifiable moment when the will to win hit me, but I believe it was the examples before me, as well as, the challenges I experienced where I had to learn to stand up and fight that taught me. I can't describe it as this explosion of passion but more of something that slowly simmered within me and rose to the surface during the biggest challenges in my life.

Like most large families, I had my uncles who were like older brothers that certainly gave me the opportunity to stand up and fight for myself. They pushed me every chance they got, to find out what I was made of and on a few occasions, they tried to break me. If they could have broken me on several occasions, I don't think I would have been as successful later in life. Family can have a profound effect on a person's beliefs, leading to the opportunity to succeed or fail. Families, at times, can provide the best example of what to do and what not to do.

I believe my most vivid lesson of domination came in sports. As I mentioned before, I was a young kid in sports who had to wear a corrective bar with corrective shoes, and was not expected to play sports, much less be good at it. Football and later baseball were proving grounds for a strong-willed kid who lived for an opportunity to compete and find the best way to beat you; not just win. I think in all of us we need those proving grounds to become champions. The potential to win pales in comparison to the opportunities to win, to compete, and find the strategy to have your arms held high in victory. In life, you don't get your hands raised every time you compete. Losing is a good barometer of how far you have come and how far you must go until you win or lose to the best. The best is looking at you over their shoulder and circling your name on the calendar before each challenge. Decide to be the one that they are training to beat; one that they fear the most in competition.

As a young kid playing football with classmates especially gave me the opportunity to compete consistently. One thing I can say though is you have to be a fierce competitor so each time I touched the football I expected myself to do something special with it. I never had a ceiling set above me that created a mental limitation. I was encouraged to go out and challenge myself and find out how good I could be. Beating you or losing to you was the only way to find out.

At the age of seven years old I remember on one occasion I was playing football in the neighborhood against three other kids from the south side of the neighborhood. It was me against the other three. It was north side versus the south side. Now, it didn't start out as three versus one. Originally it was five versus five, and with the game tied, eventually, four of my teammates went home, while two from the south side followed suit. I thought to myself, I know I can't guard them all on defense, but I concluded that they wouldn't be able to stop me either when I get the ball. The best I could do was a draw, and the worst would be to let it play itself out with me doing my best to beat all three; regardless, in either case, I would not lose.

If I had sat back and looked at the logic of playing against three people by myself, it would have been absurd even to try, but I had to defend my turf, and there was something inside me that I had to prove. This challenge would help to shape how I see and approach every test I would face later in life, truly understanding that giving up or giving in to even the toughest of circumstances was no option.

The real challenge is that everyone comes from a different background and environment. You can take two people from the same environment, and their experiences and how they define them are completely different. One may use a tough upbringing as an excuse to emulate the environment from which they came; using examples of what not to do as the path to temporary success. The other, an example of something they don't want and are willing to do anything to get away from it. So, it's important to understand the elements of what may influence a person to choose to dominate, to excel and find a personal and professional expression of success. An expression that mentally takes them beyond the influences of their early environment or what challenged them during their youth. Remember, you can't always control the condition just the response or more precisely, the effort within the response.

Whether the conditions are ideal or not within your control; you own the response.

Desire

It is part of the human condition to have needs, wants, and desires. From birth, we cry to communicate that we need some basic needs met. As we grow, our desires change as our basic needs are met, and our wants become more complex between security, comfort, personal expression, and fulfillment. There are a few of us though, who desire personal fulfillment, purpose, and to express the ability to conquer, create, or subdue something at a very young age. This is not to say that late bloomers don't hit their stride as late as their 40's, 50's, or 60's to do great things in business and society. In my early 40's, I was finalizing what I wanted to do when I grew up. Now at an age north of 50, I have a better understanding of what I want, need, and have been purposed to do.

I want to inspire, advise, and assist others in executing life in a dominant fashion. Part of writing this book is the urgency in my soul to continue the quest to dominate in every area of my life. There are hills or possibly mountains to climb, but it means seeking and accepting new challenges, as well as, mastering my current conditions and business commitments.

Desire is merely a strong feeling to have something or wishing for something to happen. This by itself means little as everyone wants something strongly or wishes something to happen in their favor. The domination kind of desire goes to the level of burning desire where there is no other course but action. The thing desired must be done, it must be accomplished, and if it is impossible, then it most certainly must be achieved. The four-minute mile at one time was impossible but one man achieved it, and over 20,000 people followed him because he believed. It is the level of wishing and wanting that leads to direct action by those who are among the committed.

The reason desire is important is because desire frames the issue. You must desperately want something strongly enough to act on it and endure the pain or process to attain it, accomplish it, or create it even after you have failed. I know no better definition of faith than to believe something and act upon it until you attain it. Desire gives focus; burning desire gives laser-like focus that creates a direct line between you and what you strongly desire. Now, of course, the process may be anything but a straight line. Lining up behind a quarterback and looking at the end zone, it was a straight line; however, in case you have ever played or watched the game, there are 11 guys on the other side determined not to let you achieve that goal. Trust me when the ball is snapped, like in business or any other worthy pursuit, it's anything but a straight line to success.

Vision

Vision is the result of having a strong desire and having spent time imagining the thing desired until you can believe and articulate it. Don't underestimate the power of image and realize that your brain speaks through imagination rather than just having a picture of something that already exists. Your brain goes after what is in focus. Your imagination is an integral part of you creating your future. Every great invention and in most cases, improvements came out of imagination.

There are times that the image is vague, hard to describe, but you know it when you see it. I am going to suggest that you go beyond vague shadowy images in your mind and that you allow your imagination to create strong, bold, and detailed images of what you truly want in your life.

Visioning is a process that is something beyond getting caught staring into space in class and being called out for not paying attention. As an adult, it's a powerful tool to engage your imagination to create the better mousetrap or the thing that has never been done before. Bill Gates, for example, had the vision to put the power of computing in the hands of the average person, thus creating a personal computer. His simple statement and desire to do this lead to a vision of what it would take to create and possess his desire. The more you focus on it, the more the desire comes clearer and sharper. The image and know-how of what the next step is must always come after knowing and articulating what you want. Where most people fail is getting an image, and quitting when they don't know how to obtain it. Some believe that Providence makes a way during the journey, and that if you walk it long enough, and far enough with the focus on end, provision along the way will be made.

The birthplace of your dreams and refinement of desire is the imagination expressed. **Developing a vision, learning to write it, speaking it, contemplating, or meditating on it and then acting on it is part of the formula for creating and possessing.** Here are some practical ways to increase desire, vision, and goal creation. Learn to honor and spend time contemplating and visioning. It may seem childlike, but the most creative time of your life is typically your childhood. It's natural for people to ask what you always wanted to be as a child. It's also natural for a child to dream about the future, as well as, the experience of the now. Intuitively, the reason is, people know that childhood is where you must connect to the deepest thoughts of self, desired experience, and purpose. Children seek this naturally without knowing the terms or even the concepts, but they know what they want to possess and what they want to experience.

On one morning during the summer break, at the age of ten, my sweet and tenacious mother abruptly asked me to get dressed. Now, there was one thing for certain, when my mom asked me to get dressed without first explaining why, I was heading somewhere I did not want to go. After a few whys from me, she told me I needed to be registered for school. It was a private school, a private school with no current football team and none in site. My only response was "no," and after a few rebuttals back and forth my final words went something like this. "No mom, I'm going to public school, playing football, getting a scholarship, and going to college!" Although my parents spent plenty of time intensely discussing the matter, after my final words, for me, it was settled. More importantly, my parents eventually agreed to keep me in the public-school system; although my mother was not too excited about that idea, she did have peace about it. Seven years or so later, I packed my bags and headed off to college on a four-year scholarship. That is the power of knowing what you want and not settling for less.

Now my mother was not trying to limit my opportunities by sending me to a private school but attempting to put me in the best possible position and environment to succeed. I was a young boy, but my mother realized there was something powerful in a mind that was fixed. As adults, we must be mindful and stay watchful of anyone that speaks limitations over us which are based on their insight. These are the dream killers whose sole purpose is to assign you a box, put you in it, and steer it toward more sensible endeavors so they may be comfortable.

Each day we should make time in our schedule for reading and contemplation. I suggest at the end of each day take some time out to assess the day. We will later address in this book about time management and organization, but it's key to take the time for reflection, active imagination, and expression of each day. Take time specifically each day to catalog what you have accomplished, then imagine your goals, asking yourself detailed questions through your five physical senses. As I began to implement this approach more consistently with my life's endeavors, I could see more of my goals materializing. After reflection, you must move toward creation, where goals and objectives are established. When goals and objectives are in place, it provides a platform and energy to fuel action and experiences. The more you can engage your senses the more your subconscious will engage in creating it, observing that it is real and move everything toward creating that experience.

When envisioning something, get as crystal clear as you can to create the image, and then ask yourself to experience it with your senses. Imagination is important because it engages different parts of your mind to solve problems and create the real experience in your mind. When your subconscious mind is locked in on something, it seeks first to prove that it is true, and either avoid it or experience it over and over based on whether it is pleasurable or painful.

The more you can engage your five physical senses with imagination in solving problems and answering questions of what your desire looks like when it's realized, the more the mind recognizes the image is real and starts creating a path to achieve it. Clarity of mind and direction leads to more accurate and meaningful goal creation. It also clarifies the actions you must take. I also believe that there is a deeper or spiritual side to you that allows you to pass your known limitations whether they were self-imposed or imposed by others. Your imagination is the gateway to your freedom. Imagination is the beginning of real freedom. Mandela, when he was freed spoke of being mentally free while he was physically shackled. Victor Frankel, in *Mans Search for Meaning,* wrote about the same concepts in the concentration camps. Imprisonment can start with the body, but freedom starts with the mind.

Decision / Commitment

Decision time is where the rubber meets the preverbal road. I have a friend who always says that potential is nothing and that productivity is everything. Deciding makes a statement to you and others, your commitment of self and resources to the accomplishment of your goals and desires. Deciding demonstrates a commitment to your purpose if you align them with the outcomes you desire. Choice and decision making is the primary key to quality of life. Decisions are more powerful than mere access. You have access to a greater life, but decisions are required to experience it.

How many people did not have the same access to money or education and yet they overcame because they were committed to the cause. You can have access to the table and still not be a successful participant. Power starts with the ability to assess information and make decisions. Many people are powerless not because they don't have access to what they need but because they have not decided to commit to getting what they want or what could be their destiny. I did not say they don't have desires: I am saying most people are not committed to the process of getting what they want. So, regardless of how simple or complex your situation is, you can't have what you want by desire alone, you only obtain and experience it by what you decide to do!

I've come to believe that success is something that you commit to over a lifetime and beyond. Those who dominate in life are not perfect, but usually do well at different things in their life. That is because of commitment along with learning there are certain principles of success, as well as, failure. Principles of success all start with a commitment to purpose. The same is true for people who fail in life. It is merely because they are committed to a process of failure and have embraced it and are unwilling to change and learn from their mistakes or the mistakes of others.

They don't see it that way, they perceive it as a lack of opportunity or that someone else had an advantage that they did not. I am not saying that there is no truth to that, but many have risen because of commitment, where many remain destitute. They say it's not where you come from but where you're going that matters. The commitment my mother made to her dying mother to become the first in the family with a college degree and utilize her knowledge to help and keep her younger siblings together is a strong example. It was no simple matter for a 17-year-old girl having to start college, help keep her siblings together, and maintain a household, but that's exactly what she did while she eventually graduated with honors from Norfolk State University. Regardless of what was before her she became blind to all potential roadblocks and remained committed to the process to attain the goal.

Obstacles are those frightful things you see when you take your eyes off your goal.

Henry Ford, Founder, Ford Motor Company

There must be real thought, and in certain cases, contemplation before a commitment is made. A commitment must be part of your underlying life's philosophy, and not just a momentary decision to do or not to do something. Once committed, you should take very seriously the decision to uncouple yourself and resources from any project, relationship, or pursuit that is not directly in line with your end goal. The easier you make it on yourself to change or correct your course, the harder it will be to quit because of convenience and unprincipled directions. There is only so much gas in the tank, and everyone has limited resources available to them at any given moment; so, no wasted movement. Going five minutes in the wrong direction takes at least five minutes to course correct, and that's assuming you didn't take some time to pause or contemplate your mishap. If we travel five miles in the wrong direction and return to the point of origin, we've invested time and gone nowhere which could be worse than breaking even.

The decision to commit to something should be taken very seriously. In God's Handbook for Success, it tells us to count the cost of building something before we get started. If you start, and don't have what it takes to finish, you will be put to open shame. Consider the cost of commitment and understand what the process of success and dominance will require of you. It's not merely an exercise to get from point A to B. I have always said that we are changed in the process as the process is changing us. When I started this process of writing a book, I was a novice, and probably still am, but by the time you read this, I will be a published author; something that I was not when I started. That is true of real success, in that, the journey is the authentic change from one state of being to another, but the transition is the grueling part. It is difficult, to say the least, to become something different from your original investment. Success or dominance then is undoubtedly the product of choice.

I liken the process to a field where the prize is not in the field but on the other side of it. You are on one end of it and realize that you must cross this field to get to the other side and grab what you want. It looks like a walk in the park, but something inside tells you that the end is just out of reach and sight; that something in the middle is going to be tough to cross. Remembering the prize, you must ask yourself how badly do you want it? If I can get through this and endure the trials ahead, if I stay focused, and don't miss the destination, then it just might be worth the fight in the middle. The field is the dash in the discussion much the way that the dash tells the story of your life when it's over. The field in the middle is life in which you labor, become, and learn to fight and win.

Your Win is Non-Negotiable

The first time I heard the words "Your win is non-negotiable." I was sitting with Brian Sabin, the CEO of Unity Business Systems, during a strategy session he and I were having a few years ago. The purpose of the session was to develop a strategy around the structure and content for workshops that were designed for existing customers. In this discussion, we would define what this meant for our customers; this powerful statement communicated a clear message to the customer and continued to resonate with me today in my endeavors.

Once you have decided to dominate, you must win at something; you must achieve and pursue it with fervor. You must be tenacious; if you don't have it in you, then it needs to be developed. You can develop that tenacity by going further into your goals each time and not quitting. Each time you endure one more rep or one more long night studying. The longer you endure, the stronger you become; the next step is transformative when you decide not to quit. If you're unable to manage the pain by yourself, it's imperative you get a mentor or coach who will push you and get the best out of you. That coach can also help you manage the meaningful rest and times of refocusing that are needed for peak performance.

It's impossible to navigate that on your own. In going through the challenge of putting this book together, I have had interesting discussions about how our beliefs and actions are formed, and how we express them. Looking back, I developed a relentless attitude because my parents certainly modeled that behavior, but it was in the trials of life, competition, and fighting that I learned that I could win; when losing was not acceptable.

When you turn the corner and begin to challenge your mind about creating the impossible or pursuing some strongly held belief that is unproven, you must understand that the mind craves certainty, as well as, new experiences. However, your mind will not fully accept any premise until it is proven. Strongly held beliefs that I can't win, or I can't lose are proven over and over again in life, and either solidify your beliefs or challenge them to be changed. Let me put it another way, the pursuit of success either proves or challenges what you believe about yourself and life. The pursuit of success reveals you, what you're made of, and what type of man or woman you most desire to become. As a young child, ownership in business and fierceness was modeled for me. As I accepted challenges, I believed that I could not be beaten, and that it might be difficult, but I could do it if I focused on it and put my whole being into it. That was proven to me repeatedly both in winning and how I accepted the losses. What happens over time is that when challenges come you become conditioned to lean into it, study it, strategize against it, and execute to defeat it. If not, then you are conditioned to back away, cower at the site of it, and quit.

Now that I believed that I could win, I then went out to prove it. Confidence is only made by proving what you believe to be true. Some people believe and are confident in their failure, and things are not working out for them. They believed, and had the life experiences to back up that belief. That is why it is so hard to change. Your mind craves the certainty of winning or losing and does not easily accept the other. Some refuse to see failure as an opportunity to learn but rather another example proving that they can't win.

You must seek challenges to learn to win from the opportunities when you don't think you can win. Losing or failing should be upsetting, and it should never feel good, but you must overcome emotional setbacks and get cerebral and matter of fact about it and find out why you did not achieve the outcome you desired. Success or failure is contagious and proves what you believe to be true already; maybe it's the best determining factor of what is going on in your inner core and how you will respond when challenged.

"Our life always expresses the results of our most dominant thoughts."

> *Soren Kierkegaard, Danish Philosopher,*
> *Theologian, Poet, Social Critic. & Author*

Winning and losing merely prove or challenge what you believe to be truest about yourself and the opportunities that surround you. If you have a losing mentality and you want to win, then there are some key steps to changing your mindset. We can start by understanding the basics of how the mind works. This is not an exhaustive study, but simply put, the mind is a massive computer that logs tons of information, whether you are conscious of it or not (This is an example of intuitive learning).

This information is then cataloged into similar thoughts that form beliefs that your mind tries to prove to be true, so you can create certainty to survive and thrive in this world. To challenge thoughts, you must dump massive amounts of information into the brain, challenging the thought patterns that are there, and create neurological connections in the brain that support the paradigm that you are trying to create. You will think and feel your way into winning or losing. The action is merely the release of energy to prove what you already believe. Action is the active side of faith and dominance.

Watching videos and reading biographies of people who have pursued success in life is purposeful learning by design. If you want to do something that you have never done before, learn the skill followed by a rigorous application. Find someone who is achieving successful points and learn from them. You may fail at the task the first time or be mediocre, but you are also changed by the task, and have begun to learn a new skill. Masters first must accept the position of an apprentice: the master's skill is forged in servitude. Serving effectively is the key to elevating in any part of life, especially in business. Some of the greatest examples of business or career successes have occurred when individuals start at one of the lowest possible positions or when an entrepreneur starts with just an idea, and with little to no money in the bank. Entrepreneurs take the risk and work their way to success.

The next step is to find someone who has attained certain levels of success and gain from them as a mentor. With technology, you can get mentors through reading tons of material generated by them if you cannot connect with them directly. Mentors model behaviors that are imperceptible many times and touch us not just on a knowledge level, but a feeling level. It is important to find out how someone did something, but that may be only a skill you have to acquire through practice. You also need to find out what they felt when they did it; what it means to them and try to find out how they are creating experiences in their mind. To model experience, you must think of it in regards to intellect and emotion. Intellect or information alone does not complete the perception of experience that can be duplicated. You will have gained knowledge, but not understanding.

You may have to do something that you learn repeatedly developing muscle memory; this is repetitive learning. True mastery can be achieved faster by learning the intangibles and philosophy that go beyond repetitive learning. It does not mean that practice is not necessary, it is, but learning the process behind that allows the "greats" to work hard and give much for their craft. The masters all had a why and you must get in touch with yours. Repetition alone does not create mastery. Learn the emotion and drive behind it. What gave them the will to do it in the first place?

If for example, I wanted to practice law; I would immerse myself in learning the law. That would give me factual knowledge, but would I have the tools needed to become a good litigator or defense attorney. If I wanted to master law, then I would have to find someone who has achieved mastery and study under them with the understanding that I am studying them; not just the law. I would find out what their motivation was and philosophy about the law. I would discover what drove their passion for the law, and how did they use that passion to their advantage when they faced down the impossible.

I would observe their speech patterns and the way they did things differently from others. Once I achieve mastery of their methods, then I must allow myself the room and courage to experience my journey and go beyond their worldview of the law to become the master that I once sought in them. Once you have obtained the essence of someone else, you must then reject it on some level to find another level of truth for yourself.

"You have to reject the perspective of someone else to find the truth for yourself."

Ayub Fleming

Lastly, you must perform new tasks physically, so you learn kinesthetically. You must change the way you use your physiology for change to take hold. Physiology, if nothing else, is an anchor to your thoughts. It's one of the reasons that non-verbal communication is important. You must change what you think, how you feel, and what you do physically to find higher levels of success in whatever you pursue. We will address kinesthetic throughout the book, but I wanted to give you some thoughts on what comes next after you decide to dominate.

If you don't come from a home with a strong family background or have mentors in your life, you can still run on the road to success. You, like most of us, have strong desires, especially in material things and relationships. These are some of the easiest ways to keep score of how well you are doing. Take the time to keep looking at your finances, health, and relationships in contrast to where you would like to be and make an honest assessment. If you are not where you want to be, adjust, keep learning, and keep grinding. Sometimes it's one versus three, but facing the challenge is a small victory in itself.

It is possible for you to start from nothing, but desire alone is not sufficient to become productive in life. When you decide to dominate, make up your mind to the point that you will not be persuaded otherwise. You are on your way across that field full of challenges but on your way to the prize as well. Once you have decided with this level of conviction that you will dominate in your life, regardless of what you are willing to focus on, commit to, and pay the price required by the process, then you will be dominant and not dominated. You will achieve new levels of success that you may have only perceived was for others.

For some, by reading this book, you will be starting new goals and coming off other successes. For others, this book will touch you at the lowest points in your life; where you are going to have to decide that the life you are living, whether by your active or passive choice, will not cut it any longer.

I believe that the turning point is the acknowledgment of what is lacking in your life, and the blending of strong desires and needs to have one cohesive, focused vision, determining what it is that you want to create. You cannot begin to be successful until you decide what you want. An overwhelming sense of what is to be achieved must become crystal clear and resolute in your mind. Until you talk about what you want, and what must be done, you will find too many old familiar excuses of why either it can't be done, or why it can be excused away until another time.

I don't want to minimize the journey from where you are or where you deeply desire to be. You must start that journey sometimes with nothing, but the burning desire to accomplish something; that for you may not exist yet. You must be desperate in your attitude to change where you are now and achieve that desire. Life is not a dress rehearsal where you wear the clothes, but you pretend as if it matters, and go through the motions of the performance. It is the performance, and every day is game day. Desire starts with the recognition of where we are going to be, but have not yet arrived; in the beginning stages, our position is often not aligned with our purpose and desires, but it must be.

One of the questions you must ask yourself is am I where I am supposed to be in relevance to my God-given purpose, my potential to achieve, and the accomplishment of my deepest desires. Once I put these together do they paint a picture of a life that I must achieve. When an individual feels inadequate, it's because they have not come to understand what they have been designed to achieve. The discovery of purpose is also when the discovery of significance occurs as well. When we discover our significance, we lay down all our insecurities, inadequacies, fears, and false realities which will lead to living an inadequate life that was not purposed for us. The responsibility is ours because the Creator has given us stewardship over our lives, innate talents, resources, access to knowledge, and skills.

"Let me show you how great I am."
Muhammad Ali

It does come down to right thinking and hard-work. If your thinking is wrong and you work hard, chances are, you won't achieve much more than someone with the right beliefs, but no work. In either case, your formula or equation is off, and you will not reach your potential or capacity. You must continue to renew your mind, polish your craft, and put in the work to pursue the levels of success you were created for. That is not the same for everyone; you must live up to the capacity you have been given.

In 1987, I played running back for Penn State. We were facing the University of Miami that year for the National Championship. We were number 2 in the country and playing what most believed to be an unbeatable Miami team. Some thought we were good enough to be there, but not good enough to win. Life is a lot like that; many times, we think we are good enough to work at a certain place, but not good enough to own it. If you are good enough to operate at a certain level, set your sights on winning and not just showing up. Your quest to win and conquer continuously must become the non-negotiable! Like you, and most everyone else on the planet, I have the potential to win and win big. If I have the potential to compete against the best, then I have the potential to beat the best. You will never be considered the best until you can face what everyone perceives to be the best and beat them. In this race, the only real competition is the one staring back at you in the mirror. It's more than anything about growing every day and transitioning into your dreams. You are changed in the process.

"Audacious-habitual thinking is the bridge to audacious living; it unlocks and opens the door to the previously unknown where we discover the personal right and privilege of deciding to dominate. This opened door reveals that we have the dominant position over our circumstances in life; that being, in our personal or professional challenges, as well as, our dreams and our aspirations."

W.H. Dozier III, Founder, UTake Dominion

Dominant Factors

1. **The act of dominating in life is not a randomly selected idea by our Creator** but rather by a designed purpose and offered as a personal choice to everyone. **Dominion must begin within us first, and then the circumstances around us.**

2. **Discovering one's purpose also offers the discovery of our value and true significance in life;** this enables us to address and overcome our insecurities, inadequacies, fears, false realities, or other shortcomings to lead us to proper life management, skill development, and mutually beneficial relationships.

3. **Mastery begins with desiring to reach a mastery level**, but of course, the process starts in the position of an apprentice.

4. **People that become champions in their life and craft will never stop asking questions to understand the "why;"** they have an insatiable thirst for understanding their purpose, gaining knowledge, and accomplishing great achievements.

5. **Consistently overcoming challenges individually and equally blazing a path for others to do likewise** should become a common practice.

6. It's essential that you **see the beginning of domination as coming into a deeper understanding of what you desire, why you desire it, and finally, deciding to obtain it.**

7. As the beast is unleashed, we begin to **know we were created for something great,** so we accept challenges, serve diligently while welcoming comfort, and we are always prepared to fight, fully aware that we are changed in the fight.

Chapter 2

The Creative Force

"Sure I am this day; we are masters of our fate that the task which has been set before us is not above our strength; that its pangs and toils are not beyond our endurance. As long as we have faith in our own cause, and an unconquerable will to win, victory will not be denied us."

Winston Churchill, British Statesman, Army Officer, & Writer

Create the one person you desire most to be, more than that, the one you were destined to be. I will make a statement that will be strange to some, but for those who relentlessly go after their dreams, it will not. **YOU ARE A CREATIVE FORCE!** How you think and the words you speak are the tools you use daily; what you choose to do with these assets mean everything! So, create is an active word, and in this book, there will be many action statements because the basic premises of this book are actions. The action that we decide to take that's in line with what you truly want and desire, not just what you are willing to settle for, provides shape to what you were destined to become. Out of the abundance of the heart, are the issues of life, from which the mouth speaks. Your mind and mouth are powerful creative forces that work together as one. They are part of your greatest list of allies in the accomplishment of your dreams or part of your fiercest enemies list that will yield crippling results.

As mentioned in the first chapter, there is a desire to compete, to win, and to dominate in everyone that I have ever met who attained measures of success or is working toward it. I have also met others whose desire was buried so deep in their psyche; it could not be unearthed. The desire to win and most certainly conquer must be specific, palpable, and in most cases insatiable. I use the word insatiable because it means nearly "impossible to satisfy." When you're making progress in achieving your goals, I think it's healthy to have balance, and find contentment where you are in your journey but never fulfillment. It's progression without a finish line, but one with points of destiny to celebrate along the way. Satisfaction leads to the point of fulfillment and the end of the line, where there is no motivation for progress. Reaching that point should never be the case!

At the end of every season in which I played football or baseball at the collegiate or professional level, I always looked forward with the thought of training hard and finding ways to improve and prepare for a more productive season than the last. No matter who I faced, the only person that I had to improve upon was me. I had the desire and the opportunity; how do I create the conqueror that I most desire to be? Looking back, I must be honest and know that I did not achieve every athletic goal that I set. By setting high enough goals, I can look back and say I was blessed with the opportunity to compete as a collegiate level National Champion and a professional athlete. I can only say that because I set the bar high for myself and I ran with it as far as I could take it. I left with quality relationships, great memories, and tremendous lessons learned.

"Desire alone does not cause acquisition; you must act. It's a simple equation that includes, desire, hard work, and a host of other actionable habits. If you are not satisfied with where you are or what you have attained in life, change your habits to change the equation."

W.H. Dozier III, Founder, UTake Dominion

Create the Vision

Create means to cause to exist or to bring into existence. That means that what you desire may not yet exist. You must want something and get clear about what that is. You must envision it, focus on it, and work until it comes to fruition. It's a process that is only for those who, by sound business practice, personal development, and hard-work are determined to create a real interpretation of what they desire; that is, to have a full expression of their life and CREATE the life that burns within them.

For us, that is why failure can feel devastating, lonely, and hopeless because we don't believe in or expect failure, don't subscribe to it, nor accept it. Failure, however, is a learning opportunity and in some cases should be viewed as a way that did not work. Failure sometimes is used as an excuse for bad behavior, diminishing thoughts, being ill-prepared, or low character and should not be dismissed, but should be examined with great determination for personal change not blaming outside circumstances. I love the way inventor and founding member of GE, Thomas Edison saw things and when he was questioned about his many failures to invent the light bulb, he responded as a true visionary and true champion should.

"I have not failed; I've just found 10,000 ways that won't work. Our greatest weakness lies in giving up. The most certain way to succeed is always to try just one more time."

Thomas Edison, American Inventor, Entrepreneur,
Co-Founder of GE

Okay, so we don't want to keep making mistakes again and again, but the reality is that we do make the same mistakes, sometimes multiple times and we do fall short of what we know we can achieve. There is a window of opportunity for each stage of life, and we are not able to turn back the clock. There is a sense of urgency in getting it right and to live our dreams before the tick-tock has timed out, and we are done.

To create requires that you first become acutely aware of what you desire. If you're not thinking about your dreams, I mean focused thought on a regular basis; scribbling all over the place or in journals then you're not serious enough yet. As we have learned from many accomplished people, goals must be specific; they should be written, read, and tracked so that you know you are making progress in achieving them.

As brothers growing up and working on their grandparents' farm, Bob and Ron Morgan had always dreamed of creating a business together. Although their plans to open a restaurant did not come to fruition, the brothers would eventually create an entrepreneurial venture established along with Rob Franklin in 1998. If you've driven in or around the Mall area in Tysons Corner located in the heart of Mclean, VA, chances are, you have seen the Morgan Franklin Consulting logo. By 2005, revenues for the consulting firm were under $20 million; today revenue climbs above $70 million annually. They have built a multi-million-dollar business that puts plenty of energy into improving the community.

For example, you will see staff members from this great company at North Springfield Elementary school annually teaching finance, business, and economics to the young students. The Morgan Franklin founders wanted to create a company that not only provided unparalleled services to its customers and increasing bottom line profits, but a company that had a strong focus on developing partnerships with the local community; they have created just that!

"Where your focus goes, energy flows."

Eric Thomas, Speaker

When you can be specific, you can begin to focus your efforts toward the achievement of singular events. When this happens, energy like a laser can be focused, and things are accomplished. Where your focus goes; energy flows. Where energy flows, the possibilities of success expand and begin to take shape. Continued applied energy begins to shape things, creates things and destroy procrastination and hints of slothfulness. One of the hardest things to do is to focus on a single idea for an ongoing period until it is accomplished. However, if this skill is mastered, then nothing can master you. Many people fail for lack of focus and persistence not lack of opportunity.

Define the Non-Negotiable

Your win must be non-negotiable, and there is no way to work toward success without a fully defined definition and image of what winning and domination look like. What does winning feel like? If winning were a terrible feeling no matter the perks, few would spend so much energy trying to obtain it. People spend their life and resources to pursue a concept of success because it is transformative and powerful. Winning changes everything.

I am not saying winning is the only thing but where does losing or mediocrity fall on the scale. Win-win, when it becomes non-negotiable, it is the only thing to be desired. What else is there for someone who wants a journey expressed by a full life?

The alternative is accepting the existence of what pain and disappointment bring. We all know at some point what that looks and feels like. The fact is, we all make assessments and assign values to experiences and interpret what they mean. Whether you are conscious of it or not, you assign a value to everything based on whether the experience is pleasurable or painful. One you seek to repeat and one you avoid.

It is easier for some to stay where they are no matter how hard it is, when the alternative is to undergo a massive change. The massive change seems to be harder and more painful than the state they are currently living. It is the only way to explain the acceptance of a life that some does not want to experience. There is never a reason to be envious of someone else, we do not know what they are going through or have been through to get where they are. We also do not know exactly what we are capable of accomplishing, that perhaps, no one else can do. We must decide to discover; to spend whatever needs to be spent, and ultimately to leave no stone unturned when it comes to our success and expression of our lives. The success of others, whether from the past or present, should be an inspiration to us.

Winning is not the same for everyone. A person who seeks spiritual growth and enlightenment has an idea of what winning is to them, but winning is why we run, why we compete, and why we as entrepreneurs and professionals spend the countless hours working and taking the criticism. It is because we want to win at everything. In God's Handbook for Success, it explains that we should run in a manner that allows us to win. It specifically says: **Do you not know that those who run in a race all run, but only one receives the prize? Run in such a way that you may win.**

No one can define the win for you, that honor is bestowed upon you. It is yours to create a precise and yet passionate vision for what you desire for your life. Tony Robbins once said that you must create a baseline for your life that you are not willing to live under; you must raise your standards. If you do not create that baseline, then it is too easy to accept something less. That should be your break-even line or your starting line that should define the very best of what you think you can achieve and the person you believe that you can become.

Start there and be determined to live above that. In any sport, if at the beginning of the season you only hope that you will have a winning season that is not the attitude or the goal that will make you a champion. Only hoping to win a few games will not lead you to ask the questions of how we will go undefeated. If you do not prepare to win championships, the odds are, you never will.

The days of training and studying at times will be long, and it is too easy to justify giving up to simply ease the pain of change. Many have defined success as the constant pursuit of a worthy ideal. No matter how you define it, for you, it must be defined, it must be personal, and it must be consistently articulated and constantly executed.

You cannot win based on the definition derived from someone else unless you find a way to make it personal to you. You only get one chance to live this life, so you must make the best of it, you must run the race to win, not just participate. Very few can win by just showing up. I would suggest buying a journal and on the very first page before you write any goals begin to think about and define what success means to you. Write at the top "Life is hard," and "Grow Stronger." Life at times demands quick decisions; think faster. Never allow yourself to think that improving your performance is not required to continue to change and get better. Your competition is counting on it.

Know Where You Are

I strongly believe that for you to be successful in life, you must have both feet on the ground and live in reality; now that does not negate faith or the idea of taking the risk, but you must understand the level of your abilities before you can surpass them. Overachievers are acutely aware of what they are told or what others believe that they cannot do. Often, it is their interpretation and their way of thinking that they must overcome. The reason they are called overachievers is that they have surpassed what was believed of them. The thing is that in our society to be called an overachiever is a backhanded slap across the face; at times, you are ridiculed rather than celebrated.

"The path of success does not need outside validation because if you seek it, you must also accept the random criticism."

Ayub Fleming

Faith does not attempt to deny reality; it chooses to not accept our interpretation of its limitations, beliefs, and actions toward something better. Belief and hard-work is the currency that you exchange for what you believe. It is the underlying proof to you and others of what you believe is coming and is unstoppable. If no one is mocking you, then your vision may not be large enough to separate yourself from them; dream bigger.

In any journey, you must know what you have at your disposal, as well as, what you are missing. You cannot just understand what the wagon is for, but what is missing from it; your trip will either be much harder than you expected or will fail because you do not understand what and how much provisions are needed along the way.

It is much like putting together a meal and not understanding that you need seasoning and not just meat. Even the best and most tender filet mignon needs salt and pepper. Prepare it without it, and all you have is a tender lump of meat with no flavor. So, learning to take an honest assessment of yourself and the resources you need in business or a personal endeavor is crucial. Here are some tips.

Always start with yourself. Those of us in business realize how fast things can change in business and technology. Sooner or later your skills become obsolete because things constantly change with technology and innovation. Your competency level over time is constantly being diminished, and you need to be aware of that. An honest assessment understands that creating value and being able to work with relevant technologies is important to your client. Everyone you serve and create value for is your client, even the person you now call your employer. Staying employed or retaining customers under normal conditions is about constantly creating value.

Make a **catalog of your experiences and skills,** and then, make a list of what the market is demanding in your field of education and experience. If you lack education, then look up what classes you can afford and take them in your schedule. If you lack experience, look for mentors or opportunities to volunteer where you can gain the experience. One of the hardest but best ways to get experience is to start a small business. Trust me, learning from the ground up and figuring out everything is enough to make a Billy Goat quit. However, as they say, for most of us, the experience is the best teacher.

With any new endeavor, once you have an honest assessment of what you need to add as skills or experience, then you must understand what you need to accomplish the goal. The two things I have always done is first meet with the client, owner or leader and define the goal and find out what the expectations are for working toward success. The next thing is to find out what resources you must have to complete the goal or task. People are sometimes the hardest piece to put together but understanding that they are your best resource; focus on getting the right people on the team for the project.

Start with understanding what you lack and where to get it, understand the goal and expectation, what you have at your disposal, and then you can see what you will need to finish the job. Professional athletics is much the same especially when it is a team sport. Each position on any team must support the other. Weak links become obvious and people that do not produce over time get exposed to competition and replaced.

The Winning Strategy

Having been a part of a collegiate national championship team in football and playing in two different professional sports in my career has not been the definition of winning but for me, part of the course of winning.

My attitude toward winning in everything I do needs an outlet for me to test myself. Collegiate and professional sports was then and now conducting for-profit, and not-for-profit business ventures is a part of what gives me that outlet today. Winning is not just a point of destination but an expression of winning along the journey.

One thing that I have seen in common throughout my athletic years and now in business has been that winning starts with having a winning strategy and the right attitude at every level. If you are a mid-level manager or director trying to go to the next levels of management you need to ask yourself what strategy is needed to be implemented to achieve your goals; what is your strategy to compete, win, and then to dominate.

Remember you cannot win if you are not competitive; not planning to be competitive is underestimating the opponents that surround you or anything that may be opposing you. Once we have determined that strategy, we either have what we need, or we are in the process of getting what we need to win, this is a part of the strategy to win.

In business, like athletics, everyone is there to compete to win. If you bring a new product to market, the day you launch, and others find out about it, you have a short period, even with a patent, to establish yourself in the market without some competing product. The competition that may be well funded and ready to innovate on top of your creativity is on the way. You must keep the competitive edge and stay hungry to continue to innovate and stay ahead of the competition and become the industry standard.

They seek to become your competition, innovate on what you have done or beat you at price points or with an innovative feature. They aim to adversely decrease your market share or even put you out of business. Become the brand name that people trust, because you have earned it with consistent marketing and surpassed delivery and customer experience.

Companies who are only or mainly concerned about market share are not thinking about winning. They are thinking about maintaining and managing marginal gains. These are not companies trying to put a man on Mars but willing to bring to market marginally superior products and doing enough to maintain. Truly successful entrepreneurs and business people who want to change things, feel that they can best do it at the front of the ship pointing and leading the way. Strong auto brands like Pontiac and Saturn may have been innovators at one time but forgot to keep reaching for the stars; they decided to produce among the herd. The thing is, about the herd, if you ever misstep you get run over and left behind because the truth is, they are not following you, they are competing against you. They are competing with you just not to get eaten; if you have no grand vision and do not exercise any leadership, then the one who is following is you.

"Our success at Cisco has been defined by how we anticipate, capture, and lead through market transitions. Over the years,

I've watched iconic companies disappear - Compaq, Sun Microsystems, Wang, Digital Equipment - as they failed to anticipate where the market was heading. Since I became CEO, 87 percent of the companies in the Fortune 500 are off the list."

"What that says is that companies that don't reinvent themselves will be left behind. I also think that's true of people."

John T. Chambers, Former Chairman, and CEO of Cisco

Deciding to Dominate is not just a call to leadership, but a mission to own, direct, create, and increase the skill and development of the individual for deeper entrepreneurship, corporate or professional growth, and personal success possibly on a global scale, but most importantly with a perpetual perspective. Domination is not about just finding a way to win once or twice but with consistency. Domination is about becoming the very best version of yourself so that you are an elite game changer. Winning and success will not just be seen along the way but is masterfully on the way. It is not just a single destination, but a series of destiny points and what remains vital throughout your journey is an ongoing strategy and execution of constant improvement.

The strategy is defined as a plan of action or policy that is designated to achieve a defined objective.

As a business, developing the winning strategy or plan has several moving parts. The first part is to understand the objective based on the expectations of the client or market. The strategy is based on outcomes. Remember, this is a plan of action that requires execution and not just a plan so that you can say you have one. I have seen many business plans that lay out various business strategies and marketing this and that, but they do not get to what we are going to do versus what we must do. It is often not clear enough on how to exceed client expectations and creating or beating the market but just finding a way to run in it. I had a person that I went to once as a young adult, and they told me point blank that they did not want to hear what I wanted to do but wanted to see what I was doing. Truly successful people are not impressed with potential, they are impressed with results.

At Verizon, a colleague of mine and I submitted a business plan for the S&E operation to the Group President of Global Strategic Services, Chief's response was eye-popping but clear. He said, "You're not here to develop projects or opportunities to generate hundreds of millions but billions!" It was the first time I was personally confronted with the "B" word, and it shook my perception. I needed to reconcile the difference between what was required and my perception. Eventually, it was settled, and so, we developed the vision and strategy that was needed to project and produce a billion in revenue. Yes, "only" one billion.

Think of yourself as an investor. It is your life, skills, time, and talents that you are investing in a relationship, person, company, or project. Is it a worthy pursuit, is it paying dividends or are you losing your shirt? The strategy should always have a win-win attached and some type of increase or profit. Win-win means that it must create value for all parties. Meaning it is not a good deal even in relationships if its benefits only belong to someone else. You must win as well. Working in any endeavor is an investment and should provide some tangible return on what you are putting into it. If it is not paying some type of dividend, then it may be time for more evaluation in what you are investing. I would take the same approach to work with any non-profit. It must be a win-win.

In business or personal life, you must create value to stay and grow. So why would you not want value to be created as a return on the investment, of our passion, time, talent, and overall life? The value must be created and received by both sides, or eventually, that endeavor is doomed to fail. Look how many companies and personal relationships fall by the wayside. They do not start out with the intention to fail, but they also do not plan to win. I do not plan to compete; I plan to win. If I do not believe and expect to be the best, I do not invest myself in it. To create value and to expect it in return, while understanding its purpose, is to expect to win long-term.

Any action plan will typically have three to five categories or major milestones that must be accomplished. These milestones have smaller goals and things to be accomplished, and then there are the smallest tasks that must be done, managed, adjusted, monitored, and documented. Putting these components into a plan will insure only the potential for success; hard-work, focus, and adjustments will insure its success, assuming it is a viable business.

Make sure that when you are developing an action plan that your thinking is clearly outlined and not repeating the same tasks in a different form. Allow someone you trust to give you some feedback. As my personal rule, I do not allow people to criticize my work though I do allow people to critique it. People that criticize only tell you what is wrong with very little or no input on making things better. People who are trusted to speak into your personal and professional life do so with motivation, with your best interest at heart, and it will help you by adding value to what you are doing, and not merely pointing out deficiencies.

"Two things that if you embrace this, you will always have success; always have a coach and/or someone you are accountable too in every key area of your life but also put yourself into a system that creates more knowledge and better habits."

Ayub Fleming

I want to share another idea that is a little different from the typical way that goals are set, and outcomes managed. I have to say that no one system works the same for everyone. Achieving outcomes, focusing on making incremental changes and habits can be very effective. So instead of defining outcomes and working backward through achieving one goal at a time, I want you to consider focusing on the consistent actions and making incremental changes to make huge gains over time.

It is like directing a ship. If you adjust two degrees a day, then your course every day does not change that much but remember the ship is going in a different direction. Over time, though, the ship has radically changed course just by making small changes every day. If you focus on making consistent small changes to adjust coarse toward your outcomes, then it is easier sometimes to focus on making smaller regular changes and gauging the effects then making large sweeping changes trying to achieve goals. Be flexible and find out what works for you.

This idea of regular incremental changes takes much more introspection and paying attention to data than normal. If you start a new workout regimen and do not track your gains and losses, then you are only familiar with the work and not the progress. You do not know whether you are making gains or not just expenditure of energy and undefined pain. The absence of a tracking system can become discouraging.

If you use technology like a "Fitbit" or some device to help track your output and another to track what you are eating, then you can begin to adjust your behavior daily to meet your goals better. Once this has become habitual, then tracking is needed less and less frequently. You merely need to become aware of whether you are staying within your system and continue to stay connected to the results. Another example is if you automate your bill paying and investments then looking at a budget daily may not be needed, tracking your outcomes such as the investments would be the focus. The daily habit of paying bills, saving, and investing is now in a system. Winning and losing have basic formulas but remember you own the strategy and the effort and can only influence the outcomes.

Execute or Get Buried

In Jeffrey E. Garten's 2001 book, *The Mind of the CEO*, he quotes Stephen Case, then Chairman & CEO of America Online, **"A vision without execution is a hallucination."** These profound words found in chapter five, I read about 15 years ago and have never forgotten it since that day. **Execution translates into finishing. A decision to start must be accompanied by a decision to finish!** The best of the best got that way with a few simple rules of execution and common items in their backpacks for the journey. Here are ten items you may find in it:

> **Desire**- It is a burning desire that leads to passion, persistence, and productive outcomes

> **Hard-work**- Beneficial in any endeavor; common among all successful journeys

> **Focus**- The power of focus eliminates a host of potential obstacles; laser focus provides a straight path to the intended target, further neutralizing potential distractions, which belongs in the enemy column

> **Strategy**- No vision can survive without (1) A pre-plan (2) Real-time planning and adjustments when everything goes live; when strategy must face the **test** of real events/reality (3) Re-launching of strategy; you must have an "Evolving Strategic Plan"

Evaluation- Ongoing assessments reveal where you are and therefore where you need to go; it indirectly provides direction; it provides the navigational options to acquire goals

Determination-Tenacity will always give way to knock down or climb over what is in front of you; even if it is you in the way if you are open minded

Endurance-The friend of Desire and cousin of Determination, providing access to longevity

Attitude- Your attitude affects and influences the very heart of your endeavors and those involved; either being positive or slanting toward negativity, attitude positively has influence

Faith- The power that moves mountains and pushes us beyond known limits, giving us access to the outer limits where few are willing to go

Risk- This is how you spell success: RISK. When you are willing to take on calculated and some uncalculated risk, new knowledge is attained, and extraordinary things can happen

Ibaka, "Son of the Congo," was an impressive documentary of one of the basketball players for the Oklahoma Thunder. I would encourage anyone who is serious about success to watch this, as well as, read biographies of the greats in all walks of life. Ibaka grew up without his father and mother for most of his formative years, and by his incredible will, he has made it to the NBA. He routinely goes home and helps his family who still lives in the Congo region of Africa. The reason that he reached these heights is simple; he had the extraordinary level of desire and tenacity that other great people have who succeed in their endeavors. Simply put, he wanted it as bad as the best want it. How bad do you want it?

In one part of the documentary, they asked him how he was so successful coming from this war-torn country, and his answer was simple. He got up at 4:00 am every morning and ran every day whether there was food to eat or not. Hunger did not give him an excuse not to run or to feel sorry for himself. His hunger went much further than his lack of food; he was hungry for success as he defined it. His success did not depend on where he was born but to what levels he could reach. America is "The Land of Opportunity," and why we must defend the dreams of the individual and their right to the pursuit of happiness. Capitalism is an imperfect system, but it produces more dreams than any other in the world.

Rudy

I wanted to include in a part of this chapter to talk about Rudy Ruettiger, number 45, who was a backup defensive lineman for Notre Dame in 1975. Ruettiger was a man of small stature at 5

6" and a 165 lbs., who played among giants. Too small to start or even make the team, Rudy played on the scout team that helped the varsity practice for games. In 1975 under a new coach he was dressed with the varsity team and played against Georgia Tech. In the only game he would ever play after having a legendary work ethic and overcoming dyslexia to get into Notre Dame, he recorded a sack in his first game.

While I cannot cover the entire story, in this book, it was later said by Joe Montana on the Dan Patrick show, "he worked his butt off to get where he was and to do the things that he did." He was one of only two players to be carried off the field by their teammates up to that point. The point I am trying to make is that Rudy did not become the greatest Notre Dame Player or an NFL star, but he was offered a contract by the Kansas City Chiefs. By the way, can you name any other defensive ends that played for Notre Dame and had a movie made after them?

You must become a student of success, and there are no better examples than those by sheer will and determination make the impossible come true. There are books in every library just waiting to be read that will fuel the human spirit. If your library does not have some of these books alongside some of the great literary works, then your library is not yet complete. If you do not own a physical or digital library at all, then we need to have a whole other discussion.

Determination

We think of our enemy as something outside of us. When we watch movies, it is called the antagonist; someone or something that contends with us and causes us problems. It is the object of our fight, for many though, it does not provoke the fight as a response but an insurmountable obstacle that becomes too hard to overcome. It is all the reason we need to quit; our Everest cannot be climbed. That is only true for someone who does not know that others have climbed Everest and that others who have died trying at least died in the site of their greatest dreams. It was once impossible until two men believed that they could. Now I believe the number is over 20,000 people have made it. From the last story, I heard Everest has a trash problem for so many people climbing it.

Yes, it would be hard not to admit that we do have obstacles that seem insurmountable. We do have adversaries in life. They can cause us to shudder at the thought of taking them on; the idea of winning becomes something else entirely. The truth though is there are always both internal and external things that we struggle with that define the experience of our lives. It promotes strength and confidence when we decide to fight them and learn to dominate them. They become the mirrors in which we see ourselves as conquerors or something else. They are opportunities for self-definition that will need self-determination to reveal weaknesses in ourselves but accept the fight anyway. A determination is perfected in areas of weakness not where we are the strongest. It takes determination to fight through our moments and areas of weakness.

It would be harder if it were only a one-sided story. In life there is also a protagonist who is the one who is the opposite of the adversary and is working on our behalf in every area of life, perhaps it is you. In a real sense, if you are working toward the success you desire and yes need the most, you are at times both the adversary, as well as, the angel. God is also your protagonist and advocate. He is ever working on your behalf not just to fulfill your purpose and guide you as you seek him but to assist you in discovering all that you can become and achieve. I heard a man say that before you travel to Florida, you must first believe that it exists.

"Remember, since God has created each of us with a distinct purpose, that distinction automatically crowns us with significance; therefore, decide to live a life of significance and fulfill your purpose to your Heavenly Father's delight."

W.H. Dozier III, Founder, UTake Dominion

The real point is that in life all of us have access to create something with our lives. **Remember, we are creative forces, and another individual cannot hold us back as we accept responsibility for our lives, its conditions, and its directions.** Again, you do not need someone else's approval to succeed in life; you only need your own! Feel free to make some mistakes, but own up to them and decide not to quit until you achieve your goals. You just cannot want to; everyone has desires, you must develop a need to succeed. **I have learned that successful living people close the gap between what they want and what is needed.** For many, they are one in the same. What is the must for you? What is your why?

To be honest, many of us have difficulty believing. It is almost embarrassing to admit, but we fail, and we quit because we do not know how to finish. When we can see no way to get what we desire, it becomes easier to quit, refusing to believe that it will come to pass. In many cases of failure, it is not a lack of information but a lack of faith and hope. Sometimes we do not believe because of a lack of information or understanding that we were created for success. Sometimes it is a lack of the vision of understanding the challenges ahead, but when it gets tough, some lose focus and stop believing that they can. We can simply lack a full measure of perseverance and steadfast faith, although we were created to conquer and win!

The one enemy that truly exists and determines defeat is the person in the mirror. You must see your antagonist like you work out at the gym. The weights are not going to change; they are merely a heavy burden that needs to be moved to make you stronger. To get stronger, you must be willing to lift heavier weights or at least lift differently because the weights are not going to change. There are plenty of stories to tell of people who have overcome outward physical challenges to become stronger people physically, mentally, and made something of their lives. Challenges, if you accept them can cause you to redefine some of the meanings in life. Redefining the meaning of things changes the possible outcomes because we see them differently and our reaction to them; it turns on the lights and illuminates. The process of redefining is not about changing the object but rather the perception in which we see the object. Be determined to accept challenges, educate yourself about them, and learn to face them. Once the light is turned on everything looks different because you can see it for what it is.

"Faith and hope are powerful weapons at your disposal; to fight against all antagonists, including when it's you."

W.H. Dozier III, Founder, UTake Dominion

Dominant Factors

1. **Be convinced of not just what it takes to win but in learning from the losses and failures** to return with the strongest most dominant response possible.

2. **Attitude affects altitude**; when you put in enough years eventually you will want to leave, be fired, or be asked to leave a company or venture, but it is the attitude you depart with that trumps the accomplishment or the falling short of the goals.

3. **You are a creative force; no one else has the credentials to define what you are capable of or who you are, except your Creator and Partner.** In this partnership, interpret and be in the defining business yourself and if you get it wrong, quickly get counsel and decide to change and adjust.

4. **Strategy gives meaning to action** so that it is not random and an unnecessary waste of time, so be specific. If your strategy is not working, ask the questions that give you the facts to adjust, but the key is to constantly evaluate, adopt, and adapt to new information, launch, and execute with renewed processes.

5. **Add courage to your list of skills** and find the overwhelming reason to do the right thing and the thing that is in your best interest, this will help as you take time to think and hone your decision-making abilities.

6. **Have a library of books, articles, and personal notes and devour new information until it becomes habitual**; God's Handbook for Success should be one of the books among your collection.

7. Understand that **desire without strategy becomes a mad scramble, strategy without the willingness to work hard is nothing but notes on paper, and action always meets resistance,** but the staying power of focus and commitment overcomes it.

Chapter 3
No Pain No Pain

"It's so hard to forget pain, but it's even harder to remember sweetness. We have no scar to show for happiness. We learn so little from peace."

Chuck Palahniuk, Diary

Pain, it is not the absence of pleasure, but the presence of something that causes physical or mental discomfort. Pain is also used as a description when someone takes great effort and care to accomplish something. Though we all experience it, we also know that it is very subjective. A reality that only the individual can interpret, but all people can truly empathize because, like love, pain creates a connection.

Champions, such as military personnel, athletes, or business leaders understand the mental and physical investment of pain and have built up a tolerance for it to push through and finish strong. Now retired from his sports career, Ashton Eaton is one of the most decorated decathletes in Olympic history. It was a tremendous moment to watch when Ashton became the Decathlon Champion of the world at the 2016 Summer Olympics. When Ashton was interviewed after the final event, he was asked how he would compete against France's Kevin Mayer. He responded without hesitation, "Honestly, I was thinking, look if this guy goes, if I have to run and put myself in the hospital, that is how hard I will run; so, I was willing to do anything!" After his performances in the last two Olympics, is there any doubt of Ashton's willingness to fight pain to become a great world champion, once again holding the title of the world's greatest athlete?

Reaching your thresholds of pain or pain points in life are the times when you must make vital directional decisions. These are critical moments which dictate your growth measurements; it may seem like an odd topic for some to discuss success and pain in the same conversation, but I think it is odd not to discuss pain while mentioning success. In simple terms, if you believe that success, in part, is the ability to make short-term sacrifices for long-term gains, then you realize that the presence of something that causes physical and mental discomfort is a part of the path to success. Then you realize that the path to true success manifests during times of pain and it is part of the process. In most things in life, there is a dichotomy that exists between two opposites that many times creates balance.

It is also true that success requires some failure, as learning does not require mistakes to be made, but the education process requires a measure of perseverance; learning is the absence of mastery that is gained in practice. Education is an internal increase in thought and awareness, as well as, an external increase in learning through doing. Success requires learning and sacrifice which means embracing the process of education and temporary pain.

In business, like in life, people think erroneously. We think that if we avoid pain, ignore it, and pretend like it does not exist, that there will be no more pain. The person who does this denies part of the reality of their life, as well as, them blazing a journey of success as an entrepreneur or anything else in life. A temporary condition of no pain does not produce a life where there is no pain but embracing and managing the pain that is transformative. Learning to get rid of the unnecessary pain is also what is required for success. Let's discuss pain and its different facets before we determine how to use pain to our advantage.

If you ask how pain is a part of the process of success, I would answer it like this. Pain is a necessary part of the process because, as humans, we require a process that changes us to truly change our circumstances. Let me say this again; if you want a change in your circumstances, you need to be the first to change. The one desiring the change must initiate the process of changing or the transformation; if our circumstances could be changed in any other way, then pain would not be required. Talent can only take you so far in your vocational experience. Preparation, sacrifice, hard-work, and dedication are all elements that provide longevity for your success. If you are serious about dominating in your life, decide, preferably today to look beyond shortcuts and simple answers. Embrace a process in life that is designed for your growth, combined with inspiring constant growth in others, to attain an abundant life rather than just existing.

"We must all suffer one of two things: the pain of discipline or the pain of regret and disappointment."

Jim Rohn,
American Entrepreneur, Author, & Motivational Speaker

When you decide to grow, the pain enters the picture because by definition it is the presence of something that causes physical or mental discomfort which is the natural byproduct of change. I would also say though, that not changing, and having unmet needs, constant failure, and long-range goals never realized are also painful. Therefore, it is false to believe that pain can be avoided. Progressing toward your goals and embracing the pain of the process or quitting and accepting a life of unfilled dreams is as painful and to some more painful.

Remember, there is a time when the process of success becomes something else. The sacrifice is replaced by the expression of the success you seek. A full life no matter what it took to get there is so much better than one that has never accomplished anything. Is it not a life full of giving and success; superior to one that only takes and produces nothing?

If you ever played football at the middle school level or higher, then you may recall that one phrase that will bring shivers down your back. That is two-a-days, or if you had a coach that was a preparedness maniac, you would have three-a-days. It is a regiment during the middle of summer, where almost anywhere in the USA it is blisteringly hot, and you have two or three practices a day during the week to get ready for the season. In the military you have boot camp, and in other sports, you have similar training camps that you know are going to be hard and either you endure getting in shape to prepare for the season or you will quit. There are no champions and certainly no championships without endurance, especially the endurance of pain.

I was told about an interview with the great Randy Couture who was a great wrestler and MMA fighter until well into his forties. He has been called one of the toughest guys in the business. He spoke of 90-minute drills where you and your opponent would go at it for 90 minutes without a break. He recalled several times when he saw grown men; strong men break and begin to cry. The contrast of this was the teammates that did not break that helped the ones that did get through it and get back up. No judgment because they remembered that next time when they are pushed beyond their limits, it might be them next time who could break. Pain is necessary to build great champions because to be the very best you must prepare that way and push until the "line in the sand" has been pushed as well. You have new limits only because you have exceeded the past ones that were created in your mind and physically about what you could and could not do.

"Most people want to avoid pain, and discipline is usually painful."

John C. Maxwell, Author, Professional Speaker, & Pastor

Two-a-days gets you in shape quick, but also eliminates many who think they want to play until the heat and the pain hits them. Having multiple practice sessions are intense; it separates those who are prepared and those who are not. Either way, all of those who pursue success is going to have to work hard and experience pain. By contrast, when you compete and for those few who can call themselves champions, two-a-days is a small sacrifice for the pleasure and honor of being the best.

The person who quits or gets cut from the team may always wonder what could have been, if they had prepared better, worked harder, or were willing to endure more pain to one day experience all that comes along with being among the best. How painful is it to carry unfulfilled dreams, regret, and disappointments your whole life?

"Dare to take chances, lest you leave your talent buried in the ground."

Phil Knight, Co-Founder of Nike, Author, & Philanthropist

Living without regret was the very reason I decided to pursue my dream of becoming a professional baseball player while still in the NFL. It was not exactly the perfect time for me to attempt such a feat and I will never forget my discussion with Stan Allen one day during our sophomore year in college. Stan and I were teammates and captains on our high school football team, and now while I was attending Penn State, he was attending Lock Haven University, proving his worth as the football team's middle linebacker on a partial scholarship as a student-athlete. I was trying to convince Stan to consider transferring to Penn State, aka, "Linebacker U."

Before his injury during our senior season in high school, Stan was highly recruited, and so I was convinced he could play at Penn State. Although the Penn State coaches were open to assessing Stan, upon hearing about his potential plans, the coaching staff at LHU was not interested in losing their star defender and immediately offered him a full scholarship. It was the next conversation and more specifically the words Stan used that I have never forgotten: "It would be a dream come true to play at 'Linebacker U.' I know one day I will regret this decision to stay here and not at least give it a shot, but with what LHU has offered me, I can't turn it down."

Regardless of probable regret, it was his sense of loyalty to his teammates and the LHU coaching staff that would also keep him from a potential transfer. Some five years later, it was that conversation and those words that echoed in my heart when I considered playing baseball. Less than 40 days later, I found myself in a Mets uniform trying out and taking batting practice (bp) off Dwight "Doc" Gooden. A year later when I signed a contract with the Mets, it would mark seven years since my last live game experience in baseball and what an experience it was!

Although Stan may have fleeting moments of regrets, on occasion, it was the ongoing experience of losing seasons at LHU that rewired his mindset. He vowed: "I will never be on another losing team again." Now, having spent decades as a highly known successful corporate executive in the Plumbing Supply space with a few large national companies; he has been winning ever since. Today, he is poised to lead and expand the growth of another multi-million-dollar family-owned, Plumbing Supply company, Northeastern Supply. He is the company's President.

If we can accept the premise that change requires some discomfort despite the best-laid plans, and that great change may require great sacrifices, then pain is an inevitable part of the process. If you understand that to change levels of growth or to add skills to talent, to forge your body like a piece of steel or your mind like a sharp-edged weapon, such change requires a process of sacrifice and hard-work, then pain is a part of the process of success and even more so, for greatness. The next logical conclusion then is to realize that anything that I need, want, and desire also requires a process to get it that will require some level of pain and discomfort to possess it.

Pain is a part of the process that you are either going through or must go through to achieve what is desired. Pain then must be acknowledged, managed, and not just experienced. Is there some pain that should not be tolerated because it might not be a part of the process or may be damaging; absolutely! Pain should not just be tolerated; there are types of pain that serve little or no purpose. If you think of a tooth-ache, that pain is necessary for a short time to tell you something is wrong. If you developed an infection without the pain, then you could see a massive infection that could kill you because you would not know the severity of the situation without the pain. If you first started feeling pain, and you took painkillers to dull the pain but nothing to take care of the infection, then the infection is going to get worse and so is the pain until you cannot bear it and you cannot medicate it.

So, the pain is not the problem, it is the infection that is the problem, and your lack of awareness of its damaging effects long-term. Pain that lingers can be destructive, and like long lingering bad relationships that are painful; they can erode the person's dignity and provide nothing of substance. The experience of pain creates the need for action to resolve it, once a decision is made to resolve the source of the pain, it ceases to provide the purpose it was originally intended, and that is for you to address the problem. So, I do not believe in lingering pain that persists. As you work harder, and elevate, you grow stronger and better at managing the process. There is inevitably more pain coming down the road that needs to be addressed.

At this point, I think we can agree that pain is part of the process and should not be ignored. Pain should be managed by making adjustments and by being sure there is not a systemic problem or something that could be done better. If there are no changes to be made, then you need to be sure that pain keeps you aware of the process you are going through but not destructive by breaking you down emotionally or physically.

During a physical workout, the soreness of your muscles lets you know you had a decent regiment. After a tough workout, there are supplements you can take, as well as, getting the proper amount of rest that will diminish the pain and start the recovery of the muscles and promote growth. If you ignore the pain and continue to train without providing the time and capacity to heal, and administer harder workouts, you ignore the pain to your detriment. Exercise without recovery would do the reverse; cause damage and not growth. The pain may increase until there is injury and that is not productive to what you want to accomplish. It is the same in pursuing better relationships, growing in business, or accomplishing any of your life's goals. The process must be conducive to the desired result.

Trying to avoid pain does not create a situation where there is no pain; it only makes the situation worse. Acknowledging and managing the pain and understanding how to make adjustments to use the pain as a gauge for balance and growth is a more effective tool. Pain is a gauge of imbalance. To find a balance to continue to grow, you should increase information and guidance from someone who has expertise in that area and takes action. Knowledge and action is the only way to counteract pain in a way that is productive. Do not seek pain but understand that it is a part of the process and get ahead of it by devising a strategy to listen to it and manage it. Being real and blatantly honest with yourself or your circumstances, as well as, giving others access, to be honest with you, sets the stage for acknowledgment and proper management to avoid regret, not pain.

"Regret is distasteful, it's not worth the attempt, and at best it leaves an aftertaste!"

> *W.H. Dozier III, Founder, UTake Dominion*

Over 15 years ago I read an article in the Investment Business Daily's, Leaders & Success section; it was dated October 28, 2002. There was a section in the paper about Jeff Bezos and his move from a productive career in investment banking to an entrepreneur during the beginning of the internet boom. When he first decided to leave his position at the firm, D.E. Shaw & Co., as the youngest vice president in the company's history, he did so knowing his move would cost him his bonus check. He juggled the regret of the bonus versus the regret of losing a once-in-a-lifetime opportunity with starting an internet related business. That entrepreneurial move, of course, was the start of Amazon, now the world's largest retailer. After putting a business plan together and raising start-up capital from investors, he and his wife personally packed and shipped out $500,000 worth of books in their first year. As of the latest numbers, today Amazon with over 500,000 employees, had a Trailing Twelve Months (TTM) revenue of over $135 Billion. Obviously, there is no trailing regret to look back at here!

"I imagined myself being 80 years old and looking back on my life, I knew I wouldn't regret missing the bonus. But missing a once-in-a-lifetime opportunity, that would have hurt!"

Jeff Bezos, Founder, Chairman, President, & CEO of Amazon

Acknowledge the Process

As I have said before too many people desire something that they are not willing to pay the price to possess it, own it, and dominate it. I have seen people envious of all types of individuals without asking the one simple question. What did you have to do to get that? I think that is why the Creator guides us not to covet something that our neighbor has. Life has a set of laws for success and failure; we have referred to them as the laws of nature. Now if you learn the patterns of success and apply them with consistency, then you could look forward to a good life. If you want to see what the other side looks like, watch the news, COPS, and other shows that show endless human degradation. If you want to see people chasing their dreams, then watch shows like Shark Tank or The Profit. Learn from their experiences, and become inspired by the entrepreneurial process. TV is not the problem; it can be used as a tool.

I was told a story about a person who wanted to write a book. The book was reviewed, and suggestions were given. They were asked what they wanted to do with the book overall and where they wanted to go from here. The person responded that they wanted to write a book. They had already achieved that; a book had been written, but the problem was that they had not articulated to themselves nor others what they wanted. If I say I just wanted to play football, and had not articulated the outcomes and experiences that I desire, then I'm not fully prepared and determined to meet success. I could have played and stood on the sidelines the entire time and said that I played football. Wanting more out of life, you must be willing to define more, work for it, experience it, and clearly discover the "why" and what you are willing to do to get it.

What they wanted was to be a published author and write several books. When they decided to write a book and accomplished that, they became something else in the process. They became a writer, but if you go further and get published or self-publish, then you are a published author. If you push even further and set your goal to publish several books and become a bestseller, then you are reaching for something that you cannot now obtain. That is how you are changed in the process, by developing goals and acting on dreams that you cannot reach without being changed into something else. That something else requires a process that is transformative. This change will certainly bring things in your life that will cause discomfort and pain, but when you endure and learn from it, it will change you and cause growth.

As Group President of the Government & Education Division for Verizon Business, Chief would often remind members of his team of certain things as he was implementing a new strategy. For some team members, a new approach as to how to conduct business, especially when communicating with customers needed to change. Chief would often make this simple and profound statement to draw a line in the sand, *"If you're not willing to transform you need to transfer!"*

At Penn State, we had good football teams but being good does not always win you a championship. Going to a bowl game was good but going is not winning. Winning a bowl game is good but becoming a National Champion and being the best is something transformative. Start out with the mindset to be a champion and remember there are milestones and goals along the way that must be achieved and the process of achieving them at times is painful and at times blissful but always transformative. There is a process to greatness, study others and find out what it requires.

Acknowledge the Pain

I know of no other singular thing that can cause more pain and disappointment than avoidance. Avoiding what is necessary to not face difficulties in life can cause many mental setbacks or illnesses, as well as, death when taken to the extreme.

"Walk toward the barking dog and embrace good and bad information the same."

Tim Lavender

Beating yourself up no matter where you see yourself, cannot be part of the process. You must consistently be willing to acknowledge that deep inside of you; you have unfulfilled dreams and desires that have yet to be conquered. If that is you, then right now acknowledge where you are. If you have previous disappointments where you may have quit because the pain of achieving it was not worth it at the time or the price was too high to pay, that is okay. It is a choice, but you are reading this book because you want to achieve something different, something more; perhaps you want to learn the secrets of why so few dominate in their lives while so many others fall short.

In the movie, "The Pursuit of Happiness," with Will Smith acting as Chris Gardner in the leading role, there was a beautiful Ferrari parked in front of an office building where he wanted a job because he desperately needed to provide for his son. When he saw the owner get out of his car, he said," I only have one question for you, where do you work and what do you do?" That is a person who understood that there is a process to get from where you are to where you need and want to be, but you must be conscious of the process. Wishing you had something does not give you a clear path to getting it. Finding the answer to what is required of you to achieve your desires is getting the right information. You then must do whatever it takes and as long as it takes to dominate your desires and achieve your dreams. I am sure either Will Smith or Chris Gardner could explain in detail what pain they endured thus far to capture their dreams and aspirations.

In the 2015 NBA draft, I heard one of the commentators ask one of the top picks what he thought about the draft? Without hesitation, the kid answered, "It made me think about all those hours in the gym before and after practice, all the shoot-arounds before the games. I am enjoying it, but I think about all the work that it took to get here." That is the answer of a champion. That is the same answer that a Larry Bird, Magic Johnson, Michael Jordan, or many other great athletes would have given. You must acknowledge the process is and will be painful; when you do, settle your mind on what must be done. Then you are ready to take your life to and thru the next level.

Remember Michael Jordan's reflection on the game in a commercial was that he made it look too easy. He missed more shots than he made. There were many long practices and sacrifices that dictated the level of his performance. That is what should always be remembered.

Manage the Process

If you are going to achieve anything extraordinary in life, it is vital you first understand what your talents are. If you have never taken assessment tests, then I encourage you to take more than one to determine certain traits you have, so you can either use that to your advantage or work on certain areas to grow. Natural talent to do something without much effort is what you are born with; skill sets to reach a master status is acquired through increased information and by implementing good solid practice habits. Remember **extra** requires **extra**, so if you desire **extraordinary** results, you must have **extraordinary** practice habits.

Managing that process is doing it intentionally and on a regular basis to determine what you need, how you are going to get it, followed by acquiring it. These principles are universal to both your professional and your private life. Think about everything you are doing or experiencing, including some of your relationships; assess not only what it is now, but what it may become in the future and if you have the talent and core skills needed to get there. If it's a relationship, are both people investing in themselves and each other to become something that is the realization of the potential of the relationship?

The process of change always starts with collecting information. Information brings awareness that there is greater potential than what currently exists and there is a process to get there. A deeper awareness should be followed up by what it is that I must do, understanding the end goal is important to you achieving it. I am sure by now you have read many articles or books espousing the need to set goals and different methods to make sure they are relevant, timely, and specific. Goal setting is the process of articulating what you desire, and so is praying and engaging your intuition and imagination to paint a verbal picture of what you desire. You are painting with images to develop the belief system to achieve what you have not yet achieved; it is called faith. Fear operates in the same manner, just used to develop the opposite effect. Faith believes and acts as if you can or will, and fear believes and acts on why you cannot and will not.

When Chief went to his first post-college interview for a promotion, he recalls being underdressed and slightly overwhelmed. On top of that, it did not help that the woman conducting the interview told him that not only would he not get the position, but he would never amount to anything in his life. Can you imagine that? Well, from that day, he decided he had collected enough information and immediately started to develop a process to change some things.

The first step to transformation began with attaining his MBA from Penn State's Smeal School of Business. Decades later Chief went on to sit in several executive leadership positions with companies within the Telecommunications, IT, and Data Analytics sectors, putting him in a position where he has interviewed hundreds of candidates for professional positions. In 2015 he left the corporate scene to venture out as an entrepreneur with a partner. Their company, Centennial Technologies, a small growing multi-million-dollar enterprise just recently surpassed 100 million in contracts. Transform or transfer, right?

Once you have started gathering information and break that down into attainable goals, then it is time to take action and have a process by which you can evaluate your results. Taking action is proof that you believe what you say you believe and have the desire to achieve it but learning to set proper goals and manage them is where action turns into results. You must be able to evaluate what you are doing to see if you are effective. If the time is too long or the results to minuscule, then you must adjust so that the results at least meet the effort if not exceed them.

Everyone needs to attempt different methods until you find what works best for you. I have seen people use vision boards, journaling, and other methods to basically engage their imagination and then connect their actions to the end desired result. No matter what methods you use to get there, the point is you must engage a system of thought and action to get there.

Managing the Pain

Managing pain is a little different and requires an adequate level of a delicacy because too much pain or the wrong kind of pain both makes you aware of something being wrong that may need to be repaired. Sustained pain without rest and recovery means things will break sooner or later and cause sometimes permanent damage to you, your business or personal relationships. Chronic pain almost always is never connected to purpose but deeper more serious systemic problems. Dr. Jim Loeher wrote a book called *Toughness Training for Life* which explored some of the top athletes and why they were successful. Among many of his discoveries was that to the level that you exert yourself over long periods of time, you had to have an equal amount of relaxation or recovery, not necessarily as far as equal time but equal levels of exertion and recovery. I encourage you to read some of his books; it may help you hone your performance game.

"Bad things do happen; how I respond to them defines my character and the quality of my life. I can choose to sit in perpetual sadness, immobilized by the gravity of my loss, or I can choose to rise from the pain and treasure the most precious gift I have - life itself."

Walter Anderson, German Writer

Managing the pain means you first listen to it and determine whether it is a good pain or bad pain. When you exercise, this good pain in the body is caused by lactic acid in the muscles which create soreness. There is also bad pain and swollen joints that may occur by overtraining that requires rest or some therapy. Managing pain means developing a strategy of heavier and heavier loads of monitored exertion but coupled then, with moments equal to the exertion in recovery. I often remind my son that we can rest or play hard after we have spent the necessary time and effort working hard. Properly managing this combined balance of exertion and recovery promotes constant growth. Constant pain over time loses all semblance of meaning.

Managing the pain sometimes is not as simple as having a strategy to grow; sometimes the pain can come from unexpected places and seemingly out of nowhere. Regardless, avoidance is never the answer, so at times you may need to

engage a process that is unfamiliar to you like journaling or engaging a counselor or mentor to listen and help you sort through your feelings, fears, or motives. Managing pain cannot be done in a vacuum you have to have some methodology for dealing with the increased load that you are placing upon yourself. Recovery and rest is only a part of what is needed; in some cases, there is a need for more extreme measures. That is why I strongly support when it is necessary, to seek a professional to assist in working through the process.

I do not believe in self-medication as far as taking pills, alcohol, drugs or doing illicit things to avoid or dull the pain. Learning to face things head on and do the difficult things is hard at times, no doubt about it, but you must face it, you must accept the fact that success looks glamorous from a distance, but it takes hard-work to achieve. Any other message is not realistic and, in my opinion, delusional. Too many lives are destroyed by people every day looking for some other way to success rather than preparation and hard-work in the long haul. Character and making the right decisions are often replaced with getting rich quick strategies and schemes that cost this country and individuals billions of dollars in non-productive time, identity theft, and other crimes that are aimed at taking away something someone else has earned.

Remember, the key to your success is seeking deeper awareness of yourself and your business. A new level is obtained by asking deeper questions, gaining information, making plans, and executing on them. Do not avoid the inevitable pain and discomfort, grow through it, and learn to manage it until it has no purpose and is replaced by something of greater benefit to your life. Here is a fitting quote used by Dr. Eric Thomas and several others, and credited to Lance Armstrong:

"Pain is temporary. It may last a minute, or an hour, or a day, or a year, but eventually it will subside, and something else will take its place. If I quit, however, it lasts forever."

Dominant Factors

1. **Avoidance is not a management strategy and leads to the pain of a different form**; always **"avoid avoidance" as a strategy** and take the calculated risk so that your talent will not end up buried with you in the ground unfulfilled.

2. **There is a certain level of pain that is required for the journey** because you essentially must change and become something else in the process to accomplish more.

3. **There are processes that lead to failure, and there are processes that lead to success**; it is vital to diligently seek the answer to what the process is for what you want and what obtaining it requires.

4. **Partner with experienced, transformative, and accomplished individuals** who have attained results relevant to where you desire to be; conduct research, consistently read books, and take courses to get informative answers.

5. **Solemnly prepare for the heavier load** by having a coping mechanism in place and not self-medication, so that you grow through the process healthy without dropping and breaking it.

6. **The desire for extraordinary results is preceded by extraordinary practice habits; extra requires extra.**

7. **Give yourself permission to be blatantly honest with yourself or your circumstances and give others access to do the same,** which will lead to the avoidance of regret, not pain.

Chapter 4

Every Day is Game Day

"Time management is an oxymoron. Time is beyond our control, and the clock keeps ticking regardless of how we lead our lives. Priority management is the answer to maximizing the time we have."

John C. Maxwell, Author, Professional Speaker, & Pastor

Have you ever experienced what happens in the atmosphere of a jammed packed stadium or arena while watching athletes and performers get "hyped" inside or just outside the tunnel with great anticipation? For the one performing, there is a vast difference between an empty facility during practice and one with thousands or tens of thousands of crazed fans on Game Day. There is something special that happens when our motivation is heightened.

What causes the difference between the two scenarios? It is a little hormone called Adrenaline! There is no comparison to when we go live with that crowd in the midst, and it is time to give the performance of a lifetime! I have had the pleasure of being clothed as a performer and a fan, but the performer wins out for me. When you experience hearing the entire student section at Beaver Stadium chanting your name in unison after a "big" play, you will understand perfectly; it sends chills up and down your spine.

"I'm a competitive person. Business is a much more competitive sport than any real sport. It's 24x7x365. I'm a business adrenaline junky."

Mark Cuban, American Entrepreneur, Investor, Author, Television Personality, & Philanthropist

I wanted to include this chapter about a game day because life is a game you only play once. In that sense, we are not looking forward to the next levels or accomplishing the next achievement to start living; this is it. Many have hoped and looked, but there is no grand reset button. You must live life as if it is your last "game" day after day. This means that it is the last time you will have this day and although keeping score in practice, as well as, in a highly competitive game is a prudent measure, in life it is not the same. It is the results on game day that are recorded and go into the history books. Now imagine what might be accomplished by having a game day like focus and execution every day.

In our personal and professional lives, we deal with challenges every day. Life should be balanced in a fashion where practice or preparation has its place and must be scored one way, and the thrill of competition or punctuated moments of achievement, should be enjoyed and scored another way. The results are not always successful because in competition someone is going to lose or at best tie. The moment of breaking through a threshold in business by launching a new ad, product, or service sometimes ends in misery and defeat, with someone, wondering why or how it did not work. We can expect some unsuccessful outcomes in life, depending on how you define them, they are opportunities to learn, not to enjoy.

"There are times you are in the process, and there are times that you must produce. There is preparation, and there is performance."

Unknown

I want to take a moment and share something about my father. My father is a highly motivated and a very competitive person; let me state that another way, he is extremely competitive, and he is not hesitant to let you know with his reactions. Without question, he was the most inspiring coach I ever had as a youngster and beyond. He is a no-nonsense, get it done type person who never backs down or accepts anything less than your best or an expression of excellence. He is a person who is consistent because he lives from a state of character and not situational ethics or emotion. His life is an expression of who he is on the deepest level.

Like many hard-working individuals, when he retired from his last position, the company needed to consider hiring two or three different individuals to perform all his duties and responsibilities. To date, the company is still trying to find the right mix of individuals to cover his areas of responsibilities. My mother does not believe they will ever find anyone or any group to match the output but perhaps when they automate the process; it will match my father's production. We should all strive for that level of service no matter what our station is in life or pursuits. The idea is not perfection or production but a service that creates value every day, all day.

My father gave me an example through his life that competition was healthy. He was not a doting father, who constantly told me that he loved me, but he was a solid man who cared deeply and would never back down. He consistently let me know that I was great and that he loved me through the things he did. His positive reinforcements allowed me to pursue life with domination in mind, not only being a fierce competitor, but realizing that whether it is today or tomorrow, winning must be a non-negotiable result. I recognize that many people do not have that type of father and too many children today do not know their fathers. I want to be clear about this, no matter the circumstance, you cannot as an adult, take the role of a victim. You must take responsibility, not the blame for your condition but your reaction to it is paramount to your future. No matter how you got here, take responsibility for where you are going. Tim Johnson, a former NFL player, aka Pastor Johnson, grew up without any real knowledge of his father to this day, yet he decided he was not going to carry the title of another victim. He decided some time ago to be a great man within his household as a husband and a father. He loves and oversees the members of his church in the same manner, with love and adoration. His decision, along with his wife of 30 plus years to live an overcoming life has also been transferred to his kids. As my father provided an example for me, so Tim does for his kids.

As I got older, looking through the glass pane of competition, it became clearer with each test, I understood its deeper meaning. I was not competing so much against others as I was with myself in becoming the best I could be and not merely performing for accolades. I never felt that I had to perform to gain my father's love. I knew he loved me; competition was merely an opportunity for me to prove who I was. I had to prove him right; more so for myself. Remember I had the slight physical challenge, but I refused to let it define me because both my parents would not let it define me. Surround yourself with people who will call not because of the mistakes you have made but will call you based on your future possibilities. Those are the ones you need on the bus. The others are on the treadmill exerting energy, with plenty of movement, but going nowhere.

"I have been impressed with the urgency of doing. Knowing is not enough; we must apply. Being willing is not enough; we must do."

Leonardo Da Vinci, Painter, Sculptor, Architect, Inventor, Military Engineer & Draftsman

The philosophy of self-competition became very clear to me when I went back to college for the second time to finish my degree. I remember looking at the younger kids in the class and realizing they were missing a connection between what they were studying and a real-life example of what purpose this knowledge could have for them or how it could be applied. Most of them were learning for the sake of grades because someone told them to and not because higher learning had a real-life application.

I wanted to compete for the highest grade in the class because I understood the deeper meaning of being there, staying on the grind, and getting it done. I understood what that would mean for life moving forward beyond that classroom. I was not in competition with them, but myself as school became another chance to prove what I already believed about myself.

"Your fiercest competition is someone very familiar to you; it's the one staring back at you in the mirror; on earth, victory over that person, how they think, and how they imagine themselves to be, is your greatest victory." Decide to Dominate!

W.H. Dozier III, Founder, UTake Dominion

Prepare for Success

Preparation almost seems like it does not need to be said, you must perform as if everyday matters. The reason is once every day is expensed and invested, it is gone, and only the results or lack thereof is the dividend that is paid. There are no do-overs in life, not days, not hours, not seconds, nor actions. I will say it again; there are no do-overs in life. Fair or not this is game day and at the stroke of midnight, that day became yesterday, history without the chance to add to it or take away from it. It is what it is. String enough of them together, and that is what puts the numbers on the scoreboard that takes a tally for both winning and losing.

As a child, when I had to wear a corrective bar attached to my shoes, it was not to walk, but to correct the deformity of my legs that I was born with. My parents were told that I would not be able to play sports. Seeing the tenacious modeled behavior of my mother and father when they did not accept this as my fate, then neither did I. With all that they endured and needed to overcome, even as teenagers, I would have no choice but to do the same with my condition, as a young child. I often cried myself to sleep and the only time I could take the corrective bar off was when I had to take a bath. I had to sleep with the corrective bar, to say the least, that was difficult as a small child. I had to grow to accept that challenge, but also find a way to overcome it. I had no intention of this becoming a permanent condition.

There are important moments when overcoming obstacles and shortcomings in life are the choices we must make. You cannot choose your immediate family or in many cases your boss or your co-workers, so the playing field is not always what you choose but often the hand you are dealt. In most cases, who you marry, who your peers and mentors are, are your choices to make and by far can become the most important choices of your life. How you interact with all these people and how you react to all the circumstances of your life is your choice and will determine the quality of the journey that you will experience, as well as, stops along the way.

The basis of preparing for a successful journey begins by dealing with you first; yes, the person in the mirror. It is hard to dominate when you are broken, or there are matters in your psyche that are not conducive to enduring challenges or perpetual success. There is a tremendous amount of talent that has not yet been realized, and unfortunately, with many people, it never will. It is not as simple as saying that most successful living people have overcome their shortcomings and most less productive people have not, but it is still true. Whether in business, athletics, those born with disabilities, or people who must face debilitating diseases, overcoming the challenge that is set before us is a turning point and it is either an opportunity for a continued journey of success or failure.

Think about it in your own life or those you have observed from a distance and look how some of the strongest, most talented or popular are merely a flash in the pan. Look at how many people fall short of making the transition into something else when they know that everything changes and nothing in this life truly stays the same. Instead, they are unrealistically holding on as if some things will last forever. The good news is preparing for the highest state of success always starts with you. It starts with committing to a strategy of personal development by adding new information, skills, mentors, and opportunities to create constant change and growth in your life.

That is what Bob Peruzzi did after he graduated from New York University with his MBA in Finance and Accounting. While he started his career in finance on Wall Street, Peruzzi was working with UBS as a Stock Analyst, covering consumer finance when he decided it was time to make an aggressive career move.

Instead of analyzing companies, he wanted to drive business opportunities for companies in the volatile and risky world of start-ups. Eventually, he did just that, and after a two-year stint with RecycleBank, Peruzzi departed from the company with his mentor and Chief Financial Officer (CFO) to bolster the finance department at LivingSocial.

As LivingSocial's VP of Finance & Global Planning for three and a half years, Peruzzi's planning would provide the path for the company's growth from operating in 3 countries to 29, with the total number of employees increasing from about 400 to over 4,000. Peruzzi's leadership and lessons learned from both successes and failures would undoubtedly prove to be valuable assets, full of rich experiences, preparing him for his next leadership role. Groupon would later purchase LivingSocial at a heavy discount, two years after Peruzzi departed for Plated.

I am an avid watcher of the program Shark Tank, which recently aired a show to give viewers an update on the company, Plated; a start-up of over five years, the company struck a deal with Mark Cuban on the show. Unfortunately, the deal with Cuban would not come to fruition, and some months later, Plated would receive funding from Kevin O'Leary. When Plated Founders began searching for the ideal CFO for their fast-growing company, they hired a recruiting firm to make sure they got it right.

Plated is a young and growing company that needed a finance leader who keenly understood the "venture-backed" world of start-ups and the hyper-growth management style. The kind of leadership that could direct and guide the finance organization with clear precision. The sharp Plated Founders and Harvard Business School alum, Nick Taranto, and Josh Hix selected

Bob Peruzzi as their CFO to leverage his expertise as Plated continues to build a world-class food company.

To further enhance its global strategic plan, Plated recently inked a partnership deal with Albertsons; it could be said that the Jeff Bezos and Amazon buyout of Whole Foods helped to set the stage and triggered Albertsons' buyout of Plated which was announced within weeks of Amazon's purchase of Whole Foods. The rumored $300 Million transaction now gives Plated the top position among Shark Tank's success stories.

Peruzzi's inner-directed approach and decision to move from Wall Street to leading start-up companies proved to be an intelligent modification in his career direction; with renewed passion, he is not providing hyper-growth expertise for companies alone, but a solid path for personal growth as well.

As you are becoming more inner-directed, and you realize that you are the greatest catalyst for growth, and not your jobs or external things, this awareness is the beginning of being prepared for a truly successful journey. By inner-directed, I mean by the thoughts and internal strength of character and integrity versus being externally influenced and more directed by circumstances. We are kings and queens over our circumstances and not subject to the circumstances. Commitment and constant action are the keys to getting the best out of any long-term investment.

I want to highlight one point about being inner-directed, and that is to stay connected to your "why." Your why is the focus or object that drives you to want to be on a successful road in the first place. Keeping your why in front of you will motivate you when it is tough. Some people think about success with their "why" only associated with material things and shallow experiences. We can have a deeper outlook on life. It is not that I do not like nice things, I do, but I do not aspire for acquisition and pleasure as goals alone.

Successful real estate giant and entrepreneur, Thomas Kyrus, aka Uncle Kyrus, now in his eighties, still to this day has a dual mission and purpose to be successful in life by always improving himself and those he interacts. Because of this dual mission, he has spent a lifetime improving himself, helping people, and generating multiple millions of dollars for his entire Greek family via various business transactions. For anyone who has had the pleasure to speak with or work with Uncle Kyrus, it is not long before he asks you that sincere and simple question: "How can I help you?" He is most excited about the people he can assist versus the net worth he has amassed.

Preparation

Preparation starts before you put your hands to any plow, even when dealing with the smallest of matters. Getting into the habit of planning and managing your preparations down to smallest detail is important. The more you prepare, the better you practice, which means the better you perform. The better you can perform in any situation, the more you mitigate or eliminate risk. I have never met anyone who did not manage their time and resources appropriately and moved in a successful direction consistently over a long period. Properly managing resources begins to secure a solid foundation that charts a roadmap with some excellent stops.

"The will to win is important, but the will to prepare is vital."

Joe Paterno, Legendary College Football Coach

In preparing, you have lists of milestones and smaller things to accomplish, all leading back to the steps of creating the vision, through to, managing tasks, and accomplishing the goals. What you must have is a commitment to a process of managing your focus, energy, and resources. That commitment to the process elevates your ability to develop habits at a detailed level. There will be times when you do not feel like doing it, or you may not be a detailed person by nature, but any improvement in this area is still an improvement. Commitment to be more detailed and managing details allows you to be more aware of, and consciously involved in where you are putting your focus. In the book, *The Power of Focus,* written by authors Jack Canfield, Mark Victor Hansen, and Les Hewitt, we read and understand the simple idea that successful living people have successful habits; therefore, where we decide to put our focus and develop our habits determines all future experiences and destiny points.

"Where your focus goes so does energy, resources, and ultimately your life."

Bethan Christopher, Speaker, Author, & Life Coach

The strategy also plays a vitally important role. The strategy or having strategic values, focus, planning, and evaluation is a favorite area of mine. Once you begin to focus, you then must be sure you are focusing on the right things and moving in the right direction. Having the right strategy is obviously more important than having a strategy. Some people are flat out committed to processes without questioning the results. They see they are not getting the results they desire but are unwilling to change the strategy. You need a system to evaluate the results against your goals to determine if the strategy is working. If you are not achieving your goals and moving toward creating the vision, then something is not working. If you prepare for each day with tasks to act upon to complete the goals, which in turn, complete the vision, then there must be systems of evaluating the results to determine if you are on the right track. If you are not achieving your goals, be keenly aware it may be time to review and consider changing some elements of the strategy, if not a complete overhaul.

In the evaluation process, it may become obvious what the problem is; however, sometimes it is more complex, and you may have to ask more questions and go down the rabbit hole to find out what the truth is. You must get down to the common denominator of your problems and then focus on changing or removing it, so that you can achieve different results. One hint; start with yourself or allow someone else to assess the results, identify your issues, and suggest solutions.

Evaluating processes, much like managing a company, is about getting good consistent intelligence about where things are, how far the business has come, or how close you have come to accomplishing your goals. Where are you with changes or adjustments that need to be made to react to the expansion and/or contraction of the business cycle or the event? Process management is the same in your personal life as it is in your professional life. You must develop an "if-then or what-if" model of life. Your behavior subconsciously is done a certain way because you are predicting the results you will get. You do what you think works for you even if that is not true; it reflects your prediction that in part controls your behavior. Predictions are based on your paradigm that is based on how you interpreted the events of your life and your reaction to them.

One of the next things that you must build into your model is a methodology of collecting and tracking information. I cannot overemphasize the importance of knowing your numbers. Knowing the analytics is a must. If you do not know the facts, what are you using to make decisions? Any good manager in any organization must know where the organization is, in perspective to its goals at all times. You should be gathering feedback on your career and the value you create on your job or in your business for its customers. You should adopt this model in every major area of your life. Do not run from feedback; design it into your life as part of evaluating whether you are getting the results you want.

Make sure it is quality feedback and not pure criticism or random information to shut you up. Most large organizations have an evaluation program conducted every six months. As a husband and dad, I decided I wanted to hear from my wife and kids regarding how I was doing in my dual role. I had the opportunity to get some interesting feedback and most importantly began to design a plan to correct the areas where I needed to get better. Whether an individual or team of people, when we decide to welcome real evaluation from those we decide to trust, it empowers us to accomplish great things.

"Greater wisdom is often derived or rooted from moments of accepting wise correction and guidance."

W.H. Dozier III, Founder, UTake Dominion

I had a conversation with someone recently about putting together and managing the team that helps them build their life and their business. Human interaction is complicated. Human decision making is also complicated. Sometimes we do things that are not in our best interest because feelings can drive us beyond logic. Developing a team must be done with logic and emotion to some degree. On a team, focused on professional success or personal development and growth, everyone must serve a purpose and have somewhat of a defined role. I say, team, because even in your life you cannot do it by yourself.

If you do not have a team, you are still in the starting gate no matter what you have achieved to this point. Until you form a team of people, you are not ready for the next levels. You must separate people that you want to have an emotional connection with you versus those who assist you in making the business or your life work. It is the difference between learning to love some people even though they are dysfunctional and intentionally choosing others who are your peers and can help you accomplish your life goals. The people you love, but do not engage, may not be the people who help you achieve in life or business that you have desired to create. Having the courage to define and recognize the difference and interact with each that way is just that; courageous.

Success and failure are at times processes of doing small tedious tasks the right or wrong way every day that helps you achieve what you desire or what you do not desire. Success is never an event. It is an unfolding process of small actions that may seem insignificant, but they lead up to a person of character or not, good health or not, or a person who is prepared to succeed in business and life or not. As you evaluate what you have achieved up to this point and what new goals are yet to be achieved, think about what process you have consciously or subconsciously followed to get here and what you must be willing to change to get to deeper and higher levels of success. If the process is flawed, so will be the results. Keep honing and re-defining the process based on results, and you will see that change and laser-like focus brings greater results. Becoming aware of the process helps you to do two things; manage the success and better manage the mental discomfort or pain to produce it, potentially on a perpetual basis.

"A man must be big enough to admit his mistakes, smart enough to profit from them, and strong enough to correct them."

John C Maxwell, Author, Professional Speaker, & Pastor

Never to kid ourselves about being great, it takes talent, hard-work, and sacrifice. If you think you will become the next great corporate executive leader or the next champion entrepreneur in any endeavor but without hard work and taking your lumps, guess again. The process is there to refine you, expand your capabilities, and to establish you with a caliber of excellence. Entrepreneurs whether CEO's, executive management, top salespeople, or great athletes become aware of the numerous sacrifices and hard-work that it takes for success. There is a process that requires that you do something with your talent and time. Learn something, acquire new skills, and develop inner toughness so that at the end of the process you are someone destined to possess or do something different, something greater. "Wild Bill" is a good example of an intense learning regiment and inner toughness applied every day. In 1984 I shared plenty of highlighted moments and high fives with Bill Emerson, aka "Wild Bill," one of our team captains on the Penn State football team. About 20 years after Bill's graduation, we shared a conversation about his position as the

CEO of Quicken Loans; when I asked him how he rose to the top position after starting out as a Mortgage Banker, his answer was simple:

"From day one I was prepared, and committed to showing up each day ready to work harder than anyone else, with the thirst for knowledge to learn everything I needed to know to be the best I could be, and nine years later to the day, I joined the company, I became the CEO."

Bill Emerson, Vice Chairman, Quicken Loans and Rock Holdings

There is no doubt that every day is game day for Bill and since he has been at the helm, Quicken Loans has been among the top 30 US companies the past 14 consecutive years. He was the CEO for 15 years and leaves the position with Quicken Loans ranked #10 on Fortune magazine's annual "100 Best Companies to Work For" list in 2017. From 2013 to 2017, it closed on more than $400 billion of mortgage volume. That is no surprise given Bill's level of commitment to the 17,000 employees, many of them, have his cell phone number. Now that's commitment! He is now the Vice Chairman of Rock Holdings, Inc, the parent company of Quicken Loans which also has nearly 100 of Dan Gilbert's Family of Companies.

Every success requires a process that changes you, and prepares you for a higher dimension of success. Short change this and when the opportunity arrives you will not be prepared, and worse yet, you may not be remembered for your successes but mediocrity or as an epic failure. Here is a thought on hiring talented people who are unconcerned with change.

"The first thing is to hang on to everybody who is talented, who is entrepreneurial, who wants to make an impact and a change and start attracting ones."

Dan Gilbert, Founder & Chairman of Rock Ventures and Quicken Loans Inc., Owner Cleveland Cavs

Blinded by the Lights

I have had the opportunity to play in many lit stadiums in my athletic career. I am now playing under a different set of lights in my business career and now the hot lights of a professional speaker and author. Now, as it was then, I was never doubtful about performing in front of the crowds because I knew that I was prepared for it and I would bring with me that tenacious and unrelenting mindset to win, as well as, creating winning environments for those that I can inspire.

Now with almost 30 post-college years under my belt, I am in my early 50's, and although some of the passion has been tempered with experience, it has not diminished. I have met a lot of people along the way who wished for the burning night lights under which to perform, but few superstars emerge claiming a piece of history in which to be remembered. I think that for most it is not only the performance and competition that they desire but the accolades and rewards of being victorious.

If you want the rewards without the fight and its preparation, then you are not serious about dominating or winning. Every entrepreneur hunts, corporate leaders and certainly leaders of a publicly owned company face the financial markets, while competitors are knocking on the door every day to gain market share. Preparing for practice is the beginning so that you get the best out of each session in preparation for the game. Not every game is the big game, but every game counts.

You prepare for competition knowing that at some point your product, your service, and your job will be tested by adversity; it is part of the champion's creed. You do not necessarily wish for it, but you know it is coming and you prepare for facing the competition every day. Before you put rubbing alcohol on a wound, you tell yourself that it is going to hurt and to brace for the pain. The cleansing solution has its purpose, and it may be painful but most of the time it does not hurt as much as we think, and the pain is soon over.

Contrast this pain with what a growing infection would do to your body without treating it. That is what infections are doing to your personal life and business if you have chosen not to deal with the pain. There may be people you need to stop associating with, but it is hard; people you need to fire from your life, but it is a difficult hurdle. The thing is, make sure you are not the one who needs to be disassociated with or fired and if you happen to be the one in charge, be sure you examine yourself before firing someone else. Be willing to put your tactics on trial first.

"Success is when Opportunity meets Preparation."

Zig Ziglar, American Author, Salesman, and
Motivational Speaker

If you embrace preparation and manage the pain when opportunity knocks, and it is time to perform, then you will not be blinded by the bright lights. You will be challenged by some form of fear of the unknown and either you will perform, or you will not. People remember those who overcome market pressure and bring new products to bear that keep the customers excited about the company. Investors remember people who make good decisions with their money and their calculated predictions of return on investment ring true through sound business decisions. We remember the athlete who does the impossible to win, as well as, live vicariously through them, and say "man, how did he do that." We remember the persons with physical limitations that warm our hearts as champions emerge by overcoming those limitations.

Our dispassionate disdain for the person who continues to lose in life and become a burden on society when they underperform, are quickly forgotten even as we wince with compassion. We move on because of those who overcome and conquer; those we heap praise and almost worship as heroes.

Remember desire alone or talent alone means nothing; it is only successful execution that is admired and cherished.

Developing a mentality like many champions who understand that every day is performance day, it is par for the course. You must have prepared for the next day before it arrives. When you wake up late, cannot find your material, and your presentation is not ready, or if you have not staffed properly that day, game, or endeavor, you are stacking the odds against yourself, when it is expected of you to win. You barely squeak by on a day that should have meant making a decisive advancement toward your goal rather than simply surviving.

You get hyped for the opportunity because you think about the long-term goals that require short-term sacrifices. You expect the heat of the spotlight because you walked the field in your mind before game day, went over every play, and executed them with precision. Make no mistake if your goals are so small that obtaining them means no change in your life, then you are spending your life's energy trying to light a 40-watt bulb. Dream bigger, accept the challenges, and live brighter. Let your life look like the bat signal calling champions to follow.

"Adversity causes some men to break; others to break records."

William Arthur Ward, American Author

Become a Perpetual Weed

I once heard someone give a great analogy about domination. The speaker gave the example of the orchid as one of the most beautiful flowers, yet it is very sensitive to its elements. The orchid, like many great flowers, only flourishes in certain conditions, change the conditions and it will die. However, in contrast to the orchid, the weed dominates no matter the condition and fights for its position until it completely takes over. It does not ask for space nor does it ask how large it can grow. The weed always grows until it reaches its full capacity. The weed chokes out the competition with ruthless precision.

Do not start to set your mindset to be competitive with anything outside of yourself. Always set your goals to grow as far as you can, even after you dominate the segment in your business, school, or anything else. Be tenacious like the weed and completely take over. Remember, it is your birthright to do so! Do not worry about the cold, heat, sunshine, rain, drought, or anything, just keep growing and being resilient until you dominate. Orchids like people want or feel the need to be liked and beautiful and there is nothing wrong with that. Many will enjoy and love the orchid. They will protect its beauty and remember it through great paintings and pictures. The weed, however, is never satisfied and grows until it finds its full potential. It does not ask for permission, and it may not even provide anything useful to anyone else, but the weed feeds its purpose, and asks permission from no one. Be a perpetual weed and prepare to dominate consistently and well beyond your intended goals.

"When you hit your target successfully, realize it's a success point but also a platform for something greater; a portal to potentially host more opportunities for you, those standing with you today, and for those to come."

"Make your quest a perpetuated one; one that continues and leaves a legacy, and eventually ushers you into eternity with a bountiful number of rewards there awaiting. This, of course, only matters when you live and operate in such a way knowing that it's the Most High God keeping the score."

W.H. Dozier III, Founder, UTake Dominion

You Can't Stop a Train

I have been fortunate enough to participate and work for or with some extraordinary teams and companies. Teams of people gathered together for one cause; to become the ultimate champion. I gravitate toward people who are like-minded and achieve at the highest level. There is something special about competitive people who can focus on greatness, while performing under the mandate to win. After retiring from my athletic career, I made my home in Orlando, FL. While there, my workout partner was one of those champion-minded individuals; he also happened to be my doctor.

"Still confidence gives you a mindset to progress, undaunted of risk and having a resolve to perform with a reckless abandonment that often brings amazing results; champions aren't intimidated nor impressed with the height or intensity of the situation. They embrace the opportunity, keep a calmed spirit, and just perform."

W.H. Dozier III, Founder, UTake Dominion

Dr. Don Colbert is no ordinary doctor. His practice has patients from all over the world. He is among the few health professionals that are both an MD and a Nutritionist; he has written over 40 books with more to come. He is a great example of what happens when you invest your God-given talents, abilities, gifts, and skills (TAGS) and apply yourself to develop and master the potential of your skill. On several occasions, I would head to his house after our workout, where his wife, Mary would prepare one of her incredible chicken dishes. Of course, it was a very healthy dish, which did not include dessert on most occasions. Now do not be fooled, Mary manages their home life, business, and ministry, and she is also an incredible speaker with a powerful message, and a recent author. An incredible couple, but something strange and amazing would occur after visiting their house and breaking bread. After dinner, while returning home, I always felt charged up and invigorated, as if I had just returned from listening to a motivational speaker. What became more interesting was there was no real defined inspirational dialog, just spending time with friends and a champion-minded couple who had a strong sense of purpose. My reaction became consistent; when I would leave their home, I always had the sense that I was **unstoppable, like a moving train**. I recently had breakfast with them, and we had a chance to catch up and talk about *The Keto Zone*, Dr. Colbert's new book. Can you guess how I felt on my way home? All aboard; this train is on the move!

As I look back to some of the teams that I have played for, both in baseball and football in college and professionally, the one thing that I learned is that winning boiled down to intense preparation. Yes, it was preparation at the highest level, and when it is time to perform, it is followed by, more importantly, execution. My high school basketball coach, Dick Ponti would call it, "rising to the occasion." When I played for the National Championship team at Penn State, one of the things that I remember most is that we expected to win. We felt we were the most prepared when we played in the championship game. With over 200 different looks for our opponent from our defensive squad, we had a legitimate reason to believe that. It is an attitude that is backed up by the grind of hard work, repetition, and preparation. Our legendary coach's strategy was to always create more pressure in a practice setting than any big game in a stadium filled with 10's of thousands of fans rooting against us.

The call made in practice on this windy, rainy day, was pitch sweep left. That was a play when the blocking was all to the wide side of the field, and the quarterback pitched the ball back to me, and I followed the blocking and took the first crack to cutback against the defense. I remember the first time we ran it, and I slipped and fell as the turf gave way under my feet as I cut back. I could not even stand up before I heard Coach Paterno yell, "DJ, you can't slip." I said to myself "I can't slip, it's raining, and the grass is wet, this man must be nuts." I guess he could read my mind because he yelled it even louder, "You can't slip." The second time I got it.

He was not saying that the conditions of competition are always what you want it to be, that part is out of our control. He was saying that you must perform no matter the challenges or circumstances. Ultimately, we were being taught that adverse conditions and circumstances gave us a sizeable advantage. Regardless of the conditions but especially in unusual conditions, for us, the glass became half full, and it was to our advantage. When you are part of a team, you take personal and individual responsibility for the success of the team. You do your part to execute by adjusting to the conditions, and not making excuses for failing in them. A wet and sloppy field was not the typical condition conducive for a running back, but after that experience with Paterno, I became a believer. Adverse conditions were no longer obstacles to our success but aided in our success. So, in other words, let it rain!

When game day came, I remember how simple our game plans were for the great teams. Our offensive game plan for the majority of teams was fairly straightforward. That is not to say that we did not respect how good the other team was or that we did not have to employ some elaborate system, it is that we came to believe in extraordinary execution above everything else. It may sound cliché, but we practiced playing perfectly. Our philosophy was to be prepared to go to war, so we are going to line up even if you could predict the play; we were going to beat you with superior execution and performance. That is how every day should be lived. Operate out of preparation rather than desperation, knowing you are prepared to compete at the highest levels.

I had a friend tell a story that every time he had a student, or someone to challenge him in the martial arts or wrestling, he would tell them, pack a lunch; it is going to be an all-day affair. If you think you can line up in front of a train and stop it once it is moving, then you have a surprise coming your way.

In your professional life, as well as, every relationship, ask yourself about the results you are getting from your strategy or lack thereof. Then go back and look at your preparation and the execution daily, until it is time to perform. If you are not getting the results you want, adjust your strategy. If you do not have one, then it might be a good time to figure out what it is, redefine and refine it so that it works to your advantage. The strategy of preparation as we have said before should be connected to purpose and purpose is connected to significance. What you do and what results you are trying to achieve should direct how you prepare ahead of time. Change the equation.

Remember the quote in chapter two, if you do not like where you are in life, change the equation.

WE ARE THE SUM TOTAL OF OUR DECISIONS IN LIFE.

As an adult, I did not always associate my not wanting to give up, when faced with adversity with my father. I realize it is a direct correlation. As I am writing this book, I remember that he is a man with an unrelenting nature. If my father said that he was going to lose twenty pounds, his mind was set, and it was done. He was a man who did what he said he was going to do. For me, maybe it was developing into the stubborn, hard-headed individual with a rebellious nature, but I, like others, hated to be told that I could not do something. My mother would describe that stubbornness as a wild bucking horse that was unwilling to submit to anything to tame it.

Most of our life is not lived through performance in front of others but performing in private; those small, private day to day decisions that shape your life more than anything. Our youth is deceptive because we do not have a strong enough sense of history. Under normal circumstances most of our years are in front of us, so we do not connect the dots that this is going to end for each of us. As we continue to grow older, we may feel a sense of being cheated and deprived, knowing that most of the history is behind us. At the very least, you will feel a sense of urgency to get things done. In a sense, it is the acknowledgment of death, which marks the beginning of life; living a full life each day, regardless of our age.

Look at what entrepreneur Harland David Sanders, aka Colonel Sanders accomplished, while in his sixties, he started building what became known globally as Kentucky Fried Chicken. When you read about his business endeavors in life, you realize he undoubtedly experienced success and failure throughout his life and eventually used those experiences to launch a global brand known today as KFC.

Any day you can pick up the newspaper or go online and read the stories that capture the headlines. They are stories of what success and failure look like. People who made consistently good or bad decisions, whose destinies were or are defined by the habits they adopted or allowed to remain.

I want to continue and introduce some new concepts about dominating that we have not talked about that will assist in living at game speed and accelerate your performance. It is a true saying that times change, and we must anticipate and get ahead of trends to be successful. I believe that, but there are some foundational philosophies that are timeless and will help guide you toward success on your journey.

Dominion

Dominion is not a word used as often in our English language anymore. It is almost a forgotten word, but it is a powerful word and concept that can become part of your foundation for building success. Earlier we described domination as someone taking control of something or someone. To dominate someone is the ability to control or have a strong influence over them. **We may manage or mentor others in life, but I believe that the first and last person that you must learn to dominate is yourself.** Our development depends on the amount of focus we dedicate to ourselves. Those who cannot influence or control their thoughts and actions are doomed to a life of instability leading to an imminent road of mediocrity or something worse that hinges on complete failure.

Everyone wants successful outcomes in their endeavors or vocation. Everyone wants to move up a corporate ladder or increase in market share and become financially independent. It is a top spot we crave and the material expression of success that says to the world we have arrived. Lasting success though once achieved is not about the sheer will and force but learning to anticipate, act with discernment, and managing the pain and the process of movement. The long road of consistently producing excellence is for most, harder than the road littered with the sacrifices of getting there.

Dominion is the concept of taking complete ownership of you and your life's work as an expression of who you are and what you find joy or purpose in doing. I say purpose because sometimes you do not always do what you love for a living but if you find joy in sales or operational management, then doing it well and taking dominion over it is a worthy expression of your life. You cannot be successful as an individual or as a team member until you take ownership and responsibility. If you are a chief, director, or business owner, and your staff does not feel a sense of ownership of the process and the results, it will reflect in their overall performance.

If they are not directly benefiting, then trust me, efficiency is an uphill climb. You have lost sight of your most valuable assets, and you may have more holes in your operation than you think. Companies should value people above everything else, and individuals should do likewise. Careers should produce the opportunities for the owner and workers to prosper, as well as, have a high valued perspective of the individual. So, ask yourself, am I taking complete ownership of me, of my future, of my work, and of the outcomes? If yes, then find a way to keep testing that to strengthen a foundation for great achievements.

"I've always considered myself to be just average talent and what I have is a ridiculous insane obsessiveness for practice and preparation. And where I excel is ridiculous, sickening work ethic."

Will Smith, Actor, Producer, Comedian, & Songwriter

If you are in the mailroom, do not take responsibility for the entire company. Take responsibility for the mail. Do it with excellence and connect to how you are doing your job affects the company. Dominate in the mail and accept dominion over your area. Dominion is ownership as it relates to the position and is responsible for that portion. A person who shows themselves faithful in even the smallest things can be trusted with larger things. Stewardship is not always ownership but responsibility for the condition now and the outcomes later. Human nature is not to take care of something as much when you use it but do not own it. One of the main conditions of ownership is the proof of character.

High character means that you will take care of what belongs to someone else as you would if it were yours. If someone borrows your car, and when they return it with no gas, it is dirty, has 2,000 miles put on it, and they hand you the keys; you quickly will regret the fact that you let them borrow it in the first place. If you own it, make it better. If you use it, make it better. In the movie the "Kingdom of Heaven," there is a line at the beginning of the movie where there is a saying written on the lintel where the blacksmith works.

"What manner of man does not leave the world better than the way he found it?"

Kingdom of Heaven

These are good words by which, to set standards. Dominion is a matter of accepting responsibility for the condition you are in, for what you have been given, and eventually the realization and manifestation of what you have inside of you. Many times, we find ourselves on the receiving end of things done to us, given to us, or broken by others, but the change is our responsibility. Ultimately the condition we end up in is in our sphere of influence and therefore we can change and thus change our circumstances.

Whether you have been victimized or not, if in any way you have accepted the position of the victim, do not read another page until you decide that you are not the victim but the victor. You are an agent of change for the better and greatness is your only destination and pure expression of your life. Therein lays the secret of the condition of mankind. It is what we have within us to possess and are willing to spend energy to accept, and to take care of that makes our lives flourish. All men and women must first take dominion over themselves. The old proverb says, "As a man thinks, so is he!" We must take dominion over our thoughts and bolster that foundation for a perpetual journey of success.

Remember it is not a secret that we do not need permission to be successful, or to vigorously pursue the desires of our heart. It may mean that no one understands what we are talking about or why we would waste our time pursuing what may be nonsense or trivial to them. Each person in this life must find his or her way and be completely responsible for it. We own the effort or the equation that will yield the principled results. Sometimes it is not the lack of effort that brings undesired results but simply, the wrong equation (focus, strategy, process, etc.) within the effort that needs to be examined and modified to yield the intended results.

Before Danny Ainge, Charlie Ward, Brian Jordan, Bo Jackson, Deion Sanders, Michael Jordan, and me, it was believed that you could not pursue and/or excel at two different professional sports. There are always naysayers who say that you cannot and more likely, should not do something, but it is only you that can or will decide to live life with regrets or not. I do not have many regrets because I learned from my mistakes and realized some things, as well as, some relationships that I pursued turned out not to be what I thought and were not for me. I learned from that, and so I do not have to look back and wonder because I tried it and it did not work.

"I tell people to look at me and understand that everybody first told me that I couldn't be a 6-foot, 9-inch point guard, and I proved them wrong. Then they told me I couldn't be a businessman and make money in urban America, and I proved them wrong. And they thought I couldn't win all these championships, and I proved them wrong there as well."

Ervin "Magic" Johnson, Co-Owner of Los Angeles Dodgers, Entrepreneur, Philanthropist

You have the authority to live your life on your terms. If you must work a day job to provide for your family or decide to go on the more entrepreneurial route because it meets a specific need, then you still should pursue your dreams or other opportunities part-time until they can provide for you monetarily. Life should be in part about a true expression of who you are, and your unique TAGS, which gives shape to the purpose God created you. Being true to yourself allows you to be yourself and people will connect to that because it is genuine. Some will not, but that means your skills and unique talents were not meant to serve them. You have the authority, the legal right to take control of the focus and energy in your life to pursue something that is great and uniquely you. You cannot subjugate that to anyone else nor can anyone else stand in your place in life. Remember having individual purpose automatically crowns you with significance; therefore, you indeed have the authority to make certain decisions to dominate throughout your journey.

Remaining watchful, whether it is a small opportunity or a large complex task, in every worthy quest there will be some level of resistance, and so, with resistance we must move forward with even greater resolve. There are things and circumstances in life that push back and will attempt to impede progress. There were times when I felt like those impediments were bigger than my desire or ability to execute. You know, like giants that were standing in the way. It was as if I needed someone's permission to overcome them. You will feel like that at times; a battle that we will have throughout life, but I have learned by doing, you do not need someone else's permission. I firmly believe and even argue sometimes with others that you cannot always control the outcomes, but you do control the effort.

"You can rarely control the outcomes, but you fully control the effort; master the equation within the effort (vision, strategy, focus, plus process, etc.) and yield the results you most desire."

W.H. Dozier III, Founder, UTake Dominion

Sometimes you must ask yourself how much dog is in the fight. Modifying your dreams is ok but before you begin squashing any of your dreams, ask yourself how much is in the seed, how much do you believe in the harvest and what can it produce? If your dreams are small, then the seed you sow is going to be small. The dream is relative to the power in which you are sowing. Sometimes you must see what you are working toward through faith by utilizing your imagination. In doing or taking action toward what you want, you are proving the power of what is coming next, not what the current condition is. The more you do and work at it, the more you believe it; however, do not let the waiting period and the people who do not believe destroy your crops or harvest along the way. According to God's Handbook, you will receive if you refuse to give up.

Many years ago, I was introduced by my friend and attorney, Rich Puleo, to an older gentleman that liked to keep things simple. I once heard him say that he would only be interested in a business idea if it could be contained on an index card. The gentleman was the late Jim Overstreet, who had only an 8th-grade education. One day while trying to assist a client with their financing needs he was told by a bank director that the bank was not interested in a loan that involved the purchase of a mobile home or the perceived stigma that comes with it. At the time, Jim owned a few mobile home locations and wanted to assist one of his potential customers in getting a loan for their home.

Now most of us would be upset and move on regarding the bank and director's stance, but Jim was so disheartened by the situation, he had a different thought. He consciously set his sights on owning the bank. That is not a simple task for anyone, let alone someone with an 8th-grade education. So, what happened years later? Well, let me put it this way, it took some time, but eventually, he owned over 25% of the Bank's stock, giving him enough controlling interest to dictate the manner in which the bank conducted business. Can you guess who was at the top of his list to speak with at the bank?

Although Jim amassed a net worth said to exceed 150 million dollars if you were to see or meet him, you would have never known it by his appearance or demeanor. Remembering my last moment with him before his passing, I will never forget the godly presence I felt when I shook his hand and hugged his neck while he sat in a chair. He clearly was a man with a giant heart who had unlimited faith to dream for himself and others. Despite his educational limitations he alone imagined himself in a place of dominance far before he arrived there.

With any endeavor, you can deal with the results, but you must own the effort first. With focus, sound strategy, and hard-work within a winning strategy, you can move closer to what you thought and what you believed would happen.

Life is continuous, variable, and sometimes does not give you exactly what you want, but you can have in general what you believe. Aiming for the bullseye and hitting a centimeter outside the center circle is a good and decent result; missing the entire board more than a few times is a different story, equation, and discussion. As a former athlete, I had the opportunity to play with an incredible group of men who became National Champions at Penn State. Like others, I went on to play football in the NFL and had the privilege of also becoming a professional baseball player. It was not possible to control the outcomes of games and thanks to my father's beloved Redskins, I did not play in a super bowl in either my Minnesota or Detroit uniforms, but I still needed to practice and play like a champion.

"Before you can be crowned a true champion of any sort or in any walk of life and enjoy the fruit of it, you must possess the heart, character, and spirit of a champion!"

W.H. Dozier III, Founder, UTake Dominion

You must make it personal, so for you not needing permission means that there is no one else who owns the effort. Coming to a deeper understanding that you do not need someone else's permission and then accepting responsibility for the effort allows you to set your trajectory for success. That is something that no one else owns and that is why you cannot blame someone else for the condition of your life as an adult. You must permit yourself to succeed, as well as, to fail, but more importantly to move beyond your known or perceived limits. It is vital we hear and come to a greater understanding of this revelation. I have had the privilege of sitting and conversing with several leaders from various walks of life; here is one of my favorite people with one of my favorite quotes:

"We are stronger together when we are strong alone."

John Owens, CEO of Prevailance, Inc

I must come back to tenacity for a moment. I see that in myself and others that I have known as a deep inner quality, never give up, even when others cannot find the strength to continue the effort. It is the quality of putting in the work until the work is done and your objective is achieved. That sounds contrived and easy, but it is not. The field of dreams is littered with failures of effort that was abandoned because it was easier to be distracted, to make excuses or to quit and walk away from what they professed to desire the most. If for a moment you could think about the thing or type of person you desire to be the most, what would you give up to achieve that? What would you do to develop yourself, so that, you had the character and the lifestyle to attract someone or something that reflected your greatest treasure. What would you be willing to do? Tenacity is the calling card, the path, the motivator, and your judge. Anytime you deal with someone who is tenacious, then you know that it is a matter of when and not if they will possess something in an area where they are focused.

"Tenacity creates the question of when, not the question of if."

W.H. Dozier III, Founder, UTake Dominion

Relentlessness and tenacity are twin characteristics that prove what you believe when you allow the answer to be based on a time of when and not wondering. These characteristics are a mirror image of each other. I imagine it as a pit bull: its effort that never wanes. Tenacity is not always expressed in the positive. Since human beings are motivated by our desires, pleasure, passion, along with pain, and fear; and, then sometimes we can be tenacious about attaining the wrong things. If you think of your mind and your life, in general, as soil that is the richest soil on earth, then anything you plant will grow. The question is, what are you planting and constantly pursuing? I have met people who were continually and inherently lazy who put a lot of effort into avoidance.

So, let us talk a minute about how to right the ship. To relentlessly pursue the wrong things, people, or relationships over time, will destroy the opportunity for a purposeful life. The consistent negative results are out of line with what you can achieve. They are out of line with what you say you want. After taking complete responsibility for your life, then you must start taking responsibility for your peers and the people you allow to influence your life.

Failure is taught at some point and constantly reinforced if you are still failing. You condition people to what you will allow and how you want to be treated. In your past, someone communicated something to you that you accepted or rejected about yourself, as well as, your worldview or mental map. Suggestions or information that you accept begins to form a paradigm and belief system. A system that will invariably affect the decisions you make and actions you take. Your paradigm is the captain of your ship who is steering the ship toward a destination you may not even want but are subconsciously pursuing.

Having the right mentors and/or people to whom, you can be accountable to as peers, ensures that you have constant feedback on what you are doing, how you are doing it and what ways might be more effective. They should be persons who are looking at you based on the outcomes you want to achieve and focused on you achieving them. No one succeeds or fails without help in either direction.

"No one succeeds or fails without help in either direction."

Ayub Fleming

I think perpetual success has a great deal to do with the relationships we surround ourselves on a long-term basis. You are not only the sum total of the decisions you have made which includes the influences you have allowed in your life. Any negative influence from the past or even the present can be upended; in moments of failure, there is never an excuse for blaming others. Negativity can influence every area of your life and dim every opportunity you pursue because of the mental programming of self-limitations.

We need to make sure we stay out of our own way. Take the position of exchanging any pessimists around you with persons who will help you follow a successful path, as well as, people you can influence and help to achieve their goals. Remember, evil or that which is inferior prevails when good people do nothing. You cannot allow constant negativity or mediocrity to exist in your life and expect positive outcomes. That is not to say that anyone can create a perfect world where negative people or situations do not exist, remember we cannot control all the outcomes, but we can influence them; we must own the effort and the decisions we make.

Negative influences at any age are hard to overcome; it is very difficult growing up around people telling you that you cannot do something. At some point though, when you, deep down, want to achieve certain things; it comes down to deciding to detoxify and overcome the influence and choose to forge ahead anyway. I have a friend who always says, "Love your family but choose your peers." Your peers are those who may influence you the most. The point is that we must actively choose our mentors, friends, and those who comprise the team to help us take the successful roads.

Ray Lewis, the former Pro Bowl NFL athlete, became that friend and mentor to one of the greatest Olympians we have ever witnessed, Michael Phelps. For those of you that do not follow sporting activities, Ray Lewis was not Michael Phelps swimming coach, but a man who has dedicated his life to helping people. When Phelps experienced a very low point in his life, Lewis was there to help guide, inspire, and mentor him. Through the book, *The Purpose Driven Life*, Phelps found purpose and what I believe we all find when we link up with our purpose, distinct significance! Remember Ray Lewis had a time in his life where he faced imprisonment partly due to the people with whom he was surrounded. It was that experience that changed him forever by making different choices about what decisions he made and who had influence in his life. Who have you decided to let have access to your life, and the power to influence you right now?

Even when the outcomes of the past have been negative, you must re-evaluate your current circumstances and what resources you either have available or need for that journey of success. At all times, if the opportunities do not exist, you need to position yourself to seek other opportunities with intense focus until you create the circumstances or surround yourself with what you need to prevail.

In the larger sense, recognizing how God can guide us in our daily lives, and what it means to seek Him gives clarity and meaning to life and what we pursue. There is no doubt in my mind that we must actively pursue and create the right types of influences around us. We also must actively pursue the presence of the Creator, as well as, a personal connection with Him to bring overall purpose and restoration to our lives. He is the big picture and the One who helps us paint the smallest details as we ultimately fit into a larger master plan. Seeking God in my life means seeking direction that goes beyond activity, no matter how important it may be. In the larger sense, we are part of a larger group that needs to come together and be a part of His significant plan, be fulfilled as an individual, as well as, fulfilling my mission in the corporate members of Christ.

I believe that God wants us to dominate in life. Our most profound influence could be from God and godly matters rather than a life defined by material things or other trappings that give us a pseudo sense of significance. With individual purpose, we are significant already; our effort and accomplishments dictate our rewards on earth and somewhat beyond, but it will not move the needle of significance at all. Again, we were significant before we accomplished anything. I believe that the goal is to dominate from a spiritual standpoint first and foremost. That means trusting in the Creator and believing that what we are achieving is part of a larger plan, with Him directing it. Spiritual fulfillment and attainment is the highest level of thinking and the strongest influence for greatness over our lifetime, ushering us to a place of perpetual rewards.

Perception

"Perception provides an image of what may or may not be true, so perception is tricky, but is most effective when it's perfectly aligned with truth. Otherwise, you will veer off course; without a course correction, you will remain off course, and completely miss the mark."

W.H. Dozier III, Founder, UTake Dominion

Aiming and hitting the bullseye is what we all strive to do in life, so our perception is vital in the process and most effective when it is perfectly aligned with truth or the laws and principles God has set on the earth. So, when we attempt to operate within a process contrary to these unyielding laws or truths, we veer off course. If we remain off course, there is a zero chance of hitting the target that has principled meaning and the greatest impact. Your direction can be turned around, but it is only changed as perception is changed. Perception is changed as thinking is challenged. If you did not have a job or you are not able to close your sales, for an extended period; at some point, you must decide that you are going to dominate regardless of what you see or perceive to be the truth. Something has got to change. That mindset that says, "I will not stop until I achieve what it is that I have set my mind and life to master."

"You must continue to study your craft and make personal mastery and improvement a life pursuit like your need for the air itself. It's not enough to want; you must do. It's not enough to do once, you must commit. Once you commit, you must pursue with passion and intention until you achieve."

Ayub Fleming

You are either dominant, or you are being dominated. An entrepreneur and corporate executive like Brian Hamilton, aka "The Marine" has had plenty of opportunities to become dominated or overwhelmed by his circumstances. In the business world of start-ups, you must be resilient and resourceful to begin to think you can succeed in such a volatile environment and that's exactly how Marines think. He is not in the military nor has he ever served as such, but his mentality is the reason I gave him the nickname. Now, like many of us, he has had his moments or months in an entrepreneurial valley when that extra push was needed. On one occasion while part of an executive team of one company, the entire team was fired in mid-stride of bringing a new product to market. It caught everyone off guard.

His position along with his healthy six-figure compensation package was gone. Now, do not get me wrong, "The Marine" may be one of the most self-motivating people I know; his wife Adrian is no slouch either. Being a former corporate member of the Healthcare industry herself, she gave him that extra inspiration and push one day, and Brian has not looked back since. I can promise you setbacks will come; what I cannot say is how you will respond to them, but I pray when they come you have a strong company of people around you.

"The Marine" is now the Founder and Chief Revenue Officer of Real Wear, a growing company which has designed the world's first voice-driven, completely hands-free, a head-mounted wearable tablet computer for connected industrial workers. Real Wear was also the Frost & Sullivan 2017 North American New Product Innovation Awardee.

At one point in his entrepreneurial career, he had worked with ten different companies and different ventures over the same amount of years. Can you imagine the mental toughness needed to get through that maze? Let me say this to bring balance. There are many things that ran the course in my life when I did not get the outcome that I wanted, even after putting in the effort. There were games we lost because our opponent was better on that day, not necessarily because we were outworked. There is a difference. If you know in your heart that you quit, then quitting the next time gets easier, and quitting if you are not careful can become habitual. If you are done because there is nothing left, and you know in your heart you have grown through the failure and have been changed, then you are ready to take on the next challenge. That is where growth has taken place. That growth, while discovering the difference, developing the mindset to recognize and know the difference, leads to more growth and change.

So, here is where the change comes in. You may be sitting there reading this, not knowing the details of how or where to start to make a change in your life. So, let us talk about domination and making changes to achieve it. To dominate, you must decide to dominate. You must decide to do something that you are not doing or to do it to a greater degree. You must better recognize areas of lack in your life, your strategy, or people who are part of your life. If you want something you do not have, then something is missing; recognizing lack is a good thing.

If you think you are okay with mediocre performances or you can achieve greater things by doing the same thing in the same way; unfortunately, you are mistaken. People who dominate do not only think what they are doing or did yesterday will get them greater success in the future; they are always looking for new ways to expand and increase; new ways to innovate and perform better.

Remember, the focus of dominating yourself is the key to an inner-directed life. Learning to conquer yourself is the key to never being conquered. I thought I was a good manager of my life until one day I took a closer look and began seeing something different. It was not a joyous moment, especially when I realized I was a terrible manager in some areas.

My management of time, finances, and business all needed to change; I was off course, and since I desired and decided to be dominant in my life, a major correction was imperative.

Correcting me began with my thought processes. It came with the recognition that I lacked something that I desperately needed. The good news is that changing the way you think changes your influence on the outcomes you get. I heard a story about a person who each year came from an eastern bloc country to America several times a year to attend seminars of people like Tony Robbins and Mark Victor Hansen. He was convinced that reading over 100 self-help and other books would change his thinking and in turn would change his life. Collecting information from over 100 self-help books over a short period was a unique strategy. He soon became a multimillionaire in business and had improved his health and life in every area. I am convinced that changing your thinking through immersing yourself in new and pertinent information is fundamental to success. As this is true, then very few people with today's technology would have an excuse why they cannot access information, increase knowledge, and change their lives. These are exciting times for all those that seek to improve themselves.

There are social media experts who are advancing monetarily online because that is the skill they have acquired and they either studied how to do it or learned through trial and error. The fact though is they learned, and they continue to learn because they want to fulfill their strongest needs and desires. It may be different for you, but for most people who pursue success, it is a deep sense of fulfillment or freedom.

Once you decide to change the way you think by introducing new information in line with your desires, you then align your activities, your actions, and your relationships with what you desire the most with your sights on achieving the most. You must develop a collective and congruent process that leads to positive outcomes. When you allow your thoughts, values, and actions to be misaligned with your stated goals, then you remain incongruent. If changing and making adjustments for life improvements are or become acceptable practices in our lives, then our time is no longer being squandered or wasted.

As a mid-level manager or especially as an executive of a small company, you must consistently adopt best practices into your life daily and improve in every area of health, business management, goal setting, implementation skills, etc. Do not kid yourself about operating or living at the next level. Either excellence or slackness permeates our lives and cannot be compartmentalized. You may be better at some things, but if you are not improving in all areas directly or indirectly, then you are losing ground. Your life and business are either moving toward integration or disintegration.

When you decide to ask yourself what you are willing to do to achieve that goal or the lifestyle you want, you begin moving toward the realization of attainment. If it is to get in better physical shape, get the detailed information on all the important factors that will equate to successful outcomes, for example, consuming water daily, reducing caloric intake, and consistent and anaerobic movements. At some point, you must look in the mirror and know that this may not be an easy process but ask yourself what I am willing to do. Am I willing to commit to the pain and process to achieve the outcome that I desire? In the process, you may have to change your peers and the people around you who want to consume unhealthy or fatty foods and move toward people who would rather train and consistently eat healthy foods. We must build a support mechanism for success. That is a matter of who and what.

Some professionals are known for their careless practices and lifestyles. Some are also known for moderate success or going broke for the same reason. The road is littered with people who without a healthy development of management skills, only experienced success on a temporary basis. Due to a lack of knowledge, commitment, growth, and the people they allowed to influence them, the journey to higher levels of success takes a detour. Some have made it out of a challenging environment only to travel with the same influencers from the old environment that will often lead to a destructive result. If you look at the people consistently experiencing success who have done it over a long time, look at the people with whom they surround themselves, and then you will understand why. The opposite is true as well.

"You have to surround yourself with people who are thinking about your success and are creating value."

Ayub Fleming

Surrounding yourself with people who are thinking about your success are the same people who are constantly thinking about their success and quality of life. Be careful not to exert valuable time with people who do not think about their personal growth and success and who have not taken the proper action to achieve it, because success and losing are both contagious. Some people have lost their way and unfortunately, lose in every area of their life and become financially supported by someone else and keep smiling as if they are winning. Sleeping in and saying you are tired, and you are dead broke; broken and being dominated is more accurate.

That is why it starts with a personal choice. Champions or winners do not feel guilty or apologize for winning; they are driven to win, knowing they were born to do so. Once you taste that, you cannot wait to taste it again. If you win a big fight, you will have some time to recover, but if at the end of that fight you are not hungry for another taste of victory, then something is wrong. Losing may not taste as good, but you can get used to it as fast. It is winning that has the unusual taste, but over time you can lose the taste for winning, and you stop trying. When that happens, then losing becomes your role to play and those who may be in your peer group. Running with winners means you are being pushed. You cannot give up; they will not let you. When someone of high caliber loses, they take it hard because they know what preparation went into winning. Losing is hard to understand and accept.

"You need to play with supreme confidence, or else you'll lose again, and then losing becomes a habit."

Joe Paterno, Legendary College Football Coach

People who dominate learn that there is a lesson even in each failure and the result is added humility, knowledge, and the building of character. Regrettably, people who are dominated learn as well. They learn that this is their station in life and that it is someone else's fault and the cure lays with someone else to change their condition. In sports, this is why the better teams historically pick lesser teams as a tune-up game. They use it as practice, preparation, and an emotional pump to prepare the team for winning. They know it is a matter of execution as much as it is a matter of expectation of winning. Do not accept being someone's tune-up game. Be a student for your success and earn your master's degree through sound strategy, consistency of character, and hard work.

If you are not winning, then the question is, how do you get to the point where you want to win more than anything else, when the condition of your life does not support that? I think this brings us to the next topic of this chapter and that is talking about taking a personal assessment of where you are; the facts. I suggest along with your goal setting that you learn to journal your thoughts and be a master at collecting and analyzing the data. No specific techniques but find a system that works for you as long as it is consistent. You must keep score almost like reviewing your budget and Profit & Loss statement to constantly know where you are. Know the facts.

In business, you obviously must know or learn the strengths and weaknesses of your company, as well as, your competition. Every brand, product, and employee has strengths and weaknesses. I have heard it said and I believe it is good advice that you play to your strengths in public and work on your weaknesses in private. Taking the position of constant assessment means that you can also adopt constant improvement and exceptionalism. Mediocrity in finance or operations should not be desired or tolerated because it is easier. Businesses lead by entrepreneurs, no matter the size should continue with an entrepreneurial model that empowers and leans away from a top-heavy autocratic model.

The "Marine's business approach suggests that you cannot be hesitant to invest or spend the money to invest in the right people. He has established successful ventures with a strong work ethic and surrounding himself with the right people, regardless of the cost of time, money, or physical energy. Larger organizations with a top-down heavy bureaucratic structure sometimes can burn through a lot of time and cash but survive even while they make ongoing mistakes. Smaller companies do not have that luxury and must address internal problems and take care of customer needs very quickly, or they soon will be out of business. For most customers good will does not go much further than the first bad experience. If you are a young and inexperienced business owner, as an entrepreneur, you should remember that, and adopt the philosophy of serving in your personal and professional life.

I talked before about the championship game in 1987 between University of Miami and Penn State. I remember in our game plan we knew the strength of Miami on both offense and defense. Vinny Testaverde and their offensive crew were one of the best in the country, and Miami had a solid defense as well. Our game plan centered around one theme. To beat them, we had to do what many thought could not be done. We had to neutralize their offense. Simultaneously, our offense had to find a way to put points on the board against one of the best defenses in the country. On paper, there was no way that Penn State was going to beat Miami. Penn State's offense and defensive schemes historically were very basic; we would have to rely on near-perfect execution.

What allowed us to matchup with Miami is that we had great individual players at each position that had played together for almost four years. We were ready to play because we had started to prepare two years before that game. Many of the players were seniors who had played when they were freshmen. My sophomore year we went 6-5 and were invited to the Aloha Bowl; the year before we went to the Aloha Bowl and beat the University of Washington. In 1984, we were invited to the Aloha Bowl, and we declined that year because we decided as a team not to play in any bowl games unless it was for the National Championship. We decided then to play for the right to be called champions and nothing else. That was our only goal. Now put that in perspective, I was a young college football player turning down $400 spending money and a chance to go to Hawaii. For most, it would have been a dream comes true, but for us, it was National Champion or bust as individuals and as a team. Our character and winning attitude were being established.

In your life, business, or career decide to be the best at what you do until you achieve that goal; to accept no accolades until you do. In 1985 we went undefeated and played against Oklahoma in the Orange Bowl. We lost that game, but we achieved our goal of not going to a bowl game unless we played for a national championship. As I said earlier, sometimes you cannot control the outcome, but you can own the effort. We set the goal, we put in the effort, but we fell short of being #1. So, we could not set the same goal again. We had to make another decision. Our decision now was to win a national championship not play for one. We learned through experience how to win. The law of progression which we will talk about again later says that you have first to desire to win and set that as a goal. Then you must acquire the skills to win, next apply the focus, and finally the effort to win. You may not win at first, but you will learn how to win along the way, collecting data while winning, losing, and making mistakes. The key thought is that you are progressing toward your goal if you stay focused and increase the preparation and the sharpness of your execution. Knowledge of what not to do, as well as, what is the result of each action is a plus. You must see failing as a plus if it is not a matter of weakness in character.

The deeper understanding is that you must win as a team. At Penn State, our fourth-year seniors with another year of eligibility did not win the championship that year. Most of them who could have gone on to play for the National Football League chose to stay because they wanted to be champions and finish that goal. As the fifth-year seniors returned, we did put ourselves in a position to again win the national championship. I did not say play for the national championship, I said, to win one. It was never our intent to play for one; we had already achieved that goal. We intended to win it. Every team or business wants to win. We learned to win through the development of a winner's preparation, attitude, partnerships, commitment, and most of all precision in execution. After designing a strategic plan, you need to articulate your winning strategy, and execute it until it is done with precision.

As a team, we saw in ourselves that we were supposed to be national champions and so we would accept nothing less. What is your business supposed to be? Business for me is a matter of personal expression of the individuals who are leading it, focused on the defined goals of the business. When you think about where your business is, or personal life is supposed to be, then you can delineate whether you are there, and if you are not, then assess what it will take to get there. Nothing else matters other than when you define where you are supposed to be, and then make the evolution and refocused effort to get there. Nothing else should be acceptable but a determined heart and mind to achieve what you have not and to become what you are not at the moment.

"Where are you supposed to be, what are you supposed to be doing or being; there is a plan and you are either there or you are not. Where are you today?"

Ayub Fleming

Dominant Factors

1. **Preparing meticulously, Practicing with Perfection in mind, and Performing with real intensity are all hallmarks of execution** on *Game Day* and Every day is *Game Day!*

2. **Become convinced Dominion belongs to you**; it is related to ownership and how you are positioning yourself; this is not only having access to it but owning it.

3. **Your ownership has the privilege of access but also the healthy burden of responsibility** and if you spend your energy getting it, managing it, and enhancing it over time to extract the full benefits from it; it will reflect the one who owns it.

4. **Embracing ownership is to embrace change and the points of success and failure you experience**; remember becoming aware of what provided you with successful results, as well as, what has caused you to fail empowers you to repeat the one you want most of all!

5. **Become responsive not like a weed but a perpetual one; be the greatest catalyst for growth in your life,** taking a never-ending and relentless approach to life's endeavors.

6. **Establishing momentum within your business endeavors starts with your perceptions,** knowing perception is a

powerful weapon that works as an ally, especially when aligned with truth.

7. Because **change is often a gateway to great achievements** we embrace change and do not run from it; if you run from the process of becoming something greater via change, what are you running toward?

Chapter 5

Your Brand and Beyond

"In this ever-changing society, the most powerful and enduring brands are built from the heart. They are real and sustainable. Their foundations are stronger because they are built with the strength of the human spirit, not an ad campaign. The companies that are lasting are those that are authentic."

Howard Schultz, Pour Your Heart Into It: How Starbucks Built a Company One Cup at a Time

With each of my visits to a Dick's Sporting Goods, the intense in-store brand battles are evident, especially between Nike and Under Armour. The brand equity Under Armour has acquired during its climb from a start-up 20 plus years ago, to a legitimate contender has been incredible to watch. Kevin Plank's emergence from his grandmother's basement is another inspiring entrepreneurial account. Similarly, entrepreneur and Nike Co-Founder, Phil Knight has emerged and is holding the top market share position among competitors which is an impressive stake in the ground. After being battle-tested over the last 50 plus years, even Nike, all the while, is still building its brand. The competition has stiffened, especially due to technology, allowing the entrance into the marketplace easier.

My first major writing assignment for English in college was writing about Nike and Phil Knight. This was in 1983, my freshman year when going to Pattee Library aka, Pattee and Paterno Library, not the internet, was customary in conducting research on campus. That assignment was enlightening for me, and I have been a Nike and Phil Knight fan ever since. Mark Parker, fellow alum, who has been with Nike since 1979, leads the Goliath of a brand today as its third CEO in the history of the company.

"Personal brand equity erodes much faster than corporate brand equity."

John Quelch, Professor of Harvard Business School

But this chapter is less about corporate power brands and more about the vitality of your personal power brand. In my professional years, branding has morphed into a part of the culture that is undeniable for the individual, and not only with business concerns. Branding has become the personal expression and signature of the individual where corporations began acknowledging a few years ago. For some companies, the personal development and branding of an individual are where a great deal of the true equity lies. First, let us take a step back out of social media and state what branding is. Branding is the name, design, expression, look, and/or other features we use to distinguish how we experience one product or company from another. Before the advent of the industrial age, when we lived in an agricultural society, branding was used to distinguish one person's livestock from another.

You must look back at the advent of new financial products as we grew from an agricultural society to the industrial age, and then look at the advent of technology that expanded the business, and personal expression through the internet that has now created the need to differentiate one person from the other. The visual brand may have very little to do with the actual person or expression. The word brand originates from the word, "to burn," that is where the brand or image was burned into the product to now give it a unique signature representing who owned it.

The brand in the past was directly represented by the owner who branded it. Whether that company's product was good or not did not play with the brand itself but the quality and reputation of the person who was willing to "make their mark." I will cover various layers of branding in this chapter. It is important because these are the times in which we live, and it is very important to capitalize on the understanding of branding if you want to expand on your success.

"It's alright to be Goliath, but always act like David."

Phil Knight, Co-Founder, Nike, Author, & Philanthropist

My parents would have easily worked one or two jobs their entire lives and looked forward to retirement. Moving from one job to another was seen as instability, not advancement. The brand only belonged to the company, as "company men and women" were produced, it was more important to comply and create lifelong customers loyal to the brand than challenge it. Our parents would have also lived in the same house from birth to death or only moved 2 or 3 times their entire lives, unless they were in the military or catastrophe struck like an entire cottage industry shutting down much as the steel industry did in the North East.

This is also the mentality that killed many retail stores and other giants of the industry of my parents' generation. They were not able to change with social trends and technology. They were not able to rebrand themselves, as well as, shift fundamental business models.

"Mass advertising can help build brands, but authenticity is what makes them last. If people believe they share values with a company, they will stay loyal to the brand."

Howard Schultz, Pour Your Heart Into It:
How Starbucks Built a Company One Cup at a Time

Times have changed; the average person from age 18 until they are 45, will move up to 11 times. The person, once they reach 45, will move on average only 2.7 times. The average person will change jobs 11 times. Job changes may account for why people move so much at an earlier age as they follow their work.

It is also interesting because we see job security more related to individualism and what we can either create or take advantage of with opportunities from other companies versus company loyalty. With that in mind, along with almost unfettered access to them to communicate with people from around the world via the internet, the individual brand has exploded. It has been created to the extent that it is hard to believe that this genie can ever be put back into the bottle. So modern branding is here to stay until inevitably it becomes something else. Do you see the current personal branding opportunity; will you be ready for the change that is coming, and can you anticipate or create the next trend?

Branding in a sense is still about the burn, the image brand or expression by which people know us. If you were to think of the brand that you are labeled, you are probably not in control of that brand; but you might have influenced the creation of it. If you think regarding what brand I want people to see and perceive, then you are in complete control of that brand, but not the perception that others place as the meaning. Take control of your brand and influence the "burn," the image, from not a visual standpoint, but a character standpoint that defines you. Understanding this arrangement is the first step to realizing we are in an age of personal branding. To some degree, it is a must for those who will attain success at anything that is public.

There are 12 things that are important in building a brand. If you are in business, these will be very familiar to you, but you may not have applied them to yourself outside of your business. If you are a small business owner or entrepreneur, then you know that relationship building beyond the product or service can make or break your business. If you are a middle-level manager or executive looking to advance, then you also know that image is important, as well as, performance. You, as well as, your product, are being perceived a certain way whether you think that it should be that way or not. There is not a successful business anywhere that is not meeting about how to be perceived more effectively and to control the event. I define an event as a meaningful planned interaction between two or more people or a business and its customers. What was merely basic interaction to buy or sell has become more of a production at every level. The more you can control the event or the experience the more you can control your destiny.

1. **Become and consistently remain aware of the perceptions of others and decide to control or influence those perception.**

Remember, the perception of the absence of what is true is the only truth that others can see, so decide to control and influence the perception of others as best you can. I use the word decide because it is not enough to become consciously aware that you are being perceived a certain way without choosing to influence and re-establish that fact to your advantage. You are taking ownership, and this is not necessarily easy to do or to even accept, especially for those who want to be who they are, the way they are, and who remain "in the way" versus on the way to change. I would say that first change is inevitable; our lives are in constant flux over time as we age and either we are moving away from our desired outcomes and destiny, or we are achieving them. Remember, we talked about the wants, desires, and needs becoming one. So, the acceptance of needing to change and making adjustments should be as equally acted upon and accepted.

Pay attention to how you project yourself both from a positive and a negative perspective. The thing that you may not like about yourself may also be picked up by someone else, especially if you comment negatively about yourself in some way. Determine to find those who will act as your "honest agents" who will deliver unfiltered details of what they think of you and how you interact with others. Here is where trust and honesty are everything; you must give them the unbiased room to say seemingly hurtful things if they are constructive. Even if you do not find truth in them, write them down, again perceptions do not have to be true, but they are true to the observer. To grow in wisdom, you must love critiquing and correction; it is the prerequisite for higher levels of wisdom and greater measures of a wealthy life.

Once you have your perception list, continue to observe how people treat you as you adjust to your work, personal life, and appearance. Collecting those evaluations may not be easy but appropriately address the issues of dress, communication, work performance, attitude, and any other area where your perception by others could be holding you back.

2. Have a personal and professional chronicle created about yourself; one not easily copied or owned by someone else based on the truths of your life.

Make sure your life story is empowering, emotional, and compelling. Never allow your story or conversations to end in the negative; learn the art of a positive spin. I am not suggesting that you should lie about your circumstances, but that you should see things from the positive and learn to redefine things that were painful or obstacles as things that were overcome and opportunities to learn, grow, and mature. The best stories are told in a way that controls the emotional state of another and takes them from one state of mind to another.

Remember, creating the professional and personal brand is controlled by you, and perceived by others. In creating it, garner assistance from others and discover and display interesting facts about yourself. Displaying your information is not about being braggadocios, but positive and inspirational.

3. Create the image in words and images of what the experience is that you want people to have with you.

Make sure it comes from an authentic place, fostered from what is important and powerful and delivered with incredible skill. Get in and remain in mental, physical, and spiritual shape, do not allow yourself to be out of shape and perceived by others as slothful. That is not to suggest everyone is going to look like a world-class athlete or dress like you stepped out of GQ or on the cover of the Sports Illustrated swimsuit edition. Dominating is doing your best in all core areas of our lives. Go to the gym or get a trainer, work out, eat right, and get the proper amount of rest. You are the brand, so the imaging starts with you. Make an effort to dress for success and over time develop a nice wardrobe that fits your body type. Consider splurging and have a few clothes and outfits tailored to make sure they fit properly. Look your best and look for constant improvement. Is it powerful, emotional, and inspirational?

Having some professional photos done may be in order. That is, not headshots but action shots as well so when asked for pictures either personal or professional, again you look your authentic best. Limit the Photoshop and fuzzy glamour pictures. When someone sees what you look like; these photos should be fairly recent. People will not take you seriously if they cannot connect the brand you have created to something of substance.

In your business, you would normally engage professional graphic artists and photographers to build your company's image. Continue to make imaging a regular part of doing business by production and distribution of information and pictures that tell the story that needs to be told. Get plenty of feedback again to see how things are being perceived. Receiving feedback is a must and should be a constant.

4. Invest in your brand both organizationally and personally to deliver on your brand promise and culture.

You must invest in the brand that is you and if an active entrepreneur, invest in your company as well. I do not care how small; you can spend pennies by regularly taking pictures and writing copy on social media or other media platforms to constantly and professionally make the promise of your brand. The promise of the brand is the marketing side that makes a perceived promise of what the brand experience will be. The operational side is where you keep the brand promise. You must look and act the part. It is so disappointing to go into a restaurant, and someone has spent a ton of money on making it look good, and the service is lousy, and the food is tolerable only. The imaging through words and pictures tells a story that made me decide to forgo other choices, and spend my money, but again the service was lousy, and the food was cold. The brand promise was made but operationally under delivered. You must be congruent with the promise you make and keeping that promise. That is how trust is built and why people decide to invest in you or your business in the long-run.

5. Make sure your personal brand is and remains relevant and strive to be "the most relevant in the room."

One of the best ways to see if your brand is relevant is to pay attention to the reaction that you are getting and ask yourself one question. Is that the reaction I was soliciting? Many times, in life professionally and personally, we are dumbfounded by the reaction we get from something that we have done. Personal development should be intentional, relevant, and constant. The results over time must be perceptible. People should be able to see the change you have made in yourself and your business over time.

When you get ready to start any campaign or make any adjustments begin by asking yourself a simple question. So, what? So, what gets to the heart of whether the audience will care for what you are trying to say? The goal is to sooner or later deliver what people want to buy; it may take some trial and error. A good read is a book, *Tipping Point*, by Malcolm Gladwell. Success spreads more like a virus over time when it is continually introduced and allowed to fester. One ad campaign usually does not elicit a large response because people will not remember it and unless it is extremely relevant to their experience, they will not respond. The competing of other ads and other viral type input in front of the viewer makes one ad standing alone difficult to remember and almost completely ineffective over time. Name recognition comes into play because they have seen it repeatedly and now suddenly it becomes a household name and thus is relevant.

6. Lead by example and be authentic so that those closest to you buy in and become the connectors and information sources that you need.

Good brands have good people that attract believers closest to them. Again, great companies, which are derived from great people, do not see recruitment or retention as their highest priority. Great companies have people clamoring to get in and stay onboard. The less than stellar companies have high turnover at a great cost to the organization. If your company has no long-term employees, be concerned. If you have no long-term friends at all and have people coming in and out of your life like the grand central station, again be concerned about what their experience is with you. It is vital to discover why you are attracting transient relationships and clients and not people who add value over a long period.

7. Deeply understand what your customers want out of the experience and make it your mandate to deliver that consistently with excellence.

Make sure that the customer or people in your personal life have an optimal experience. Realize that it is the perception of the one having the experience that matters. I would suggest from time to time that you ask them and gauge your performance with their response. I have always asked my superiors or people that I work with, as well as, friends, "What are their expectations?" From time to time, I must ask if I am meeting them and if not, how I can improve? Remember, lasting relationships are about creating value.

Do not try to overachieve but meet them at the point of their expectations. If you do that consistently, then you have done all you can do in increasing the brand experience. If you treat your friends, as well as, your co-workers and customers from a brand experience perspective, everyone wins.

8. Make modifications to deliver a powerful and optimal brand experience with supreme consistency. Be as honest as you can be and give others access to be honest with you!

If you followed my advice, then you are becoming more aware every day of people's experience with you personally, as well as, your product or service. That means you are making adjustments wherever you must make them, to increase the brand experience. In your personal life and business, there are no sacred cows; you must adjust if you want to meet your goals. I am not asking you or telling you not to follow your values, but your values are just that; yours. For example, the religious expression should be done with humility in the spirit of love. So that, you do not live in a state of compromise, but make sure you reflect a Creator that wishes that no man should perish. Change whatever needs to be changed for the experience of others to be the best that it can be; serve them by resolving their issues, become a "problem server" and you will increase.

9. Be present everywhere your target audience is, but in a way that is inspirational, informative, and emotionally delivering a clear, genuine, and relevant message.

How do we get people to pass thinking about us and feel confident enough to invest in us? One of the quickest ways is to establish and build trust. Trust in the promise and the experience so that others know what you stand for, your drivers, as well as, what your business delivers. Trust is the long-term goal that will pay dividends over a long period. When you lead with promotion, you must back it up with delivery on the promise. Securely executing on this simple yet vital process is how trust is built. You make the promise and delivery relevant by meeting certain needs and making sure you change as the needs of the customers change. In your personal life and every relationship, it is about making a promise and keeping it. It is simple, but it does require hard-work. In the book, *Radical Trust*, author Joe Healey acknowledges how global competition has forced organizations to adopt the need to become more collaborative, building partnerships with its employees. However, if an employee cannot be trusted to collaborate with other team members, any number of degrees and years of experience, the employee moves toward being worthless to the organization.

10. Move from promise to promotion; cultivate and remain faithful to the promise of your personal brand and become worthy of promotion and utilize God's Handbook for Success to position yourself.

I remember a line in the movie, *Troy*, when a young boy who was sent to find Achilles, he said he would not fight because he was afraid, Achilles told him that is why no one will remember your name. Yes, even your relationships need a touch of marketing but a lot more of character. Self-promotion via delivering on the promise, not aggrandizement is important. Telling people the truth and delivering the message with regularity is not taking the position of delivering a fairy tale that exalts you while diminishing others. Keep your name relevant, and you will not be forgotten. In the account of Joseph and his brothers, when Joseph was in prison with the baker, he utilized his gift from God to help the baker. Joseph told the baker not to forget him when his position is restored with Pharaoh. What is interesting is that it was not the reminder that promoted Joseph out of prison; it was the utilization of his gift in operation that ultimately promoted Joseph from prison to the palace.

11. Be an organization or a person that people can care about, do good work for others, treat your peers fairly, live a clean life and be upstanding in the community.

Protect the brand by delivering on the promise of substance. Expand the brand by using word of mouth because others have bought into the brand and act as your free advertisement. Remember people will not only connect you to others but vouch for you when they believe in you.

12. Deliver the brand with a long-range purpose in mind. Have a resounding reason why it is important for others to remember your name; over a lifetime and beyond if possible. You want to have a lifetime value approach with relationships that highlights a long-range purpose with your audience.

Develop the important "why" that gives everything you do reason, meaning, and overall significance. For all the things that have no reason, eliminate them or delegate them but do not tolerate them. Activities and things of little purpose serve no purpose. Beyond the brand is the development of meaning and character. That is the substance that will deliver the promise of a brand experience. What will people find when they get close to you or experience your product or service; answer that question before you expand your marketing. It may be time to slaughter the sacred cows and become something meaningful in the marketplace and your life. What do I mean by sacred cows? These are the things about you that are not discussed. They are the things that you do not think about because they are accepted as the way you are. Remember, change is about collecting the facts first, facing them, accepting them, and finally deciding to put measures in place to bravely change them.

I want to continue this discussion by talking about personal development. I think that this subject, other than a personal connection with God, is the most important thing that we can talk about. What are you and who or what are you becoming? Constant improvement so that as you become the commodity that people need, want and desire due to the value you create, your stock increases. Your world changes because you change. People may invest first because it looks good but may not continue investing unless it creates enough significant value. I would suggest again to mentally consuming large amounts of information through reading and studying. Remember the example set by the gentleman who read over 100 self-help books, who today is a multimillionaire. Exchange habits that are more beneficial and in line with your long-term dreams and values with ones that are not. As you grow philosophically, begin thinking about how you conceptualize the work and give each opportunity and person in your life meaning.

How you interpret the world has a great deal of how you experience and participate in it. Your preferences, as well as, your prejudices, will color your world and allow you to see the world in monotones or an array of color and textures but it is up to you to broaden your thought life and experience, which equates to your current and future perceptions.

I have mentioned journaling in this book in a few places and if journaling is not for you then having some other method of discovering your thoughts, feelings, desires, and giving a voice to your internal world becomes critical to your maturation process. Complex concepts should be broken down into simpler concepts until most experiences and feelings can be shared and expressed in short phrases if not a single word.

"The fact is, there are many facts in our life that can change, but the truth has no such flexibility; so, when we seek, find, and detain truth, even while surrounded by overwhelming facts, the truth remains the gateway to the ultimate place of strength and dominance."

W.H. Dozier III, UTake Dominion, Founder

It has been my experience the long-winded explanations of things cloud our true intentions as the mind overshadows the heart; what we seek is a balance between both. Enriching our lives with simple concepts for love, the satisfaction of achievement, and its expression is where life is clearest and uncomplicated.

Dominant Factors

1. Understanding **your personal brand is your story**; it is the prepared and scripted description of what you are and what you are becoming. It is the relevance of your life and how you affect others.

2. **Your personal brand is one scripted out of character and not self-promotion** for either your company or yourself, knowing no matter how good the image, people rate the experience.

3. Understanding **people are drawn in by imagery, and your promise** is important **but it's character, consistency, and deep experiences that become solidified in the emotions** that keep them coming back for more.

4. **Implement a Lifetime Value strategy or approach to branding and building relationships and partnerships**; it highlights your long-range purpose to the marketplace.

5. **Provide experiences that transcend money** because of its life-changing effect; for example, the price is a secondary condition at the finest restaurants; it is the experience we crave most.

6. **Build perpetuated brand trust** by making a promise and keeping it. Remember the greatest is the one who serves the most and MJE aka, Magic Johnson Enterprises has built a brand, in part, by serving and establishing a trust relationship with those who have the greatest needs.

7. **Invest in thyself;** it takes an investment of Time, Interest, Money, and Energy (TIME), so decide not to leave it to chance, it is your brand to own and control!

Chapter 6

Dominate Via Leverage

"The gig economy is empowerment. This new business paradigm empowers individuals to better shape their own destiny and leverage their existing assets to their benefit."

John McAfee, British-American Businessman

The act of leveraging anything useful encompasses all the parts necessary to create leverage to move an object. Those components are identified as the Fulcrum, the Lever, and the Applied Pressure or Force. As individuals, when we become aware that our greatest tool for leverage is the one staring back at us in the mirror, we will experience greater movement with maximum outcomes. For example, if you are the fulcrum in a given situation or equation, as the central part of the leveraging process, you provide the support and the ability for the lever to pivot. In the act or process of leveraging something, all parts have a vital role, but without the fulcrum, there is no foundation, and results are severely hindered without a firm foundation.

As the fulcrum, you must be solid, trustworthy, and sturdy, providing a real opportunity to move something of size, assuming you will have a reliable lever and enough force to create movement. You are the key element to the process of leveraging; regardless of the role within the components. Leverage is often relying on something or someone else and not yourself, but I believe it is your role that must be seen as the top priority in your mind; the key leveraging factor to gain maximum results.

"Give me a lever long enough and a fulcrum on which to place it, and I shall move the world."

Archimedes, Greek Mathematician

Employing your survival instincts in any setting, especially in an adverse one, is a normal part of the process and progress toward succeeding. Being instinctual is true for either the inexperienced or the most experienced. Whether as a young entrepreneur, an old veteran in a corporate setting, or just life in general, most people are motivated and driven to self-preservation.

We do not necessarily need to learn instincts to survive; although we can learn from our instincts, we are naturally born with them. Utilizing leverage is largely an instinctual tool and the more we understand its power and how to prolifically and effectively use it, the greater the impact we will gain and witness from it. When we activated our natural survival instincts, along with what we have learned from those instinctual experiences, and capped it off with what we learned from other people's experiences (OPE), there's extraordinary potential for impact.

"Entrepreneurship is like a computer game in which you have to master every level before achieving success. Start-ups repeatedly stumble and must go back to the drawing board. The best way to skip some levels and to increase the odds of survival is to learn from others who have already played the game."

Vivek Wadhwa, American Entrepreneur, Academian, & Author

Leverage is a real part of any success story or one of failure. It is used every day, but many are unaware of its existence or its potential impact, either to our advantage or our demise. Leverage is simply the mechanical or an instrumental tool used to move or affect an irregular object or one that would normally be too heavy to move without it.

The tools or assets that we utilize can be anything such as, but not limited to: talent, money, social media, reputation, friendships, structure, strategy, contacts, networking, or even a decision that can facilitate or affect a situation to the advantage we desire. We all have tools or a set of tools, but do not often utilize or fully utilize these tools to our advantage in many cases. I want to talk about leverage and how to use it to dominate in your field, career, or personal life. Here are five simple points about leverage.

"Adaptability and constant innovation is key to the survival of any company operating in a competitive market."

Shiv Nadar, Indian Businessman

1. You must decide and become aware of what you want to affect in your favor. What is it that you need to create or increase? What do you want to do that you currently cannot or believe that you cannot do? Consider this; if you can do it on your own, the task may be too small to create the success you desire the most.

2. Create your BHAG (Big Hairy Audacious Goal) and make every decision to support that desire. Articulated desires create clarity. Clarity added to passion creates a clear path and fuels the energy to get up every day and walk it with intentionality and purpose.

3. Talent, money, knowledge, reputation, skills, structure, strategy, a decision, or anything that is unique to you or within your sphere of influence can be used to generate leverage on your behalf.

4. The outcome itself is achieved by using something you may or may not have been conscious of to complete something that you could not reach without it.

5. Leverage is a tool used to increase force; add greater speeds to the equation, and the force increases exponentially.

"I tell people to look at me and understand that everybody first told me that I couldn't be a 6-foot, 9-inch point guard, and I proved them wrong. Then they told me I couldn't be a businessman and make money in urban America, and I proved them wrong. And they thought I couldn't win all these championships, and I proved them wrong there as well."

Ervin "Magic" Johnson, Co-Owner of Los Angeles Dodgers,

Entrepreneur, Philanthropist

Ervin "Magic" Johnson, who grew up in Lansing, Michigan, leveraged his passion, knowledge, and desires to design a vision for Urban America by bringing greater brand experiences to these forgotten neighborhoods. He established a business model that today and the days ahead will strongly affect millions of lives. This focused business model would also assist in amassing him a net worth of over $500 million. Magic did not just have an excellent idea posed by a single person with undoubtedly a big heart but has repeatedly proved that he is a savvy businessman with expert level status. Magic, who was one of the greatest assist men on any basketball court, also developed an unbeatable team to help create more championships off the court.

Through this leveraged endeavor, he executed on his purpose to show corporate America and the world how to invest and get a solid ROI in a previously overlooked demographic. It's one of the prominent investment strategies that landed him as a partner/owner of the LA Dodgers, Dodger Stadium, a television contract, parking lots, and land around the stadium, according to New York Times. He is a former professional athlete who has not only proven to be a successful entrepreneur, but also a rising and inspiring philanthropist, or what I would call an entredoneur. What is an entredoneur? It is a word that I am branding and a description of an entity or someone who takes on the responsibility and the risk to create opportunities to give and change lives in the world through non-profit endeavors. They are dedicated to being successful in an entrepreneur experience and with the same tenacity and insight; create life-changing innovation in the non-profit arena. Remember every business or company began as an idea which evolved into an entrepreneurial venture. Similar to the origin of entrepreneur, the French translation of this new word, entredoneur is "to give."

We are moving into an area of domination, as we again, learn to do things with purpose, awareness, and as execution becomes paramount to dominating in every area of life. There should not be activities in your life that you are not acutely aware of the outcomes desired, to be achieved, and experiences to be gained. Every situation should be moving you toward a win-win situation where it is a good deal for others, as well as, for yourself. Cheating or decreasing value for others while increasing it for you is not a viable option and over time does not create a great life, just more stuff to be measured by and fewer meaningful relationships.

Several years before the Turkish invasion in 1974, Uncle Kyrus moved from Cyprus to the United States; he had learned valuable lessons from his father who was a very successful entrepreneur in Cyprus. He recognized from his father as a young teenager that trust was paramount for a successful journey in life. As a real estate broker, Uncle Kyrus acquired the reputation of always putting the deal above his gain. Honesty, relationships, and serving people were his priority, and eventually, created a tremendous amount of leverage for him. While working in his uncle's restaurant, he developed strong and healthy relationships among several of the local farmers in Virginia Beach. It was his honest brokering with the farm property owners throughout Princess Anne County that would eventually propel him to large financial gains. Those gains positioned him to leverage even larger deals. Owning commercial properties zoned resort in a city like Virginia Beach, means owning the primmest of real estate. His elevation from selling farmland to owning restaurants, shopping centers, banks, and hotels is a tremendous example of leverage, and this was just the beginning.

"As the broker, I wanted to structure a deal that was fair for both parties. In the long run, it's trust from others that allows you to dominate in terms of respect, so always be honest, domination will come out of respect."

Thomas C. Kyrus, Greek-American Businessman and Philanthropist

Ask yourself in every relationship, business deal, or investment what you expect to get out of it. What is it that you desire the most in this situation? If you have not become aware of what you truly desire in every situation, I suggest that you make that a base part of your overall success philosophy. You must become intensely aware of what you want, work toward achieving it, and decide nothing will stand in the way of hitting your target! You want to build a platform for a life that you want on purpose, rather than being caught up in idle activities and wondering where the time has gone or the life that I wanted. You do not want to find yourself asking the question, why didn't I work harder toward what I wanted rather than leaning on how others defined me or what they wanted for me? But instead, you mentally announce, I am going to accept the responsibility for creating the life that I desire; so now, it is a life on purpose and consciously done. This desire, which leads to decisions, should be accompanied by wisdom and guidance from others outside of you.

Once you have decided what it is that you desire, now it is time to become more aware of what you must bring to the table. It is necessary to assess what you have access to, who you have access to, and how these assets can all be used to manifest something greater than what you could have done without them. It is an awareness that you must generate leverage now to get what you want and to create more leverage along the way.

Look at it this way; some people do not utilize others as leverage, while others overuse their relationships by attempting to involve them in many things, to the point of being inappropriate. What I am saying is that we all have a purpose; therefore, every relationship should have meaning; some are just waiting for you to ask and would not mind vouching for you or helping you leverage their relationship on your behalf.

At age 89, Uncle Kyrus has not changed; he still has those two simple goals in his life. Improve yourself and help people; until it was recently sold, every Friday at lunchtime you could find him at his family restaurant sitting with his friends and international philosophers discussing world events and solving its problems. Uncle Kyrus is the type of person when he asks you how he can help, he truly means it; like other giving individuals, he will often jump in and offer his assistance without the ask. Trust me; my family represents just one of the many families he utilized his resources to strengthen and improve lives. Again, he is another great example of the evolution from an entrepreneur to the status of an entredoneur. He may even be the recipient of the first Lifetime Entredoneur Award!

How do we improve or increase our leverage? With the equation of leverage, there are several calculations or elements that can increase your position; sometimes it is a strong decision that marks the beginning of that leverage. Recalling the one example with Chief's 1987 ordeal with a woman in HR who was interviewing him for what would have been his first supervisory position at MCI. She, point blank, told him that he would never be anything and would never amount to anything.

With that negative yet awakening response, he vowed never to be underleveraged again; he began plowing through and reading the WSJ (Wall Street Journal) daily, left the company and went back to school to get his MBA to give him a sense of being more relevant to the world. There, he would hone in on his communication and analytical skills. His goal, moving forward would be simple: always be prepared with the most relevant information or knowledge, be the most prepared in the room, have an insatiable appetite for knowledge, and a keen focus on leveraging that knowledge with every possible opportunity. Based on my personal experiences with him and observations, he hits the mark. I have witnessed his evolution from the locker room to the boardroom, which was all started with a decision.

"When you decide to dominate, your decision itself becomes leverage, and winning emerges as a non-negotiable quest and result; so, the quest doesn't conclude until your win is recorded."

W.H. Dozier III, Founder, UTake Dominion

Whether as a Group President of a major corporation or President of Ashburn Youth Football League (AYFL), Chief always proved to be a masterful leader. Leveraging his experience from his youth, his philosophy and vision with

AYFL was to assure that every kid had their best part of the day while among the staff and coaches. It is an organization that has produced countless numbers of positive experiences, and a solid group of college-bound athletes. Among them is Trace McSorley, one of the most exciting quarterbacks in Penn State football history.

Here is an astonishing account, since the year 2007, there has been a high school football team from Ashburn, VA participating in the Virginia State Championship Game every season. That is 11 straight seasons with one of the four Ashburn high schools having a presence in the final game of the season and winning 6 out of the 11 appearances. The effects of good solid leadership are never hidden.

"Our goal is to make it the best hour of that day for each kid and also to keep us aligned with the high schools to teach them the stuff they need to know to be successful players, to teach them good sportsmanship, how to win and to lose, and how to be overall good kids."

"AYFL strives to help its players succeed both on and off the football field."

Troy "Chief" Cromwell, President of Centennial Technologies, Former President of AYFL

As mentioned in the first chapter, about 30 years post-college, Chief and I were leaders of Verizon's Global Strategic Services team. Chief held the Group President position overseeing a business unit with a revenue target of just over $4 billion, while I headed the S&E Vertical. We would eventually learn that the Cisco Sports & Entertainment business unit was on pace to generate over $100 million in revenue in the same year. Cisco's S&E business unit had come about after John Chambers had conversed with the author, Ron Ricci about Cisco having a division solely focused on Sports. Ricci would become Cisco's VP of Corporate Positioning and his brainchild unit which focused on S&E, immediately brought in 15 different experts for the new division. In less than 120 days, the group had built a multi-million-dollar business unit by a leveraged internal collaboration with Cisco's sales and marketing team to win contracts with Arizona Cardinals, New York Yankees, and the Dallas Cowboys.

At Verizon, we also learned that our counterparts from the company's Networking team were assessing the cost of upgrading the technology within Verizon's sponsored facilities. It included stadiums, arenas, ballparks, and Live Nation properties across the US. With a budget of over $300 million to upgrade these facilities, we found a vital leveraged component to design a shared cost model with customers and began projecting an ROI.

One of our stops would include meeting with "Magic" Johnson and AEG. Although today Magic is partnered with the investment firm, Guggenheim Partners, as an owner of the LA Dodgers, a few months after our executive Cisco meeting, we were sitting with Magic discussing partnership possibilities as he was developing an opportunity to own and operate an NFL franchise and the new stadium in Los Angeles.

Magic understood how to leverage his money, connections, and yes, even his name. We must be adamant about discovering what our leverage is and what leverage is needed to move heavier obstacles for greater achievements. Learning how to network and develop those leverage points of money, business, contacts, social media, relationships, recognition and then executing on those leveraged points to dominate is imperative. Execute with forethought and preparation to increase maximum force; in other words, have a plan and work your plan to perfection. If you do not achieve it the first time, continue and learn and adjust from experience.

Whenever I have asked an entrepreneur or top executive of any small organization the "million dollars" question, I have done so to effectively plan, and establish a strategy to fulfill the vision. It is a simple question that takes some real thought. That question is, "Do you want to establish or grow your company by $1 million, $10 million, or $100 million?" With each level, the overall strategy, and the leverage needed will be modified. The type of relationships and potential partnerships vary at the different levels and are assigned different targets, as well as, methodologies to hit those targets.

Using leverage starts with a mindset that current levels of achievement may or may not be sufficient with what I have now, but I must take what I have been given and what I can access to create greater leverage to move heavier opportunities. Passion, people, and certainly purpose are a few vital determinants of personal leverage, but we must become consciously aware of everything that is within us first. Work to uncover assets that you may not have tapped into; create systems of daily preparation and study to increase your personal leverage. Take inventory of your talents that you have not developed yet because you think they are not marketable. They may be the key to taking you to the next level.

The writing of this book means I am a published author. Being a published author is exciting to me. As a publisher, I have additional leverage in fulfilling my purpose, as well as, creating new avenues to network and help others. Make a list of the things that are external, including, for example, people who can create leverage on your behalf; find out how they best fit and engage their assistance.

Developing a superior philosophy about life and your vocation is a long-term leveraging point that might be the most important in your life. The key is understanding what you truly believe and adjusting for maximum levels of success. I have seen many people who are ready to argue and defend their positions and many times they are just dead wrong but will defend their position no matter what. For example, if they had simply put more effort into studying or seeking mentors to help them, they may have achieved much more success, because of their commitment to cause many times, is unparalleled. Your chosen philosophy is your guideline and roadmap.

Having the wrong road map obviously leads to the wrong destination. How do you know if it is wrong or not? Are you where you want to be or where you set out to be in your journey? Adjust the map; the destination has not changed, though the direction you take to get there often does. What if you had access to the One who knows all things with nothing hidden from Him simply because He created it? Now imagine if we could leverage portions of His knowledge and understanding. Would you be interested in having access to that powerful lever? Think back to George Washington Carver's experience with the peanut.

By the time I had entered the second semester of my senior year of college, I had spearheaded four different mini entrepreneurial ventures. I had a marginal profit with one venture, broke even on two others, and had a considerable loss on another. But before my departure from the university, John Shaffer and I once spoke to a group of about 450 Penn State Business School students, and my theme centered on God is an entrepreneur; the original One. Since then, 30 years later, I have also discovered He is the greatest entredoneur.

Although this message was received by some and thought-provoking to others, I am not sure what was more surprising to the group, the message, or my attire. I had been told that this was a radio broadcast, and so I dressed comfortably for the occasion in my athletic sweat suit gear. Remember, I was a senior college student; the problem was it was not a radio broadcast, and I had to enter a hotel ballroom full of students "dressed for success." Now, looking out into that sea of "coats and ties" how do you think I set up an opportunity to leverage that ordeal? I started my presentation by asking the question, "Why is everyone so overdressed," of course.

We can create great success by leveraging outcomes via better systems based on the immutable laws of business, as well as, success in our personal life. Developing Standard Operating Procedures (SOP's) and/or defined philosophies like entrepreneurship in your organization or personal life can generate a tremendous amount of leverage. As an owner, if you think for a moment that you could convince all of your employees to act as if the company were theirs and that their behavior directly affected the success of the company, they probably would view their jobs differently; especially if you demonstrated your appreciation for that behavior. Many do not see a direct correlation between their individual effect on the team winning or direct reward for doing a good job. There is no win for them, so they just work in a job where they are not willing to overextend themselves to make someone else rich; that is a sad commentary but true. It is also a point of leverage that is not being utilized properly. If you are an entrepreneur, CEO, or top manager and you do not find a way for the team to buy into the success of the company, but just performs tasks, then I believe you have missed a great point of leverage to create an innovative and exciting organization.

At Prevailance Inc, John Owens is a dynamic CEO and thought-provoking leader. When you sit down with this Retired

Navy Pilot, regardless of where it might be, make sure you are prepared to take notes because you are about to go to school. While many detest or attempt to avoid change at all cost, John's vision for Prevailance is built on the spirit of change. He has a strong focus on its' employees; the company rewards change via a series of awards for leadership, customer improvements, and discovering new and efficient processes to operate.

"Companies that value change don't suppress innovation, they channel it."

John Owens, CEO of Prevailance, Inc

At every level in business, you can see yourself as an entrepreneur who is powerful in creating a better company and your skill, talent, and work creates value for both the company and the customer. That insight alone can create immense leverage by causing a shift in thought and core values. Some companies have consistently struggled on how to get employees to buy into the overall success and increased profitability of the company. Companies with a short-sighted vision and executives who operate in that manner do not consider it because they have decided not to see or believe that the employee is their best or greatest asset for success. In down economies, people need a job and will be loyal to a paycheck more than the culture and meaning of the job experience. Therefore, employees are expendable and turn over as a regular business expense.

I do not personally believe that, and this book does not espouse those values. I believe vision is the prerequisite that affects the trajectory for all endeavors, and therefore, sets the tone for the experiences during the journey. Creating a great work culture and deciphering a way of sharing profits, providing long-term benefits and retirement is crucial in establishing a path for great experiences and lays the foundation to build a successful vocation and company. Leverage requires discovery, failure, and the concluding of a process that works, as well as, a process that does not. Learning to leverage failure by learning from it increases your probability of success because you can eliminate what did not work. It is not that we fail on purpose or dismiss it to create leverage; we accept that sometimes failure is the only path to finding a solution.

"Your workforce is your most valuable asset. The knowledge and skills they have represent the fuel that drives the engine of business - and you can leverage that knowledge."

Harvey McKay, American Businessman

I hate the concept or idea of failure and choose to see and translate it into a learning opportunity. Leverage is increased from learning because you have narrowed the field by the process of elimination and you are now unafraid to try something new or ask exciting questions about what is possible. Taking the position that you learn from failing moments and not quitting because of it, further positions you to seek solutions rather than excuses. Innovative solutions are derived from both failure and great successes. Embracing the idea of both, with leverage in mind, leverages the removal of the fear of falling short and prepares you for dominant actions and outcomes. Thank God, inventor, Thomas Edison was an entrepreneur on a mission and refused to see failure as a stopping point during the many times he did not discover something miraculous and inspired many others to think and do likewise.

"Be courageous! Whatever setbacks America has encountered, it has always emerged as a stronger and more prosperous nation. Be brave as your fathers before you. Have faith and go forward."

Thomas Edison, American Inventor, Entrepreneur, Co-Founder of General Electric

There are very few industries where half the businesses do not fail within the first four years of the startup period. By year 10, more than 70% of businesses fail, that is a staggering number. Now because of innovation in technology, and behavior of the consumer, long-standing businesses are failing because they have not leveraged technology and embraced change. Also, I believe many businesses, and individuals fail, in part, due to not leveraging knowledge and imagination. Imagination used in business is not an entirely new concept, but it is underutilized. We do not like the soft skills, but these skills are invaluable. Imagination allows you to innovate and create beyond the known facts. There is nothing in the material world that was not created by imagination. The imagination is the ability to picture what does not exist or seeing something in a new way that does. It is the key to innovation and leverage.

Most people who are going to be entrepreneurs are going to fail, but many of them have technical skills to produce, provide a service or sell a product but not the skills to run a business. I would encourage you to check out www.sharktankblog.com and look at some of the failure stories and near misses that are there. There are a lot of interesting stories of why some companies did not make it even though they have increased their leverage by taking a partnership with the sharks.

To understand how to leverage business, Shark Tank is a great example of good ideas and bad ideas where some work and many do not. The premise is that the entrepreneur has the technical expertise and may have manufactured and sold some number of products in the marketplace trying to prove that the business has some potential for increased sales. While on the show, they are requesting money but what may be the greatest commodities are the knowledge, experience, and contacts that the Sharks have due to their success. Couple it with the exposure to the show's large viewership and the potential is exponential! Sometimes it only takes one experience, a contact, or one deal to have a major impact on your situation. During one Shark Tank program, here's how Chris Johnson of Rapid Ramen Cooker responded after he and Mark Cuban agreed verbally on a deal.

"Making a deal with Mark Cuban is huge for me. To build wealth, it's all about proximity. If you hang around four broke people, you will be the 5th. If you hang around even just one billionaire, that proximity can impact your life!"

Chris Johnson, Founder, Rapid Ramen Cooker

Chris is correct in the concept that the type of feathered friends you run with matters immensely. In his case, with a one product idea, he was on a path to interact with a seasoned billionaire entrepreneur that was a game changer. The exposure Chris would have with Mark Cuban and his staff would be short-lived and for various reasons, the deal was not solidified, however, due to the leveraged power of exposure during the show and some strategic partnering, even with a "no deal" Rapid Ramen Cooker sales moved higher. Rapidly higher!

The first level of leverage is understanding not just how much expertise you have, but what you are missing. It is an assessment where you check your ego at the door; you must understand that a pure idea person, which is a great gift to have, does not always have management or great organizational skills. Idea people are normally more imaginative by nature. They spend a lot of time talking about their ideas and normally need to seek more logistic orientated people to figure out how to do something and to keep it on task. These are more engineer types. Engineers do not usually make good sales professionals, so now you must get with someone who is a great connector and communicator to learn how to sell the product.

You must remember your constant need for facts, honest feedback, and evaluation as the process unfolds. This is not an emotional quest as it can feel like one, but more a fact-finding expedition that you must embark upon to run a successful business. Most businesses fail because people who start them do not leverage information and constantly look for what someone else can do better than they can. The smartest guy in the room fills the room with people who are talented in different areas, can be trained, or are smarter and more talented than they are in areas where they might be deficient. Intellect always needs influence and leadership. In the beginning, the entrepreneur would be better served to focus on the team more than the product. A review of the team at the outset of each new goal makes sense to make sure you have what you need in personnel to achieve the next venture. If you have already started, keep going, but you may want to slow down long enough for people to jump on the bus.

This brings me to the second part of business leverage which is that of getting the right people on the bus. If you go back and look at the statistics, most of the problems with businesses surviving are plain old mismanagement and incompetence. There are times when we do not know that we do not know something. Bringing in the consultant or finding a mentor in a similar business may be able to help you evaluate whether you are maximizing your potential. There are also classes that you can take or take advantage of programs like SCORE (Senior Core of Retired Executives) which is part of the Small Business Administration. They can offer great advice when you cannot afford to hire someone on staff or a consultant. Many cities have business assistance teams through the Mayor's office, Community Redevelopment Agency (CRA) or other business development departments.

One of the most crucial areas of business is financial management. Often companies are not properly funded to manage cash flow or lack thereof due to long periods when you may not get paid. Some larger companies which may have a great deal of operating cash will still pay slowly. Many CFO's see slow payables as a financing tool and pay slow, so they do not have to borrow money to manage their cash flow. The other reason is to earn more in interest on their invested capital before having to pay it out. A financial process that hurts many small businesses that lack the understanding of how working with much larger companies can sink them, especially if that is their only client. Managing payables through fractioning or by having enough money for slow payables is critical. Operating reserves can act as a leveraging tool.

The business owner no matter the method used to ensure that they have the capital to provide the service, buy materials or sustain the marketing and sales efforts must make that a constant chore of the business. Managing payables and debt is as crucial as any other phase of business. Being under leveraged where you do not have access to lines of credit or small loans can be as bad as being over-leveraged. Either way, it can be difficult to function if your business is over or undercapitalized.

Leveraging Your Vocation

Creating leverage in your vocation is important to most accomplished people because they see opportunity as a ladder to climb and not a bed to lie in. Employment is a matter of climbing from one position to another as supervisor, manager, director, maybe even a President or as a partner of the company. What does your personal growth plan look like? Most want growth, but we must decide what our plan will entail and how we will finish, time permitting? When dominating in a business setting, it is imperative to assess, reasonably understand, and address ourselves as individuals before we size up situations.

People at all stages in their vocation want to feel needed and feel that they contribute to the bottom line. It is difficult to do that over time without moving up in the company because most have an entrenched bureaucracy that does not allow for true individualism and entrepreneurship. I am talking about real growth that allows achievers to continue to increase in knowledge and reinvent themselves for the coming changes in the marketplace, not those who want promotion only on seniority.

As the Chair of Wells Fargo's Board of Directors, Betsy Duke is a fine example of what happens when you actively pursue personal reinvention and personal growth. Before her work in the banking industry, she was in hot pursuit of an acting career, but when I first met Betsy, she was a founder, executive, and board member of the Bank of Tidewater, headquartered in Virginia Beach, VA. Uncle Kyrus was also an important board member of this successful local community bank and his role in endorsing Betsy became crucial to her executive elevation. The opportunity for Betsy eventually to become the President of the bank came when her mentor and CEO, Burt Harrison suddenly passed away. However, it would be Uncle Kyrus who recognized her amazing talent, ability, and work ethic. He, against strong resistance from other board members, recommended to the board that instead of hiring an outside executive to become the next President, Betsy had developed into a fine bank executive, and she should be given the opportunity to serve in the top position.

"I think it's great, the fact that more women are brought in at such a high-level, especially in this industry. It appears to be a pattern from my perspective; it's inspiring!"

Jessica Phillips, Control Specialist, Wells Fargo

Looking at where she is today, there is no doubt she took care of business every step of the way. A Fortune Magazine piece by Bloomberg from August 2017 on the Most Powerful Women, mentioned that by her obtaining this position, it caps one of the most epic climbs by a man or woman into the financial industry's top echelons. Betsy has become a tremendous role model for men and women in the financial industry, but especially for women. I have spoken to women who work for the company who testify and are inspired by Betsy's climb. What an amazing journey.

"Knowledge is the power that ignites self-mastery and dominance."

W.H. Dozier III, Founder, UTake Dominion

Experience is the first place to create leverage for long-term growth in a company. Many HR departments are not set up to look at skill sets as they are at educational level and on the job experience. These are important, but I have met many industrial people, as well as, multi-millionaires with little to no formal education. True education is both acquiring more knowledge, skills, and making people more aware of the talents that they already possess and how they may use them to their advantage.

Experience is an important tool to use in separating yourself from others. The traditional model is to look at what people have done and compare them to see who has the most experience. That is not the best way to look at experience. The problem with this method is people think that the number of times doing a task makes you more competent in doing it. Repetition is a great teacher but what if you are repeatedly doing it wrong or without enthusiasm and creating a mediocre product? Experience can also hinder you because some believe it does not qualify you to do something new and they do not see the skills behind the experience as transferable.

A truer sense of the word experience must go deeper into what are the components of the task and what parts are transferable to other things that may make a person as good or better at doing something else. Getting people to realize that they are more gifted than their experience brings extra resources into the business and gives the individual an added advantage by recognizing transferable skills where others do not. Allowing this mindset to flourish will also create more opportunities for those who can cross-train or add additional skills. Andrew Moses, a gifted, hard-working young man, is a great example of what can happen when a company adopts that mindset. Shortly after beginning his career, Moses was completely caught off guard when he was part of a company-wide workforce reduction at KPMG. Whenever he is faced with adversity, Moses thinks about his grandfather who escaped Nazi Germany at the tender age of 15 and after immigrating to the United States, worked tirelessly to build a successful business overcoming countless challenges along the way. Faced with the adversity of being cut loose by his first employer, Moses, now young, hungry, and carrying a chip on his shoulder, sought and eventually landed with a group that knew he lacked certain prerequisites but simultaneously saw a young man with transferable skills.

Moses, who has already been recognized as having the skill set to be a great c-suite leader, at that moment decided there was something to prove to himself. With almost a decade of experience later, Moses holds a vital leadership position overseeing sales and marketing at that same company, Morgan Franklin Consulting, one of the fastest growing private companies in America. If you looked at his experience only, you would have missed what he had the potential to become.

Awareness and increased information no matter what subject you are talking about makes you superior in the conversation and endeavor. Become a person who is in the moment, prepared, aware of himself, and who increases knowledge in many areas as a lifelong pursuit. Knowledge and experience many times are transferable from task to task giving a person fewer limitations than what is traditionally believed.

"Leverage is figuring out where or what makes you different, putting that difference to work, and making yourself nearly impossible to get rid of."

Andrew Moses, Director of Sales & Marketing, Morgan Franklin Consulting

Building a resume or dossier is your calling card for opportunities both in your current position and all future positions. Your Dossier is you, not a vague someone of whom you are trying to describe. Make it about the facts of your experiences and your skills but also make sure it is a good representation of you. Even if your experience is diverse be creative and descriptive; hone it into a skilled message about who you are and the skills you possess. This may be how you present your skills on social media sites. Resume development is a part of the branding process.

Interpersonal work relationships are good for many reasons, but like business relationships, become your best tool for leverage. Let us be clear, people and your relationships are always your best assets or worst liabilities. On your job, you do not have to be the life of the party, but you must be a person that can get along with most people. Loners do not make good supervisors and many times are overlooked because they are seen as not having social skills. We as humans naturally overlook the people we do not like. Personal prejudice and just having a general dislike of people can affect how we hire and fire. Who would disagree that bosses have favorites or people they like. I call them a group of untouchables.

Mastering interpersonal relationships should be a goal as a business owner or someone looking to move up and be successful in any business. I have always said that eventually, someone is going to ask about you. If the consensus is you are lazy, incompetent, or just a bad person; whether it is true or not your days are probably numbered. The influence of others on what is being said behind your back can make or break your career. There are plenty of books that can help you build work relationships but let us talk strategy for a minute.

Develop and maintain an influence diagram showing who in your company from your supervisor to HR, co-workers, and other people could have the most impact on your position in the company by either positive or negative feedback. Those are the relationships you need to improve or at least understand how they affect you.

As a strategic goal you should be at least cordial to these people, and over time seek to know them and allow them to see the employee you are and an all-around great person. You cannot win with everyone, and in some cases, you should not try, but you should be aware of who may have the most influence in getting you where you want to go. I am not suggesting anything other than building an office environment that is cordial and that these people would have the opportunity to get to know you and your level of commitment to the company through your hard work. Nurture all relationships where possible; even those who are challenging to work with, remain strategic. That also may mean distancing yourself from certain associations that could hurt you.

Owners should see every position and person as strategic because they are the most important commodity. Getting and retaining good people with ability who are faithful to the company is everything. Do not allow toxic people to stay even if they do a good job. Engage them, but if they are poisoning the well, they cost you money in the long-term in moral and trust.

This next subject is somewhat debatable. I have heard a lot of differing opinions. Many people believe that the best way to advance over the long-term is not to have too many weaknesses. They spend most of their time trying to get better at what there are not that good at and what may be draining them of further productivity and creativity. Having glaring weaknesses, on the other hand, will not get you the Most Valuable Personnel (MVP) of the company either. Your weaknesses can be a stumbling block and slow production for the company if it requires others to pick up slack for you.

I want to share an article that I came across that brings an interesting viewpoint.

"Think back to your last performance review. What do you remember most? The feedback you got on what you did well or the feedback on what you didn't do as well? If you're like 81 percent of the workforce, you focus more on your weaknesses and don't give much thought to how you can use more of your strengths in the workplace. According to research from the

Marcus Buckingham Company, 59 percent of the workforce believes they will be most successful if they focus on fixing weaknesses rather than leveraging strengths.

It seems lots of us are more interested in what we don't do well, and we take our strengths for granted. Marcus Buckingham, a leader in the strengths-based movement, has done a lot of research that proves this approach doesn't offer any long-term success. Buckingham describes a strength as not just something you're good at, but something you consistently do to near perfection and that gives you strength. A weakness is a task that drains you and makes you weak. Buckingham believes, and I agree, that leveraging and amplifying your strengths is the only way a person or an organization will excel; it's never by fixing weaknesses.

In 2007, 198,000 workers were asked whether they had the chance to play to their strengths every day. The findings showed that those who strongly agreed that they did were

- *50 percent more likely to work in teams with lower employee turnover;*
- *33 percent more likely to work in more productive teams;*
- *44 percent more likely to work in teams with a higher customer-satisfaction score.*

Despite this kind of research and the fact that smart companies like Yahoo, Intel, and Best Buy are publicly committed to a strengths-based culture, there's lots of evidence to suggest that many people don't know how to do it. It's simple: If you're currently employed, identify the specific work activities where you feel strongest and intentionally and strategically focus your job around these activities. When you do this consistently, you'll gradually tilt the playing field so that the best part of your job becomes the biggest part of your job. If you're job hunting, now is the time to clarify your greatest strengths, ensure that you can articulate them, and know what to look and listen for when you meet with potential employers.

For more information about how you can better identify your strengths and weaknesses, check out Buckingham's online and printed resources at www. marcusbuckingham.com."

Story written by Caron Vernon, Associations Now, November 2010

Here is the one thing that I would add to that. I believe in constant improvement, and that is not just in getting stronger but working where you are not strong. I just believe that a lot of this should be done in private. Life presents many opportunities that I view as combat. When in combat, your weaknesses are what are first exploited; that is what the enemy is looking for in you. Strategically preparing for battle is easy to fight where you are strong, but areas of weaknesses are where you will be attacked so why not lead and spend most of your time getting your enemy to fight you where you are strong and in your private time work on your weaknesses, so they are not apparent. Personal development should be something we do across various areas of our lives, improving on our strengths and weaknesses, but spending most of that time performing in our strengths.

"Spend most of your time working where you are strong, work on your weaknesses in private so that you are complete in your offense and defense. Be competent in all areas of the fight. "

Ayub Fleming

Investing in yourself consistently and over time is the best way to leverage you in your business and career. When a true leader with a heart to serve his people invests in personal development tools, that process also enables a greater potential impact upon his or her entire team. Improvements among team members will produce exponentially. When one goal is accomplished, rest or celebrate or allow that occasion to pass only long enough to mentally put it away and set a new goal to achieve.

In football or baseball, you win one game at a time, and whether you win that week or lose, you put it behind you, and prepare for the next as if the season is a long haul. Remember your eye is on the championship, and nothing short of that will do. In chapter four, we discussed Bob Peruzzi, and how joining the championship team at Plated as the CFO was beneficial for both him and the company. Here is the thought of Plated's co-founder regarding hiring Peruzzi:

"We're thrilled to welcome Bob to our team and leverage his expertise in financial planning and operations, as we continue to build the world's best food company."

Josh Hix
Co-Founder, Plated

You may be using what you have and acquiring what you do not have as leverage, but now that we have discussed leverage you can do it with intentionality. Strategize, plan, and execute using leverage of all types for your advantage. Leverage accelerates your endeavors and allows you to pursue larger and loftier goals. Leverage your life for greater success.

Dominant Factors

1. **Leverage or good leverage levels the field**; when you utilize it properly you can achieve great or even miraculous results; look how the internet has provided leverage for individuals and small businesses worldwide.

2. **Impose purposeful action to consistently improve personal development**; this action works as the cornerstone of long-term success arranged by a consciously planned effort to openly enhance your strengths, while improving on your weaknesses in private.

3. **With mentors, developing Standard Operating Procedures (SOPs) and a superior defined philosophy for life and business is a long-term leveraging poin**t that will act as a guideline and roadmap.

4. **Become your strongest point of the leveraging equation** for the endeavors in your life.

5. **While improving you, make it a goal to improve, influence, and inspire others** to live at a higher level of thinking, action, and overall purpose.

6. Education is acquiring more knowledge, more skills, and becoming more aware of the talents that you already possess and how you will use it to your advantage; remember; *"Knowledge is the power that ignites self-mastery and dominance."*

7. Prepare to go beyond brand management to improve the brand moving toward brand domination and expansion. Leverage your past experiences and push into new territory. Continue to expose the brand, solidifying its effects on your personal and professional life. People **who dominate seek larger exposure of territories to influence**.

Chapter 7

Raining on My Adversary

"If I run at the same time as my enemy then I realize that he runs under the same sun and moon; I can only defeat him if I rise before him and run longer; that is what creates space between us."

Ayub Fleming

The definition for adversity is to have difficulties and misfortune. The one thing we know is that in life all must face some difficulty and misfortune at some point. I have never heard of a life that was not inspired, shaped, or broken by adversity. I am always surprised and sometimes shocked at the stories of the lives of people that I have known, but did not know the background of their journey. I have also met others who would not let you forget their troubles. "Woe is me" is their calling card to gain your attention rather than your respect.

I would rather have your respect than your attention.

I am writing this chapter because it is as important as anything else to understand that life has difficulty and adversity. Life is hard. I have had people close to me who have lived with passion and grace and died with the same humility in which they lived. If you too are touched by the feelings of your infirmity and that of others, you know that you may grieve for a season, but death teaches us many things about how to live.

Adversity is similar; it strengthens us and teaches us how to grow as the metal of the man or woman we are made, tested, and proven. Trials bring multiple layers of opportunities. Patience is one example; patience gives us the ability to remain calm and level-headed to assess the reality of our surroundings or circumstances and effectively decide what should happen next.

A few years ago, on one occasion, I began advising two small companies, a construction company and a back-office provider which also happens to be service partners. Unfortunately, due to a financial setback, the construction company could no longer make payments to the partner managing the administrative and other functions. As it is with many small business start-ups, the construction company provided 85% to the administrative company's bottom line. This financial setback was a near-fatal blow. They were able to bounce back and learned a valuable lesson about diversifying their pool of clients. Adversity strengthens us and teaches us important lessons we could not learn in any other way. When adversity comes, we must first decide to respond constructively. If you do not know how, then ask yourself how you can respond that creates a win-win situation. The quality of the question is directly linked to the quality answer that you need. Ask empowering questions that allow your mind to seek creative solutions. Then you must be resolute to stay in the fight until you find the way to win. You must pivot and not become rigid in your thinking. I listed nine things that this company did to pivot in adversity and create a winning solution.

1. The owner of administrative service company decided not to panic but instead took a moment, prayed, and quickly decided what their response to the challenge should be. Response should be calculated but never hasty.

2. They began to randomly research to find other opportunities to service clients within the real estate and construction industry online.

3. Within days, they located a small construction company online in need of administrative services. The company was the ideal size that they could service and build small commercial and residential projects.

4. Through some investigative work, they found that the owners of the small construction company were members of the same church; however, they were selling the business and moving out of state relatively soon.

5. Instead of looking for work they looked for an opportunity to purchase the small construction company. One tip is to never limit the opportunity, look at how large you can go or grow and not to merely get through adversity. Look to grow through it.

6. The two parties could not initially agree to terms on a partnership; however, owners of small construction company had a hard-moving date. Continue to not accept no for an answer. Remember there are always opportunities that arise when you do not quit.

7. Tenacity paid off as discussions continued about what opportunity could take place for an equity position to be established with the small construction company. The previous service partner and owner of the construction company became interested in purchasing the small construction company only if the owner of the administrative company is a partner in the deal going forward.

8. The purchase was finalized with the owner of the administrative company having a 30% interest and the remaining interest secured by construction company/partner.

9. Although the acquisition of small construction company was finalized at the beginning of the fourth quarter in a down year, it provided additional revenue to top previous year's revenue by 20%.

"Adversity can breed fear, doubt, and unbelief; fear tears down hope, doubt holds back growth, and unbelief stifles all visions. Deciding to take a stand and being positive about what happens next in any crisis like situation, lays the foundation for exceptional possibilities."

W.H. Dozier III, Founder, UTake Dominion

I shared earlier in the book the story of practice one day that it was raining, and I slipped on a pitch sweep and could hear Coach Paterno from across the field yelling at me not to slip. It was a great lesson for me because I learned in life that adversity is part of the game. A lesson learned in the preparation to win and just not to compete. It had rained, and I expected that slipping on a damp field was part of the game but Coach Paterno did not; he would not allow me or any other athlete to use that as an excuse or it would have become part of my mindset. He trained us to see any weather-related or adverse condition as to our advantage, and so it was. Regardless of the conditions, it was our execution that came close to perfection; it made Penn State champions.

To dominate something is to overwhelm and control it. I remember in Desert Storm the military had this term called "Shock and Awe" which meant to use overwhelming force. It was impressive to see such a display of force from the TV. Think about it, how you would react if you were on the ground and you were being pounded day in and day out for extended periods and trying to hide with nowhere to rest. You would have been glad to see allied troops walking in, as you see there was little resistance when ground troops arrived. War is hell on earth, and do not think for a minute it was easy for the pilots dodging the flak or what would have been done to them if captured. The enemy's troops on the ground must have suffered tremendously in the onslaught and yes, faced tremendous adversity, bringing them to the point of laying down their weapons and quitting.

It is possible that you will experience, as a result of your shortcomings, "shock and awe" during your training and preparation for the next evolution of your life. You, on the other hand, should never allow yourself to be overwhelmed. You must find a way to manage the situation, so you are not overrun. Your senses, intellect, and emotions at times must experience the pain of shock and awe as you work toward perfection through repetitive action and pushing passed your known limits. One more transformative rep at a time as you tell yourself; I must take it, I have got to take it, just one more rep. They say real growth starts when the pain starts, and you continue to push through it.

I believe our lives are driven by underlying hidden philosophies, mental maps, and paradigms that we may not be conscious. Through these patterns of thought in the subconscious mind, we are put on autopilot. It is not until adversity, and something unfamiliar arrives that we realize something is wrong, because emotions now come to the surface to alter the course and influence our decisions. Pain makes you want to quit, even with the best-made plans and loftiest goals.

There should always be the expectation of hard-work, training, unexpected setbacks, change in the market, and a host of other things. An appropriate response as a general plan for adversity should already be in place. You should plan a response because you should expect the adversity. However, as human beings who love certainty, we are often caught off guard by the change which should, in general, have been anticipated. Adopt as a philosophy, that no matter how things appear; change is a constant.

Who in business would not think ever to have an attorney they can call or would not provide insurance for their business if dealing with the public? Who would not do background checks on employees and have tight hiring practices to minimize risk and expand the opportunity for great service or productivity. We must plan for and expect adversity. When you develop your SOP's, remember that people are your greatest tool but also the weakest link in the chain. My goal when creating systems that work consistently is to anticipate issues such as trust or mistakes that cause the system not to work properly.

Employees need to be continually trained, evaluated, empowered, and managed to be developed into a cohesive team. Employees alone are not the system but must be considered an integral part of it and must learn to work within it to optimize performance. The system always breaks down when people fail to understand how important they are to it working. When they see their interests apart from the system, overall team breakdowns are guaranteed.

As I have mentioned before, you cannot control but you can influence the outcomes; what you can control is the effort. Being prepared for challenges is the most basic part of being successful. It is not always an even playing field, and sometimes your opponent has advantages over you, and at times you have advantages over the opponent, which is life and you must accept that. Planning, of course, is part of our preparation, but there is a distinct difference between having a plan and learning to be flexible in adversity. You must learn to change and improvise to be successful. Scenarios should be thought through, so you can anticipate problems and prepare for them. This is planning in real time.

Our first twelve offensive plays of every contest at Penn State were always scripted and called in order regardless of the circumstance. Each play had a specific purpose to gauge the defense's response and provide a loose strategy for the remainder of the game. I will never forget the comments made by Bob Bergman, a Warfare Strategist for the military; he describes planning and preparation this way. **"The process of planning is of extreme value. Going over and simulating countless scenarios is an essential part of the process, but regardless of the arduous details of the planning process, one major truth will always remain. No plan survives first** contact of the enemy; it's the development and execution of the real-time plan that decides who will be victorious."

"Wherever there's destiny; there is also resistance, so we all contend with some measure of adversity; a champion's nature is always to fight adversity, follow the path to victory, and maintain the position of dominance."

W.H. Dozier III, Founder, UTake Dominion

Adversity is a force with an agenda that works against us. Self-imposed or not, one of the things that you can expect in the pursuit of your goals is opposition through people and other opposing forces that can and will align against you. This could come in the form of your health, relationships, finances, and many other things that create obstacles. I lump these all together and look at them as adversaries to be overcome. Phil Knight's journey of success with Nike was anything but simple; when you read his book, *Shoe Dog*, you will discover various details to that fact. Regardless of the adversary's tactics he stayed true to his calling and pushed the brand forward.

Your adversary creates adversity. There's no doubt about it; your adversary is trying to defeat you or at least distract you from your mission. It will push you off course so that you are ineffective, if not altogether defeated. We should always consider adopting a philosophy in our business and personal life that the adversary creates an opportunity for change and growth. You should expect the challenge of the competition because the presence of winning brings a higher level of competition and growth with it. Any great athlete will tell you that when you think you are unbeatable, that is when defeat is nearest. Winning attracts greater competition. It is only a matter of time before the competition has caught up with your skill level and without growth, on your part, surpasses it.

Be aware of and prepare for resistance before you feel it. Understanding that all movement will have resistance or friction, so constant or consistent pressure and force are needed to prepare for and overcome it. Whatever your endeavor, constant application of focus, effort, and strategy is needed to overcome resistance. Adversity is inevitable, and so must preparation and real-time planning be to combat it. If you want to get in the best shape of your life, and you are serious, then put all the pieces in place that put you and keep you on the road of success. For example, here are some items you would associate with an exercise plan: healthy eating, nutritionist, trainer, reading materials, and a gym, gym-like, or anywhere conducive to reach your goals. The level of detail determines the level of seriousness and therefore sets the equation and the tone for the results throughout the quest. Preparing with the smallest of details for adversity eases the suffering that it can cause. The good news is most suffering continues only until something is done to address it.

When accepting a new challenge, always look to get ready mentally and emotionally before making any physical changes.

Remember, you are the source of your effort; God is the source of your perpetual success. Make no doubt about it; you must make an effort. Prepare for the long journey ahead internally first, then externally. Awareness of resistance is first, preparation for resistance mentally and emotionally is next, followed by the implementation and execution of the whole person, mind, body, and spirit. I have seen others, as well as myself, get through many challenges. When you take the time to accept the price that is required to obtain it, think through it, and then plan and strategize against the thing trying to stare you down; it is not so scary when you are prepared to meet the challenge.

Developing and growing in faith in my life must be a constant, faith is the realization that something can and will happen because you are acting on principles that are derived from the Handbook for Success. Knowing that a personal relationship with the Creator provides an unshakeable foundation; His desires for us to be victorious in life is an important truth. Faith is developed by immersing yourself in information, prayer, imagination, and His presence to give us a full measure of strength against everything in life that would attempt to drain, challenge, and oppose us. Faith is the ability to believe and know something good will come to pass, which gives us hope along the way. Faith is put into action when we properly take the constant and consistent action to bring it to pass. There is no faith without the effort to achieve it; so, action and movement are vital.

As a quick tip, get someone you can trust and who will be supportive and honest to whom you can be accountable. Coaches and accountability partners can push you past and through the rough patches. Having some encouragement and direction is a must to achievement. Build your internal and external resources for the journey that lies ahead. When we strive to be in the best physical shape possible, we can aid in our success. It is hard to be serious about success if we are abusing substances or involved in behaviors that cause our body to become weak and our mind dull. We should first identify our body as an instrument of success to prepare it for the stressors and challenges which we will inevitably face.

I do not want to get into the politics of judging people by their looks, but in all honesty, many of us do that. When we see someone, who may be overweight, but they dress sharp and appear prepared, we think more of them than if they are in great physical shape but sloppy and inappropriately dressed. The other part of the external success is putting the right pieces in place to help deal with adversity. Be sure that your peers who support you are also there, to a certain degree, to hold you accountable. A relevant group which is made up of family, friends, and acquaintances who are in place to help you manage the process, give you advice, delegate tasks, as well as, be an escape and stress reliever is vital. Build your internal and external world and design it on purpose for lasting success.

Study the achievement and success of others in particularly how they faced and overcame adversities in their lives and businesses. Gain wisdom from the rain that fell on them and figure out if they did slip and fall, how they got back up. How did they learn to adjust and not continue to make the same mistakes? Glean wisdom from others and not only from your experiences. Learning from others is nearly free; learning from your mistakes can be expensive and set you back. How about learning on someone else's dime? This is what I remember hearing from Dave Truitt, the father of one of my collegiate teammates, Greg Truitt. Dave is a wise and successful entrepreneur and investor, and that is what he would say to those who were planning to enter the entrepreneurial arena. Before you own and operate your own business, it would be wise to work first for someone else in that field. During that time you would get paid while learning from their past and present achievements and mistakes, and then at an appropriate time launch your entrepreneurial endeavor. This is sound advice from someone who has earned his stripes and given back to his community. As your challenges and your successes pile up, be careful not to become arrogant because of prior or current successes; always be teachable.

"We realized success had covered over mistakes, and we had begun to lose our compass."

Charles Schwab, Founder, Charles Schwab

Now that we have gotten past the awareness of resistance, as well as, an adversary to our progress and success, it is time to create movement. There are going to be people and circumstances that can appear to be negative toward your progress. Why, because they may not see the larger picture of what you are doing, and the destiny God has upon your life. Sometimes it is a matter of them having a blind spot because they have not reached that level in their life or you are going against their rules and expectations of you. Remember, it is your brand! Some may envy your success because of their pain. Be mindful of the enemies of progress.

What about and where exactly is the enemy in the camp? There is always an internal antagonist, as well as, an external adversary that creates the opportunity for failure. Continual movement requires the need for us to continue to conduct personal assessments to discover where we are in the process, not only from preparation and a real-time management plan standpoint, but also from a spiritual perspective. We have a responsibility to live, as well as, think in a way that is in line with why God has created us. He has created an opportunity for dominion; to take possession and be a creative force for good. Regardless of the enemy's location or tactics, that creative movement or force for good will demolish all that opposes you and resets a place for you at the table of dominance. There are a few principles we can touch on at this moment, and one is that once we have assessed where we are in a position to God, keeping spiritual awareness in mind, then we must make some tough calls at times because our behaviors and associations often need to undergo modifications. Sometimes we must sweep the entire house clean. We cannot continue with the same behaviors, keep the same associations, and think that this will not affect or spill over into our business and personal lives; it will. Think for a moment of how many people who are succeeding in their vocations, whether they be attorneys, businessmen or businesswomen, athletes or clergy that had a great deal of material wealth and success in their vocation, but personal weaknesses destroyed it. In many cases, the adversary was staring them in the face every day, while they were shaving or putting on makeup unaware.

Change is necessary, and it is inevitable if you are serious about forging a successful journey. Now once you have begun to make some changes that are more in line with your vision and goals for success, then you must undo and replace the bad habits with habits, as well as, associations that support the successful path that you desire. You must sweep the house clean, and then fill it with the factors that equate to successful outcomes. Your mind is where it all begins, if I can attack you there and keep you flustered or stressed out, and then I can get you into a state of confusion, fear, and doubt. You are distracted and in a mental state of lingering frustration, and now hopelessness can take root. If you are hurting enough, you may take the opportunity to seek unproductive alternatives or engage in harmful behavior to avoid the pain and the hard decisions that you must make. We are never without hope; do not avoid making the hard choices or the changes; seek and learn to embrace the transformational process. This is where healing can take place, where victory is won, and dominion has its beginnings.

I would imagine that some individuals, if not most, are convinced that God is their biggest critic or antagonist, when He is our most powerful leader, advocate, and gracious partner. Thus, prayer and acknowledging Him should be a lifestyle as opposed to avoidance and self-medication. We learn to see and operate in the positive, as opposed to operating and thinking in the negative. When you are positive and congruent in your thoughts and actions, God is already moving on your behalf before you are aware of what you need. It is a matter of connection to God and seeing yourself connected and possessing what you want, rather than being disconnected and separated from what you desire. **Choose to be overwhelmingly positive, so that a clear vision and various solutions can be more readily seen and accessible.** Negativity is a filter that limits our view of what is possible, stifling our true and overall destiny.

This is the law of representation: everyone must think of themselves as representing someone or something. The question is who or what do you represent so that your thinking and your actions are consistent with that which you serve? This process assures that your thinking and your actions are consistent with what you represent. We are not perfect, so when we make mistakes, we must give ourselves the grace to do so, learn from them, and get back on track because of whom and what we represent.

What does my company represent? Who is my boss and what does he or she represent? How do my employees describe me and what am I showing them that they represent in working for me? Work with the philosophy that your thoughts, actions, and outcomes are consistent with who and what you describe. Create a mission statement in writing and keep it visible as a reminder. If you are an examiner of God's Handbook for Success, it acts as a guide and reminder of who physically created you, along with an important purpose; this is who you truly represent. Create core values and post them so that your employees and customers know where you stand and then invite your employees to follow them, giving guidance for conducting business, as well as, how to treat each other. They represent you.

There is power and an increase in efficiency where there is agreement. When the employees come under that represented leadership, then the blessing is in the alignment of the vision. When your business or your personal life is most efficient and flows best is when and where you operate in defined authority. Those in positions of authority are not always right, and there is a place to rebel against that which you know is wrong. Character, however, is the important point and the expression of character in strength, with understanding, is the responsibility of the employee. You are not representing yourself only.

When developing yourself as a real person of character and you express core values that you adhere to, there are not a lot of things that can stand against your success. You must become a person of honor where your integrity is not questioned. People will come to trust your word and your work. Trust speeds up productivity and increases profitability. Trust creates synchronicity within your team and begins to attract the right people because of the trust and integrity. Trust in character, but also in the skill to do what you say you are going to do, when you say you are going to do it.

Lack of trust is created by lack of character and the skill to perform. Mistrust erodes our personal and professional life and must be addressed first with us, our peers, our co-workers, and employees and continue until it is removed from our lives. Untrustworthy people are like cancer that should be eradicated as much as possible. It is like chewing food with one tooth, and that one is broken. A hilarious image, but a truth somewhat paraphrased, from Proverbs in God's Handbook for Success.

Joe Healey, who is a CEO, consultant, and entrepreneur currently leads Faster Asset Solutions. In his book, *Radical Trust*, he goes into depth on the power of trust and how it relates to core values and the building of character, which leaders must possess. As a consultant, he assisted Marconi before it became Ericsson, on how to tie compensation to character and core values. A commitment to integrity was at the top of the list.

You must be more committed than your adversary because it does rain on the just, as well as, the unjust. It is raining on my adversary, but what am I willing to do about that. Am I willing to work harder, prepare longer, to become a person of character and play to my strengths; all the while, working on my weaknesses in private? Am I willing to learn consistently and build trust and demand it from others only when I know that I have earned it? I have heard it said that character is the Champions Gate, through which, all who would achieve greatness and longevity must enter.

"Establishing sustained success with character in mind is what we should strive for, but also being mindful of not allowing our prolonged successes to become a prerequisite for a string of failures; always be prepared for the next goal and transformation."

W.H. Dozier III, Founder, UTake Dominion

"Every adversity, every failure, every heartache carries with it the seed of an equal or greater benefit."

Napoleon Hill, American Author

Dominant Factors

1. **Remembering in life, we all have challenges and adversity; it is how we choose to respond and deal with it that separates us** and determines the trajectory of what happens next.

2. **Fall in love with stories of overcoming adversity**; it acts as a cornerstone to build hope and mental toughness, serving well in hard times.

3. Understand that **adversity creates mirrors in which we examine ourselves more closely than in times of success**; always expect success but realize it can cloud your perception and vision. It is adversity that more accurately teaches us who and what we are.

4. We must **be careful not to allow prolonged success to become the prerequisite for failure**; it is only the continuing reaching for the next challenging goal that we continue to transform, not in performing and creating success in the familiar.

5. Realize that **the deepest changes occur when we accept the challenges of what we see or perceive as impossibilities** but decide to accept the challenge anyway.

6. **Remain more committed than your adversary**, because it rains on the just, as well as, the unjust.

7. **Work extremely hard to keep your name off your list of adversaries**; stay out of your own way!

Chapter 8

Grindors Master Potential

"When you look at people who are successful, you will find that they aren't the people who are motivated but have consistency in their motivation."

Arsene Wenger, French Football Manager

In chapter seven, we gained some insights regarding our adversary in real life. The chances are, if you, like my kids have joined the fan base of the multi-billion-dollar box office hit-movie series, Transformers, you have seen the work of Grindor. If you are not a true fan, you should know Grindor is a fictional adversarial bot; a Decepticon from the Revenge of the Fallen franchise. He is known to be a master strategist and close combat specialist. According to link, https://tfwiki.net/wiki/Grindor_(ROTF), Grindor can predict his opponents' moves before they know it themselves; relying heavily on his instincts. Although this fictitious character is an adversary on the side of evil, it is his list of mental and physical attributes where I want to focus. Other than being a master strategist, Grindor is a close combat specialist, able to predict opponent's moves, and highly instinctual.

Real grindors employ "the grind" daily, so it is a constant application as a strategist, who is completely aware, equipped, and prepared to combat all that opposes them. It requires all your attributes and faculties; that is, from a perspective that includes the strengthening and use of the whole person, meaning your mind, body, and spirit. So, it is a combined mental, physical, and spiritual grind, that I believe, introduces us to true mastery. The focus of attention and implementation of all three of these aspects of your being, give you the ability to reach the highest level of mastery and become a master of your potential.

I also believe, in God's eyes, we were all created to be far more important and far more valuable than our potential. In other words, we were created with potential, and not for potential. So, we were created for a designed purpose, giving us significance, and having a great amount of potential. Our goal as grindors can only be to utilize our entire being to master potential.

Grindors, therefore, are fully equipped with combative weapons, value the understanding and implementation of the strategy, as well as, the full potential of the human makeup: mind, body, and spirit. It is an overall combination that imminently leads to a full portion of mastery and execution.

As you could guess, I am a legitimate 'Big Screen Movie Fan,' and there is plenty of fictitiousness to be seen in that setting; however, moving in the direction of mastering potential is anything, but a fictional quest!

One of the important elements of any strategy or any set of strategic plans is built on daily structure. But before we get more into daily routines and habits, I have a question for you: Have you ever wondered what some people are doing each morning when you get up and start your day, feet on the floor, trying not just to lay back down and snooze for a few minutes more? I sometimes wonder if others who are the best at what they've been called to do are motivated to get up earlier than others, for the sake of the grind. You know those gritty, sometimes hard as nails moments, when it is just plain hard. It is where victory does not seem like a victory, but shallow, empty moments of hard-work. I mean, you are up before the rooster kind of grind, when you can hardly motivate yourself to arise, but you rebel against the lack, and start your daily routine anyway. If you are one of these, you have the mindset to set the pace of an official grindor.

I am writing this because I have struggled at times, but I find solace in the moments after the grind is over, when I am euphoric because the work has been put in, and the damage was done regarding who I used to be. My dreams that once seemed more than a country mile away, must bow down, knowing I am getting closer with every possible moment; knowing that I am one step, one giant step closer to dominating in what I do. I am grinding passed my potential and stepping into my dreams. It is the grindors who master their full potential in this life. You will not know what that is until you have been pushed well past what you think that is. That push past your known limits does not start in the body, but the mind and the spirit.

"I can't rest because it's based on a lifestyle. I've got to grind. Grinding is my rest; I taught my kids that, you start something; you finish it...You got to be willing to walk in a storm. That's what I tell people all the time."

Ray Lewis, Retired NFL Pro Bowler, Author, and Mentor

Spirit, or spirituality, is many things to many people. In times past, science has had a hard time quantifying or ever accepting the existence of something spiritual, but cannot deny that in life there are things that cannot be logically explained; however, it can be a spiritual experience. Love is one of those things that is a deeper experience past logic which without it can turn life into a grotesque experience. Success in life has a spiritual component that mastering the basics of successful principles will set you on the right path but the deeper experience of meaning and fulfillment is hard to grasp without confronting the fact that there is an intelligent design in the universe and that we were created with purpose and significance. To not make this a part of your journey beyond the strategies and the grind is to miss the mark altogether.

"What would it profit a main to gain the whole world and lose his own soul?"

Mathew 8 v 36

Domination is the purpose of this book because expressed excellence through a life that is divinely inspired and lived is the journey not just the goal. It is the call of every man's life to find and fulfill the purpose of why he was created and to live that life to whatever extent he chooses to make himself skilled and becomes a person who creates value. A great deal of that will be unscientific things like loving his family and his neighbor as he loves himself.

Structure

If you have not developed the practice of putting daily structure and disciplines in your life that prepares you for the daily challenge, then you are most definitely limiting your potential and now is a good time to leverage structure around the 1,440 daily minutes you have. In 2016 we saw the end of an era for Kobe Bryant, a masterful player who was beloved but also hated during his career. Maybe it was his prowess or nearly unbearable arrogant attitude as some described him, but for many, they love and hate the standouts in any field. Maybe at the end of the day, he was a winner, and you hated him because he was not on your team.

You cannot have his life's experiences and purpose. Those millions, the cars, the houses, or the screaming fans that bid him farewell as he hit 60 points in his last game, it was allotted for him. There is no shot at that kind of success in life without talent and the work that he was willing to put in. He was the first one in the gym, working hard, and most times by all accounts, the last one to leave. Putting in the long hours is a trait that all the great champions in all fields have, whether it be homemakers, entrepreneurs, teachers, or athletes. You must put in the wrench time to become a classic.

I heard some say that after a playoff game some years ago Kobe missed a winning shot that would have given them the victory. He not only apologized to the team but went out with one of the trainers and shot baskets until 1:00 am in the morning. He did not have to do that, but he understands the grind, the moments of hard-work when no one is watching that makes you one of the best. When you prepare like this, you can perform at the level that he did for a time.

So, what is a simple definition of structure in your life? I am defining the structure as the habits that shape you the most in your life. It is not just the moments like Kobe's ordeal when you cram for an exam or a presentation but the study or self-development of sound work habits when no one else is around. How are you grinding it out on a regular basis? A friend of mine who is an example of one of the best commercial real estate professionals I know provides a good example of structure. He is very disciplined in numerous business pursuits and successful at almost everything he does. His work ethic is real. The grind for him is not easy but is a necessary adversary. Jim Rohn said you should be working harder on your dreams and yourself than you do on your job. You should have a different structure and goals for your off time.

Your day starts the day before. If you stay out late, do not eat right, and will not exercise, then why complain about getting subpar results? Your habits determine your direction and quality of your life and endeavors. Your daily habits must be connected in a real way to what you want to achieve, your vocation, and your dreams you are chasing. If you are not grinding beyond the average workday, then you are not transforming your life. If part of that time is spending it with your family, then bravo, you will reap the results of a good marriage and home. Too much time not working, and you will be the conductor on the poverty train. Work on everything you perceive creates value for your life. Then at the end of it, it was what you chose, and not what someone chose for you. Trust me; you will be screaming all aboard for there are plenty of passengers, dare I say your family and friends and folks you do not know will hop on and ride your success to the end of the line.

A long time ago I heard Ed Cole, minister and author, say that **balance** is the key to life. Balance for me is about training yourself to make small adjustments in response to forces pushing against you; forces that may be pushing against you even when you are not aware of it. When you think that you are on course, you are slowly drifting off course. I equate it to a ship that is sailing for Hawaii from California and heads west on a certain coordinate and lets the ship run on its own toward its desired destination. If the ship without course corrections is only off just a little, it will miss Hawaii all together.

Without any storms to blow you off course, the currents will continually push against your ship pushing you off course toward somewhere else even though you knew where you wanted to go. You were equipped for the journey but flipped on autopilot hoping it would reach its destination. You must have a system of evaluation daily to make sure that you are on course. You must accept the fact that currents pushing against you are pushing you off course and with small deviations unchecked you will miss your desired destination altogether. You can be just five degrees off course and over time you will miss the entire Hawaiian Islands. Your diet, exercise, budget, relationships, and everything else in your life are like that. In the martial arts, there is a belief that when you think you are throwing a kick correctly, that is when you are doing it wrong. Perfection is not about the arrogance of doing it right in your head but feeling the kick and gauging the results.

You are only doing it right when you feel that you have thrown a great kick versus thinking that you have done it correctly. If I throw a hard kick, but it does not affect the target maybe I am not throwing it as hard as I thought or maybe my form is off. You should never be satisfied but in pursuit of constant improvement. The moment you are satisfied rather than content with the effort, you have reached the end of growth. Be content with your current status, but never satisfied with that status.

Break your life down into its separate tasks that you do daily. Look at what you eat, how you study, how you perform at work, your relationships and how you handle each. If you have done your best, be content with the efforts of the day because you cannot change them but always learn from them. Go into your affirmations and state your gratitude for each day and the efforts that are connecting you to your dreams. Then focus on how you can make it better by making small adjustments. Remember swing small miss small. Swing big miss big.

To truly be balanced you also must get stronger in every area of your life. Sometimes it is not a constant gentle push that gets you off course, but a shove in the wrong direction. When we look at people slip and go through all kinds of gyrations without falling, we say "wow, they have good balance." If you can get stronger in all areas, you can create balance in your life because you have no glaring weaknesses. It is easier to take the hits when you have good balance.

One thing we talk about in this book is owning the effort. The hard-work is yours to do. It takes massive action to change the course, but you must be balanced to grow stronger. Let me give you a great example. If you are married but also the CEO or mid-level manager with a fast-growing company, then you know what long hours and dedication to your craft are.

In business, learning to work hard yet smarter separates you from those who are not willing to put in the exhaustive effort or work within a productive environment. Remember this, to the level that you are willing to work, is to the level or intensity that you must find rest. If not, you will eventually break. Here is where you must find a balance because while mastering your craft you also must put in real time building a good relationship with your family and develop real intimacy. Do not grow into a casual passing from day to day; remember it is your family members and their support that you are going to need through some tough times, besides business does not keep the bed warm at night. Find balance and invest in what is important. Do not be enamored with short-term gains only but become obsessed with building a great life over the long haul and beyond. Choose your priorities that will create a perpetual platform for your life's purpose.

I always tell people that when you are working out do not complain about the weights. Gravity is a constant and so the weight stays the same. If you want to lift more weight, you have to grow stronger. In life do not ask for it to be easier, ask how you will become stronger. Muscles are not built by lifting heavy weight; they are torn. Muscles grow during the resting period not during the effort. Balance and longevity are finding the will to make small moves and adjustments between two extremes. A perfect effort must be matched with the balance of a perfect amount of rest to achieve the best results. To dominate in life, you must become and/or remain balanced in your work and your personal life, or you will inevitably sacrifice one or the other. Find balance by spending intense time in both but keep them separate. Choose to love both because when you love something you cherish it, protect it, and provide for it.

Expansion

At every level of your life, you must provide greater details, analytics, and a more precise process to the structure to be able to handle more stress or mental exertion and maintain balance, if you want to create more success. Some believe that exertion cannot be avoided, this is certainly the case from a physical perspective, but in either case, it must be managed. If you want to climb higher mountains and achieve more, then you must grow stronger and learn how to handle the challenges that come with it. Think leverage! The structure is another tool we use as leverage for execution.

So, let us talk about expansion. The expansion is the intentional means and methods put into strategy and action that allow for managed growth. I use the term managed because improper management of growth can end a business, and execution of a good management strategy will enhance any endeavor. Executing on strategy provides results or you can get into unrealistic promises to the customer that you cannot deliver. Adding massive amounts of debt, and inventory shortfalls that you cannot overcome, will put you in a horrible place.

I use some very strategic words with expansion because first I think it should be intentional. I say this because I believe that you must develop the skill and temperament to manage every area of your life. Pain and displeasure are good indicators that you are unbalanced and unhappy with choices you have either actively made or passively allowed. The decision to expand or not to expand should be as routine in your evaluation process for your life and business as anything else. Expand with intention.

In evaluating your business or job, it is also important to realize how your personal life is affecting it for the positive or negative. Your insensibility to pain or displeasure can and will affect your business or management decisions. Spend some quiet time with a calm mind getting answers to your questions, as well as, hearing clearly what is going on in your life. I also would recommend journaling to help you give voice to things that are going on in your subconscious mind. Once your thoughts are clearer, a plan to address any imbalances can be put into place. Balance makes you more productive.

If possible develop a mastermind team at work, as well as, an accountability structure in business and your personal life as an outer gauge of how you are doing with achieving your goals. When you and another invest in each other's lives there is a synergy that is real and authentic and can take you to those next levels. There are some things in life that we do not see clearly. Meet on a regular basis with an agenda. Go through the results as part of your evaluation process. Use this to come up with new ideas and make needed adjustments. The high expectations of others when structured in a healthy accountable relationship can push you further than you can push yourself.

Develop strategies that provide a vertical continuum to the next level and beyond. **Next Level Living** should not be the new buzzword that gets you motivated. It should be a mission that is clearly defined at every level of achievement. What does the next level look like, feel like or mean for you? Not for someone else, what does it mean for you? Define it, practice seeing it, positively infecting your subconscious mind and soul with the confession of it, until it begins to germinate and take root in the deepest part of you. When it is real to you, then strategize as you would with anything else looking to what you have, where should you start, as well as, what you must do to achieve what is missing.

Decide to expand. To plan the expansion, you must know you have the resources and are willing to make the sacrifice before you get started. There is a principle in growing crops; know what is in the seed, as well as, the soil. The good vibrant seed has what it needs in the DNA to become what it has the full capacity to become. A tree grows as tall and as large as it can become and is only affected by its outward conditions that it cannot control. **You may have the DNA of greatness inside of you but be careful where you plant that potential**. The farmer also knows the seasons in which to plant. He also must look carefully using his resources because he must finish what he has started at the right time to have the best chances of reaping a healthy harvest. You may be desperate but planting in time of drought and famine will not feed the family. You will need to go where the land is fertile and able to yield a good return.

Develop an Action Based Philosophy

Banish any thoughts that there is a level of success in life that takes little to no effort. As you grow stronger, and more proficient, that climb in front of you may become easier, but you must realize there are mountains that you have not climbed yet. Once you set out on that course, you will be tested in new ways. Many people who have made major mistakes will tell you it was because they underestimated the challenge in front of them.

You must be willing to cut all ties with negative people especially those who do not share similar values and would hold onto and practice other philosophies that are not in line with yours. You do not have to agree with every point, but you do have to spend time with people of like mind or with people who have been where you want to go. Your philosophy in life must include action and expend resources.

Develop habits in line with your purpose

If you can pair yourself with others who have achieved or are achieving goals similar to yours who are either in the same business or have transferable skills, it makes it easier to create synergy with them, as well as, consider them as a resource. You must develop your skills and daily habits in line with your purpose.

If I began to emulate someone who is working toward being a teacher, and I adopted their habits and studies, then I might be preparing to become a teacher, but it may not improve my chances of being a great financial advisor. There may be some commonality, but the point is that you must develop habits that support your goals and your larger purpose. Do not adopt the habits of a long-distance runner if you are trying to become the world's strongest man. Develop the day to day habits that support your goals. If you do not, you will build a body, life, or habits that will not support your deepest desires and failure is assured.

Feed Your Subconscious Mind

One of the daily habits that you absolutely must form is feeding your subconscious mind. I do not intend this to be a philosophy book or a book on the law of attraction but let me tell you why I am adamant about this. Each one of us has an image that is made up of our thoughts about ourselves or business; this is our self-concept. This is what we think about the limits of ourselves and our businesses. This begins to shape how we feel about ourselves or business. We have come to know this as self-esteem or how we feel. What you think about something or the meaning you assign to it has a lot to do with how you feel about life and the opportunities it presents. Thoughts and feelings shape deeper beliefs that guide and profoundly affect our performance. They also profoundly affect your state of mind and ultimately the decisions you make.

Great pioneers in human behavior such as Tony Robbins, Jim Rohn, and others have shown us that our emotional state can greatly affect our reasoning and our actions. These come together to form an image; a strong self-image that is impossible to go beyond because this is who you say you are. Some have likened it to a thermometer or a governor that shuts down or revs you up to meet that limit. It is the same in business or any endeavor you choose. You cannot go beyond what you think, feel, and see as the opportunity. However, and more importantly, you can go beyond what you believe, how you feel, and what you see as your life.

It is a different thing to grow beyond your initial vision. That happens all the time, but you first must believe that you can grow farther than you can see. If you are an entrepreneur, you have a natural inclination to believe what you cannot see. Your subconscious mind creates a map called a paradigm that guides you without you knowing it. It is one of the things that creates certainty and allows you to get up every day and perform. Certainty, however, does not like change, and it can also be the thing that is holding you back and causing you to reject opportunities without giving it serious thought and analysis.

Tony Robbins once said that you could only grow to the level of uncertainty that you can allow yourself to experience. I believe you can create new neurological growth and patterns in your brain by introducing new experiences, as well as, new information that challenges what you may already believe and feel.

You must decide to gather new information, read new books, watch videos, attend seminars, and turn over every rock to find answers or solutions to help you grow. This must be done with intention, and it must be done daily. New information must be sought and assimilated daily. New experiences like networking must be done even when it is uncomfortable. Trust me if you hate public speaking, your mind will pitch a fit if you must talk yourself into taking a speaking class or accepting a presentation to speak in front of your peers. This creates uncertainty and is the only environment in which you can grow.

Develop habits to speak constant short affirmations that are charged with emotion. They must have a meaning to you and no one else. They must be clear and concise and repeatable repeatedly. Do this as your mind comes back to it all day and night under your breath and when you are alone aloud and charged with emotion.

Learn to use your physiology differently. Learn to do simple things like dress nicer, purchase new clothes and shoes. Keep yourself neatly trimmed and looking like the money you wish to make. Dress and act like the champion you are becoming. Also, you must use your body posture differently, how you use your body to help create an emotional state. Next time you watch a sporting event look at how elite athletes use their body to support the emotional state, both when they fail and when they succeed. I would also suggest that you take your physical activity to the next level by setting new goals for your health and fitness and finding something challenging to work toward.

Developing the "Will to"

I listened to a message recently from a great motivational speaker that was truly inspiring. He was teaching personal trainers about how and what he felt was the most important part of the training. He said that it was relatively easy to show someone how to do something and get them to repeat it. What he found astonishing was that there were so few who decided to demand something of themselves that seemed impossible. It was a challenge that could not be accomplished by reading a book or gaining the "how to," but them learning to exert the mind of the "will to." Most people will not push past their perceived limits. If they do not already believe they can do it, many will not even try. They do not take on life-changing challenges that will cause them to excel because they must endure the elements that often come with a chance to do it.

How does one person with the diagnosis of cancer or someone with a debilitating physical condition decide to live and accomplish things that experts and many others believed to be impossible? How do others with exposure to the same type of information settle for average results or just quit altogether? Some do not quit when they are challenged because they never accepted the challenge in the first place; there is no fight in the dog.

Once you get past the initial desire of deciding what you want, you can expect resistance. After you begin to pursue your goals, you can expect conflict and at times failure. I believe that both are part of the maturation process that allows for some to achieve their goals while others are defined in the opposition as failures. You literally must become something different to achieve something different. That is not a cliché. I am becoming an author as I write this book. That means hours of formulating ideas, research and working to bring my thoughts and passion into physical form. Everything worth the pursuit requires sacrifice and the discipline of will, then it's hard to quit!

You must take time to become more aware and sensitive to how you are feeling mentally and physically. Develop a fallback plan when you feel tired, take a break, eat a snack or meal, hydrate, or take care of the physical need to replenish yourself so that you can go on. Have a plan that allows you to react to how you feel and become more creative and stronger by addressing the need rather than quitting because it is hard.

Get rest. When you train hard, you must rest between sets. The heavier the weights, the longer the rest period between sets because heavy training is greater mental and physical exertion. You must mentally prepare to lift heavy weights because any bodybuilder will tell you; you have to visualize yourself completing it before you do it. Doubt will make you fail. If you want to get in better shape, reduce the time between sets, but it may require longer rest after you have completed the sets. The key is to have a plan to do it and then evaluate and make changes to make the execution more effective.

The Discipline of the Conscious Mind

I have had the privilege of playing professional sports, as well as, working with leaders in various industries. One of the things that separate less accomplished athletes from the great athletes who attain longevity is the discipline of the conscious mind. In life, success, if ever obtained, can be fleeting, if you do not learn to master the ground you have conquered. It is the reason why a lot of lottery winners have the same desire and drive for financial security we all have but once achieved; they tend to lose it very quickly. The phenomenon is elementary. Most people are not prepared for longevity or in most cases managing success when it is achieved. This is not an act of will to gut it out but the preparation that is geared toward managing success. You might be prepared to work hard or take a chance to get something you want but be ill-prepared to maintain it once you get it.

I would dare say for every great basketball player there are a thousand with incredible talent who lack the fundamental skills and character to manage success over the long-term. How did Kobe Bryant build one of the best careers in basketball over the span of 20 years? How does a Tim Duncan in 2016 playing in the finals at age 40 and have one of the most stellar careers in league history? How does Lebron James play at an elite level after 15 years of being the "King" of the NBA? How do others with such talent burn bright for such a short period or never live up to the promise of greatness that their skills gave them and fail? With some, because of their character and not putting in the work they could not fulfill that promise.

I firmly believe that discipline of the mind and character of the person and not the perfection of the skill are what build longevity. We must all learn from and embrace the indiscretions of youth, and the maturation process that requires the sacrifice of short-term pleasure for long-term gains. I do not know if there is anything worse than seeing individuals of middle-age and beyond acting as if they are 20 years old and still making the same youthful mistakes.

We must accept sacrifice as part of the maturation process. When it is required, expect to give it as part of the process. This is not just the effort but also your behavior and the disciplining of your thoughts. If you are serious about success, you will make the sacrifice to go to bed early, so you can get up early and put in the extra time to master your craft. Then what you value the most will create the life that you want. Do you value over-sleeping more than what you are telling yourself? If playing video games for hours or going to club nightly is the limit of your discipline, your talents can only take you so far, but that lifestyle will not build longevity. You must only look at the very best to see that this is true.

You must master your craft and become a student of success. It is not enough to be strong physically and mentally; you must be smart. You must seek and acquire constant information and motivation to become the absolute best that you can be; I said that YOU could be. You must find your limits and become the best version of yourself by developing yourself mentally. That is both intellectually and emotionally and without discounting your physical and spiritual development.

You master the art of focus and become singularly focused on one thing at a time to the exclusion of everything else at that moment. You must be dialed in and present at the moment of experience to get the greatest expansion of the experience. The thing you focus on the most expands. As I have shared in previous chapters, I have heard many say that where focus goes energy flows. That is true, but they do not state the fact that the item that energy impacts is changed. Focusing on anything causes energy to interact with it and assist in changing the state of it. Learn to focus, this is harder than you think, but it is a key skill to learn to amass greater results. So, whatever you focus on expands, meaning the state of it changes. You want a greater result in one area focus on it with intense thought and equally intense action.

Learn to hone your mind by controlling your thoughts. Learning to keep single thoughts in your mind for longer and longer periods of time is essential to getting more profound results. When an opposing thought comes into your mind you must remove it. At first, it is difficult but becomes easier over time. The more you meditate and take time for focus and singular thought as an exercise, the more you will become aware of the effects of your thought process on your daily life. I would suggest learning to focus by using your imagination on one thing for 10 minutes at a time and then increase it. Ask yourself questions about it until you have a full sensory experience even though it is an imaginary event. Do not waste time on nonsense; use this exercise to focus on the things you want to experience.

Until you can control your thoughts and learn to perform at peak levels, you will never know what you are capable of becoming. Your thoughts control your feelings and your actions. The more you can quiet and discipline the mind, the more influence you will have on the success of your future.

Playing To Your Strengths

Playing to your strengths is not about knowing your strengths as it is about using what comes naturally to you as you discover other strengths or developing those that you do not currently have. The best fighters fight their style and not the one their opponent is trying to impose upon them. When you have competition for a job, or you have a competitor trying to take business away from you, you must realize what separates you from the competition and use it to your advantage. If there is no difference between you and your competition, I suggest you learn to create bold and unusual differences that you can use to create advantages for you.

A larger opponent sometimes does not move as fast as someone smaller in business. That does not put the smaller business at a disadvantage; it means that they both have advantages that they need to use to gain and retain customers. For example, the larger chain business can provide deeper discounts because of buying power. However, the size of a business also creates bureaucracy and sometimes it cannot make decisions as fast nor provide adequate levels of customer service. A good example of this might be Ace Hardware compared to Home Depot. Ace Hardware, since it is smaller, provides better customer service and may be able to get specialty items that Home Depot may not stock. Home Depot, on the other hand, may be able to provide better bulk pricing because of its buying power but many times the customer is not able to readily find someone to help them on the sales floor.

This is not to knock the big box stores. I use them because of their product selection and price.

Take the time to not only recognize your uniqueness but try to document it and quantify it. What am I good at and how can I use that to my advantage? How does that separate me from my competition?

You have a distinct purpose, so you should never consider being like someone else, even though you may love what they do. Learn from them, but always assimilate information into your style. Learn to direct things in ways that are comfortable for you and place you in the best state to perform. Things that you are not good at, practice them in private until you become proficient. Adding new skills in areas beyond where you are naturally talented does not bring you to greatness because you cannot be the best at it all. However, as I have said before, never have glaring weaknesses, or they will be exploited.

Defend the Weak Points

There is an old saying "Never let them see you sweat." You perspire many times not because of expenditure of energy but out of fear and incompetence. You must learn how to defend the field where you are weak. Lately, in basketball, you see that the three-point shooter reign supreme but that will change because a balanced game is preferred. There was a time when the big men ruled the court, but that evolved, over time, as well. If a team is weak at shooting from the 3-point line but can get stronger at defending it, then they have a shot at winning. If they can stop the other team from making 3-point shots, they have a greater chance of winning. Every sport and business are like that; you must learn to defend the areas where you are weak.

Get stronger by delegating to someone else that may be better in an area than you are. Do not dismiss it because you do not like it, remember great managers manage information. Also, you must remember that delegation of menial tasks is needed to free you up to do something more strategic at the time and allows you to get more done. Being mired in task work is the pitfall of any great manager or leader.

Get a mentor or bring in a specialist who can help you with your backhand if it's weak. Many times, the smartest people had to have a tutor or study in areas where they were weak to graduate and move on to and thru the next levels. This notion, which supports the belief that you do not spend any time in your weak areas, is nonsense. I would agree that you do not lead or focus on your weak areas versus where you can be competitive, but you better learn to keep your hands up in a fight, as your defense, or you will be taking a nap.

Continue to learn and get better at every area of your life. Remember small course corrections between two extremes keeps you balanced. Standing on one side where you feel comfortable does not bring balance but weakness. Have you ever seen a weightlifter who has a huge upper body and skinny legs? It may be genetics, but most often it is because people spend most of their time doing what they perceive adds value to their lives; even if it does not. Yes, bang the upper body and show off those guns but work your legs with equal passion and be pleased with the effort if not the progress.

Accountability

One of the greatest secrets to success is realizing that you cannot do it by yourself. I have had many times where it seemed as if it were me against the world and yes, those times made me stronger. To be honest, I could never have experienced what it was like to be a national champion without the other members of the team.

In baseball, as in many sports, it is you against your opponent but performing at your best is having a coach and team who bring out the best in you. Coaches can see things about you that you cannot see in your personality or performance. They push you harder when they see greatness and add valuable instruction in areas where you are doing it right and sometimes in areas you need a lot of practice. Increased competence is necessary to win at any level, and it is the one thing that you cannot achieve by yourself. Your teammates build in accountability. You must accept responsibility for doing your best for the rest of the team to win. If you are in shipping, and a sales slip comes through from the sales department to send something out, and you get around to it two weeks later, you may have lost that client because one person on the team did not perform with the same expectation of what it takes for the team to win.

Invite a team of persons both in your professional and personal life to be accountable for your desired level of performance, as well as, task management. It's important to do what you say you are going to do, as well as, the level you will perform. You cannot muddle through work and be great. Greatness performs great. Greatness prepares and practices great. Have regularly scheduled meetings with an agenda, action items, status reports, and time to comment on what needs to get done. Invite people who have reached successful levels and can add valuable comments, as well as, connections to others who can be a resource.

When others and you hold yourself accountable, you perform at higher levels and get better results. The psychological side of that is when you know that you will have to give an account of how you spend your money, your time, and the effort put forth to achieve something, procrastination and frivolity are gone. If you continue to make excuses and waste your resources like others who do not excel, you know that you have not truly decided yet to dominate.

Making New Promises

In my opinion, one of the worst things in life is to lose trust in a system or especially in yourself; you can go out and live a life of your choosing and get great results at what you pursue. Regardless of your circumstances, never lose hope. It comes down to whether you can influence or change your circumstances and achieve what you desire. Nothing is done in an instant; you must keep learning and chipping away. Entrepreneurs and those like-minded take the risk, and they learn from each failure. As it is often said, "you only have to get it done right once."

I heard Dennis Kimbro say once "Life is what you get from God; the lifestyle is how you chose to live it." That is a powerful statement and very true. So, then the question is how to restore or maintain trust in yourself and eventually the opportunities in life. It is my opinion and that of others that real trust is built on making promises and keeping them. It is the ability to create certainty in the know; it is the precursor of faith. Remember faith is what you believe strongly enough in, which you act as if it is true, witnessing it going from an idea to the manifestation of the thing desired.

Whatever promises you have made to yourself in the past, it does not matter if you have achieved them or not, no one can look continually in the past and drive forward. You must be able to learn from your successes and failures, and once you have achieved them, you must make new promises to yourself and decide what that next level of living looks like.

Making new promises to me is the first part of the change, much like thoughts are the first part of faith. I would suggest taking some time each day and first, conduct an assessment of what resources you have for a new journey. It may not be much but trust me you have more in the tank than you realize. Then begin to record whether in writing or voice your thoughts on what you desire the most for your life. Then you must act without hesitation and with an all matter of fact attitude, and with an emotional thrust, you must start acting on those new promises you made to yourself. In that declaration, make a promise to yourself to do whatever you need to do legally, to achieve it.

Wrap strategy and action around what is in your heart. It does not matter your past failure or achievement at this point, when you know how to fail and succeed the most important trait is taking time to build character. Capture the strength to stand against adversity and difficult times and maintain the fortitude to push through and do what you said you were going to do. Here is where you have made a promise, and needed the discipline to keep it. If you can do that, then you would build greater levels of confidence and trust in yourself inwardly, and then watch your external world change.

Healing the Emotions / Emotional Intelligence

You may read this section and say well what does my emotional life and what I am going through have to do with me being successful? It has everything to do with my emotional life. There was an outstanding book called *Emotional Intelligence* by Daniel Coleman, which said that Emotional Quotient (EQ) is more important than Intelligence Quotient

(IQ). If you have not read the book, you should add it to your library and reading list.

The most successful living people often are extraordinary at being empathetic to people and learning to lead them authentically. Jim Collins' work on describing level five leaders of great companies shows that the intellect or charisma alone will never make a good company great or build a sustaining one. The greatest leaders are not perfect by any means, but they are people moving toward wholeness and balance in their intellectual growth and emotional health. They are people who can empathize, think, feel, and lead others to better themselves, as well as, to achieve, what seemed at one time, impossible dreams.

Learning to forgive others and yourself from things in the past lays a powerful platform. Continuing to learn from your present condition all that you can learn and when you are finished kicking over the garbage can, clean up the mess and move on.

Look at the results of your life, either you are getting the results you want, or you are not and should admit that you created them. If you find yourself blaming circumstances from your past, or your present, and you think you cannot resolve these issues by yourself, get help. As an adult, you are the sole creator of your experience in life. God provides each of us the gift of choice and the opportunity to be transformed.

Power of Vision

The power of vision, the ability to see using your imagination is limitless. I do not know of many great discoveries that had nothing to do with someone using their imagination to see something in a new way or something that did not previously exist. Imagination drives innovation. You should foster this in your life and the life of all around you especially your business.

If you ask someone how we can do this better or reduce costs, then it takes some level of imagination to do something with the expectancy that you have not done before. Imagination is the power of vision and the heart of creativity. Once you can dream it, believe it, and define it, you can achieve it.

Use vision boards and/or journals in your life as an articulation of what you want and are working toward. The setting of goals is no more than the pieces that you believe will get you to what you want. They must be in line with your vision.

You must have a vision statement and mission statement for your life. We talked about this in an earlier chapter. Here the point is that the vision and mission should be cultivated to a level of this is who I am becoming. This is what my business is in a mature state. This is what I believe my purpose is.

Therefore, I must achieve this. Your vision statement, therefore, is your purpose statement. It is a good idea to articulate your "why I must" statement. There are many great techniques with personal development authors like, T. Harv Eker, Bob Proctor, and John Assaraf that can be used to develop the continuing skills needed for visioning.

Developing the Will

This may be the one part that makes or breaks you in your conquest to achieve everything that is in your heart, what you have purposed, and have the capacity to do in life. Where the rubber meets the road is where you must have the will to overcome obstacles and pain. There will be both in life. Developing the will to do, the grit in life to keep going when others do not believe in you or your dream is essential because there will be times when you and your company do not grow. Times when the economy is stagnant, if not in a recession, and you must figure out how to drive sales, fulfill them and find the dog in the fight to keep going and believe against all the odds.

Champions work through the pain and know that rest may mean recuperation but even when your knee is repaired do you believe that you can still perform at a high level or has doubt taken over. When your company does not get the contract, or you do not get the promotion, can you still perform when some may think you do not have what it takes or maybe it is just not your turn? It is unexplainable why some overcome great odds, others quit, and some decide their fate even before they get started.

John Warren is a former Managing Partner & CFO of Highground Services, a small engineering firm out of Franklin, VA. In 2010 when the company was facing the challenges of a slow and dipping economy, John decided to call a meeting with the entire company. His single purpose in calling the meeting was to explain to his employees and furthermore to set a mindset among staff that Highground Services would not be participating in the slow and dipping economy but decided to grow despite the recession. That year while other companies dipped with the economy, John's will and strategy proved to be extremely effective, and the company had a significant increase in revenues. John later sold his stake to his partner and retired to spend time with his wife and volunteer with his church.

Developing the will exposes the true power we have of choice and making decisions. It is sometimes a matter of saying no more to certain circumstances and saying yes to the potentially unpopular or difficult things, bearing down, and choosing to get it done. It is pressing through the long hours of study or enduring workouts to hone your craft and gut it out, but you get through it and get it done. You make the sacrifice to play for the win and then comes the glory.

Dominant Factors

1. **Cherish both the daily grind and the time of rest in your personal life** but keep them separate, while remaining balanced in life.

2. **Developing the practice of putting daily structure and disciplines around those vital 1,440 daily minutes** is preparing you to oversee your daily challenges and uncap your potential.

3. **Focusing on daily habits (good, bad, and ugly),** knowing habits are connected to what you want to achieve, your vocation, and the dreams you are chasing; however, it is the grinding beyond the normal workday that advocates the transformation of your life. The structure is a vital tool to harness those habits.

4. **Feeding your subconscious mind to influence and shape a healthy self-esteem** results in the effect of your overall performance, but also realizing that you will not achieve your purpose on your own.

5. **It is the discipline of the mind and character of the person first and foremost and not the perfection of the skill which builds longevity;** we must accept the sacrifice of short-term pleasure as part of the maturation process.

6. **As the CEO of your life, you are solely responsible for the experiences in your life**; God (Chairman) gave us all this top position to choose and change when necessary.

7. **Having a distinct purpose, you never consider being like someone else even though you may love what they do**; you only learn from them and always assimilate information into your style.

Chapter 9

Vertical Evolution

"In High School I was blazing, in college, I was fast, in the pros I was one of the slowest on the field. Everyone is fast at the next level."

Unknown

What is Vertical Evolution? It is life's upward development and advancement of the quest to take a dominating position. It's imperative to prioritize the evolution in your life internally, then over your endeavors, responsibilities, and finally through your assigned purpose to impact the world. Vertical evolution has perpetual consequences or benefits. Never-ending and perpetual mean the same; when I say, "the world," it is not to suggest everyone will have an impact on a global scale, but more so, regarding the people you are intended to influence in life. Whether that circle of influence is simply in the neighborhood or around the world, your world includes those assigned to influence you as well. Since this quest and impact on the world around you are measured on a perpetual scale, it is a large scale. That being said, this unending approach to success, will come at a steep price.

Due to the heavy cost, some choose not to pay the price; if you are too comfortable, it signals that you have conformed. You have found an area where you are barely noticed; to survive, you have pulled the bodies on top of you to insure you will not be noticed. Even if you have conformed to what is expected in the trappings of the good life, you have still conformed. I do not believe you are in that category because you would not have made it this far in the book. Of course, I am assuming you did not skip a few pages or chapters. If you are still reading this book, it is because you have **Decided to Dominate** in your life and you are seeking the answers to fulfill that call.

We have touched on what it means to have a burning desire to accomplish something to carry our badge of significance on the earth. That burning desire acts, in part, as fuel and energy to not only go to a higher level, but burn thru upcoming levels and continue to evolve. I say burn thru because when you have an element that is hot enough, like fire, it will not lay idle, but consume or remove everything in its path. Unwanted or not, it will not be denied access, progress, and continuous execution. I am talking about the kind of fire where it is continually stoked, refuses to burn itself out, and has every intention of advancing; overtaking all obstacles to sustain its evolution. So, we must be all-consuming in our progress.

This whole book culminates in the last two chapters with the understanding that transforming or evolving is necessary to effectively reach higher vertical levels, which are awaiting your challenge! Becoming someone else is the prerequisite to succeed at every increasing level in your life. To compete in business, any operating system must be precisely honed to make sure it's efficient, not just in a vital area like technology, but also in our paradigm about life.

We are in the process of constant change and have the opportunity for constant growth. While in that process, do not focus too much on where you are moment by moment, but how you respond to the challenges and continue to create value. Steadfastly, take ownership of the life that you are building and eliminate as many distractions from your intentional goal as possible. It has been an incredible experience for me to witness the growth of "The Marine" as an entrepreneur. He learned firsthand that the evolutionary process is everything if you are going to move vertically. The change was imminent, and the consistent maturing thru life's experiences delivered greater understanding of the true value of time and why the type of people around him needed to change as well.

"There is at least one point in the history of any company when you have to change dramatically to rise to the next level of performance. Miss that moment and you start to decline."

Andy Grove, Hungarian-American Businessman, Engineer, Author & Pioneer of Semiconductor Industry

If you have had a team exercise where employees talk about improving the company, they usually start with systems and processes and often get bogged down there. Task-oriented people no matter how bright, like to talk about tasks. For you to get better and perform thru the next level, start with the team of people you are working with first, then look at the processes. Jim Collins coined the phrase to "get the right people on the bus first." He was right. Good fighters who want to rise to a new level and beyond cannot train as they do on the level where they are. Elite fighters will add a coach or change camps all together so that they are changed in the process.

You may have to go and run with another pack to see how fast you can be, not just how fast you are today. The athletic "greats" like Michael Jordan did this after losing to Detroit. Jordan added weight training and added weight for their punishing style of play. Michael Johnson in track began to train with weights to be a stronger runner over the season; all "greats," regardless of the field, must evolve and grow continuously to compete at and move thru the next levels.

The fact that the competition is tougher as you move higher, you must advance to manage and compete with more increasing precision. Once you understand that simple concept, along with the fact that it is a daily progression and it will not be easy, you are ready to take on the complexity of a higher level of management and competition. You are ready because you have made up your mind that evolutionary change is the only path to greatness. Previously, we talked about the competition is better at the higher levels, and it is, but recall, the truth is you are not competing against outsiders, but yourself in personal and business development. Change must dictate change.

The greatest fighters or boxers in the business are only out in front until someone catches them and figures out how they fight. Remember, styles make fights. All the "greats" lose eventually, in part, because they make the competition better until the competition equals them. If there is no law of equality, I just made that up. Two things of different pressure will seek to interact with each other until the pressure equals and homeostasis is created. Have you ever seen someone who is partnering with or competing against someone who is clearly not on his or her level? One may try to pull the other up, or the other may try to pull the higher down to their level. Eventually, one is going to rise or fall to the level of the other. Find mentors or coaches who are greater than you in their craft and allow their wisdom and example to guide your vertical progress.

Why does one prosper?

I think people have always asked a few basic questions to create understanding where we have a hard time accepting the obvious facts. If you take two people that had similar upbringings, went to the same schools, had the same opportunities, and access to education, but one prospered, and one did not, you can perceive the differences in outcomes to explain the disparity. The difference is created by outward conditions, or inner preparedness, and certainly better decisions were made more by one than the other.

In real estate, for example, I have seen people with the same opportunities have huge disparities in income, and performance. From a distance, you think that it is because one person had an advantage over the other but when you look closer and study both times and again, the same things begin to show up that created the disparity in success.

It has become somewhat cliché, but most people who are successful in business do think differently than others. A steady mindset of preparedness and tenacity to execute among other things are essential in any successful endeavor. Why, because we know success is not easy, let alone the philosophy and execution that creates perpetual success. Cultivating a mind that counts the cost and says I will do this, without fail is necessary to move at higher levels. **Remember, a decision with a strong commitment can be used as leverage to yield results if the correct process is in place!** People who put it in their hearts to climb Everest but will not train to overcome the lack of oxygen, cold, and pain are delusional. Once again, in the book, *Mind of the CEO,* authored by Jeffrey E. Garten, we learned that vision without execution is a hallucination.

So, to think we can become wealthy "just because," we are fooling ourselves. Looking at the success of someone and just saying I can do that without some understanding of the process that leads to execution, is like looking at a mirage. A more intelligent response may be to find an experienced mentor or group of mentors and start asking questions regarding how to get it done.

Successful paths require a mindset that will prepare you for the sacrifice and hard-work ahead. I have paid people to mentor me in certain areas where it would have taken too long to gain the knowledge through my own experience. I saw the benefit of taking advantage of an opportunity to learn and glean from their years of experience; that is wisdom.

I think you develop a mindset that you currently do not have by employing mentors who have accomplished things in areas you desire the same and ask them what price they paid for the celebration of reaching successful points. How did they develop mental toughness before they were tested? You do not know how tough you are until you are pushed to the limits, so maybe they were not aware of how strong they were or their true potential, but they soon found out.

That is exactly where Chera Reid found herself after graduating with honors from the University of Virginia with a degree in education. She recalls certain people taking an unusual level of interest in her future and future decisions. At some point during her post UVA graduation, she realized that any opportunity ceiling placed on her vocation was self-produced. There were lots of moments when she would ask herself regarding attaining great success, "why me," eventually she settled for the idea of "why not me!"

It would be mentors, both with decades more experience than she and peer-mentors who would assist in shaping and uncapping her potential in her mind. Since then, over the last 16 years, Chera has made stops at Phillips Academy Andover, America's oldest and top high school; collected her master's degree from the University of Michigan, and a Ph.D. in Higher Education from New York University before landing at The Kresge Foundation. The foundation was founded by Sebastian Kresge in 1924 when he gifted the organization with $1.6 million. Now as the foundation's Director of Strategic Learning, Research, and Evaluation, Chera leads the organization-wide work to grow the foundation's learning endowment. Throughout her professional climb and having to deal with multiple transitions her mentality to adapt has been instrumental.

"Whether its organizational changes or changes of behavior, it's your adaptive skills and qualities that get you promoted, not your technical skills."

Chera Reid
Director of Strategic Learning, Research, and Evaluation, The Kresge Foundation

Vertical-minded people at some point after they are mentally prepared, begin to understand the physical regimen necessary to accomplish their goals. Many successful living people even though their success is not physical, often work out or adopt different eating habits because it is with the body and the mind that they must perform. So, understanding the mentality, you must have and modify how you use your physiology to your advantage is an important element. Every detail matters.

As we talked about in an earlier chapter, we must be prepared for the battle emotionally. You must have emotional support as part of your success regimen. I have friends who spend time every day getting into a strong emotional state and feel it is their job to stay there all day to manage and compete at the highest levels. It is hard-work controlling yourself mentally and emotionally while staying in a peak state of performance, but that is why they are some of the best at what they do and perform with consistency.

The next thing is to launch out into the deep end of the pool because you are ready. Some of the roads will be revealed to you while you are moving. Every step reveals new things on the path that was invisible 15 levels ago, but now is coming into focus. Commitment to purpose is what is required of you because now you are out there and there is no turning back;

you keep going until you reach your goal. You are in the grind now, and as Eric Thomas, the Hip Hop Preacher says, "Thank God it's Monday, you have to grind for grinding sakes."

This is a winning mindset because he and others like him look forward to getting to do the work of building the lives they want. Grinding for a better life is both a privilege and a responsibility. We need to maximize each moment we have to achieve as we say in an earlier chapter "every day is game day." Hard-work means you must be willing to outwork any other performance bar set by another, as well as, your previous self. A better version of you does not ask to lower the weight to change the effort needed to resist the force while you are training but realizes that this is necessary to grow stronger.

Champions are not born as such, but they are those few who accept the challenge and decide to compete against themselves. Many are gifted, that fall short of their potential, or because of unproductive choices did not receive another chance at an opportunity to prove their true worth. Others have not been able to recognize the opportunity. When you are blind or lack knowledge of the equations of success, you cannot discern or see even while standing next to greatness.

You must learn to compete against you. The things you may hate to do such as, reading, studying, or employing a healthier lifestyle may be the very thing that you need to do to transform into someone unstoppable. The reason you hate to do it is that you perceive it is painful, but that pain is the path to change. If you hate to read, but you know it is the missing ingredient that is needed to feed your mind to become a multi-millionaire, would you do it? Could you become passionate about it? What about getting up at 4 am in the morning, so you had time to study and work out, would you make the sacrifice? Most people would contemplate the effort because they see beyond the pain. They choose the level of effort that matches the level of pain they are willing to endure.

Do not avoid pain unless you have done the cost-benefit analysis, but be honest, do not procrastinate. If you are not willing to make the changes, then you certainly should not exercise your right to complain about the mediocre results and the life that awaits you, while the same person from the same place with the same opportunities has the life you want. You must lean into it, become motivated or find a bigger why and become inspired. Listen to audiobooks, read blogs, and watch success videos to feed your mind until everything means nothing to you except the identified areas of success.

Look pass the other person, learn to compete against yourself, but you do have to put yourself in the fastest crowd to run faster. You are the one who must eat right, work out, rest, and embrace the grind. You must study and find purpose in the most mundane things if it means training you to be better. Pursue personal perfection, but you must be willing to practice with perfection in mind because that is how you are going to perform.

Why have a mentality of counting thousands when you want millions? I became conscious of the fact that when you are in business, and you start at minimum wage, you count dollars. It is because that is the value you bring that is represented by the dollars. When you start to supervise employees and operations, you become more valuable because you are managing thousands if not millions. When you start working at higher levels, closer to that vertical peak, you can talk about millions and multi-millions of dollars. That is because you have learned the law of use.

Law of Use

The Law of Use means that when you use something repeatedly, competence should be gained or granted through repetition. Use and repetition mean having a specific focus of energy which always coincides with a natural process of evolving and expanding. When you are given a talent, at first, it may be natural to use it, but to be the best at it; you must practice it, as well as, be taught by individuals with more similar experiences who can help hone your talent. When energy is expended in one specific area more competence is acquired, and you can do it better, faster, and with more skill.

In martial arts we practice with form, then power, then speed, and in that order. Talent alone is never enough to win over time. You must hone your talent and skills to move closer to expert levels.

An increase in confidence, speed, and skill creates more capacity to execute, which is part of evolution and expansion. The same is true for not using something, especially if it were certain body parts. Therefore, over time atrophy sets in and the lack of relevant activity or use creates a disease to your talent and lack of confidence, incompetence in performance, retreating skill reduces capacity until there is little to nothing left. You must use your talents and add skills to those talents to expand.

Developing the mindset of expansion means mastering where you are while adding things to your regimen that are new to expand your competence. The mastery of what exists solidifies the neural network in the brain, the introduction, and mastery of the new create new neural networks, which continues to grow the capacity of the brain. These new things should add new skills not just be connected to your purpose. There are many skills that are transferable from one type of job to another, so adding new unrelated skills expands your person. If you want to become a master communicator, then take classes and master speaking through preparation and repetition. Not speaking makes you incompetent.

The new thing you could add is a foreign language. At first, you are going to have gaps in your ability, but through study, preparation, and repetition you are going to master it and expand your capacity now by being a professional speaker in two languages. When the rest of Uncle Kyrus' family first came to America, like many immigrants, several of the family members could not speak English. It is amazing what we can accomplish when we are given no other options.

As mentioned in previous chapters, Uncle Kyrus' mission is simple and can be presented as more of a question. How can I help you? Every time I have ever spoken to him over the phone, at some point in the conversation, he would ask, "How can I help you?" He has built a life on assisting entrepreneurs, charities, and other nonprofit organizations and in almost every case, having nothing apparently to gain except a thank you. In your endeavors, some will question what you must gain. Their questioning is meaningless; your life must have a distinct purpose and meaning to you.

When he left Cyprus for America aka the "land of opportunity," he arrived young, rich in expectations, and low in cash. On one particular day, he desperately needed $1.90 to wash his clothes but did not have one penny to his name. Thousands of miles from home, his only support was his uncle who gave him $1.90 and not a penny more. That was a day that would set the stage for all the days ahead. Uncle Kyrus vowed that his life's mission would be to help those in need and if he became successful in business, he could help numerous individuals.

After his two years in the US Army, he returned home to Norfolk, VA and turned down an opportunity to take over his uncle's restaurant; instead, he got his real estate license and eventually gained ownership positions in several commercial properties, shopping centers, banks, and hotels. Today, if you have ever seen him in an office or public event, people are still surprised to hear him ask how he may help them. Amazing!

Can't Change the Game

I want to mention this because some people do try to change things that are not in their control. As we mentioned earlier, you can own the effort, influence the results, but you are unable to control them. Sometimes in life, there are setbacks.

I have learned that in life there are opposing forces; much like our immune system fighting against free radicals trying to make us sick. You get sick sometimes when your immune system is compromised in some way, by either what we eat or overwhelming exposure to a disease, stress, foreign pathogen, or just a lack of rest. That is life.

In sports, when both teams are competing, and one team thinks there is an infraction, many times they will stop play and argue with the referee. They do this while the other team takes advantage of that and often scores on them or at minimum prepares for the next play. There are going to be bad calls, let your coach handle that you just keep playing and stay focused. Rarely can you be defeated if you realize that there will be setbacks and mistakes and that you must stay focused and keep grinding until you win. I said until you win. Remember, when you decide to dominate, winning is a non-negotiable result, so the game does not conclude until we win.

That is the law of stuff happens. The tough-hearted keeps the non-negotiable in mind until they get the results that they desire. I do not know why bad things happen to good people and while two teams cannot win the championship outright, but

I know that only one can win even when from the outside it seems like they may not deserve it. Often in life, you have dynasties that capture your youth, and if you are blessed with long life, you will live long enough to see them fall, be dismantled, and yes, rebuilt. Walk into any school gym, and look at the records, the banners hanging from the ceiling, and the retired jerseys. You are standing where past moments of greatness were created. A moment to be awed and inspired; but, it is the past. You must decide that you will be a part of creating new championships and it is your jersey that will be retired one day.

You cannot change certain laws in life, learn to accept that and learn to create great effort and leverage within the rules of the game. List your name among the "greats" by having the attitude that you will accomplish your dreams or die trying, which will prove to make the difference.

"For the timid, change is frightening; for the comfortable, change is threatening; but for the confident, change is an opportunity."

Nido Qubein, American Lebanese-Jordanian Businessman, Motivational Speaker & President of High Point University

Dominant Factors

1. **A steady mindset of preparedness and tenacity to execute among other characteristics are essential for any successful endeavor.** Why, because we know success is not easy, let alone the perpetuated version. **Cultivating a mind that counts the cost and says I will do this without fail is necessary to move at higher levels.**

2. **Winning comes down to the choices we make**; it comes down to your level of study, investment, focus, and effort that others may not be willing to make, so keeping "easy" out of your vocabulary is just a part of your mental growth and what will separate you from others.

3. **Align your desires with new thoughts that support you getting what you want.** You must design your core values consistent with what you want; **announce your intentions by writing them down, live them, be accountable to them and do them!**

4. **The Law of Use or repetitiveness dictates the Law of Increase**; with an intense focus of motion, it produces energy, evolution, and expansion which, eventually provides you with the credentials of an expert or master.

5. **When the Law of Increase and Expansion becomes part of your mindset, it means mastering is present**, yet be prepared to add to the regimen to expand to even greater levels of mastery.

6. **Time management is the key to all solutions**; developing a greater sense of the detail of self and how to manage our lives, with a keen focus on our time. It is apparent that those who have mastered their minutes have mastered several other things.

7. **Deciding to Dominate is deciding that winning is non-negotiable** and therefore nothing will conclude until we become the winner!

Chapter 10

Time to Dominate

"Sometimes when you've gone in the wrong direction the thought of starting over seems hopeless. You only lose hope if you keep going in the wrong direction. It's never too late to make a life-changing event in your life. It's a do-over for me with whatever I got left; with whatever's left in the tank. Quitting is not an option. It's time to dominate!"

Ayub Fleming

Now is always a good time to choose to journey through life with a sense of purpose in a prevailing manner. Of course, we are not able to go back in time and change the past, but we can compile the experiences and lessons learned to date and add it to our asset column for the benefit of positioning our wins to influence our present and future endeavors. It is time to Dominate, not spending another moment with unfulfilled needs, wants, and desires, finding the strength of character to reposition ourselves for the long journey ahead and lay the foundation for a beautiful success story.

"We have to live life with a sense of urgency so not a minute is wasted. In every day, there are 1,440 minutes. That means we have 1,440 daily opportunities to make a positive impact."

Les Brown,
American Motivational Speaker, Author, Radio DJ, Ret. TV
Host, & Ret. Politician

It is rare that I tell people that they should compare themselves to other people, but there are times when we need examples of achievement that we cannot always find within ourselves. We need to be able to look at other examples of success for present inspiration. We need to read the biographies and study the lives of people who have overcome their obstacles and reached successful points; this provides opportunities to investigate their lives to observe and glean the secrets of success and gain inspiration.

As much as possible we must control the input into our lives, meaning we must govern what we are exposed to because it affects us positively or negatively. It is not the same for everyone; what may be inspirational for you may be depressing for another. People are influenced by the exposure and environment that they are subject to over time, so controlling that access to your life is to influence the trajectory and course toward your destiny.

We witness not only the examples of success but also of failures. In this case, I think there can be a healthy comparison to assess where you are, what you need to do to build the right strategy, and add some of the values and other elements that put you on a successful path. From a distance, this may provide the mentorship that you may not currently have in your life. I especially would pay close attention to what methods they put in place to understand where they were mentally and how well they paid attention to the cobwebs in the corner. It is interesting sometimes how we do not see the ever-growing spider webs until they become obvious, catching our attention as they wistfully blow into our eyesight.

We need to develop a greater sense of detail of self and how we manage our lives with a keen focus on our time. It is apparent that those who have mastered time management have mastered several other things. I believe time management is a key to many solutions. It may be time management for me, for you, it may be your health or paying more attention to managing your finances. Whatever has the most impact in your life, decide to focus on it, move toward it, and execute. We can glean a lot from others who have walked the path before us and have left breadcrumbs for us to follow. Here is how the #1 most influential leadership expert in the world, John Maxwell, calls it:

"Time management is an oxymoron. Time is beyond our control, and the clock keeps ticking regardless of how we lead our lives. Priority management is the answer to maximizing the time we have. The secret to your success is determined by your daily agenda."

John C. Maxwell, Author, Professional Speaker, & Pastor

Some transitions in life are forced. You don't always get to ponder change; sometimes it is forced upon you, and therefore, your focus is dictated by the circumstances. At the time of me working toward completion of this project, I was released from an executive advisory position with very little notice and no severance. We were in the middle of expanding operations, with solid momentum behind us, but I could not ponder the change. I was thrust into taking the helm again, and steering the ship to a new port of call, of which, took a few months to define clearly. Crisis creates the demand for change; challenges like this, demand the need to refocus and keep pushing toward a life defined by our decisiveness and our deepest desires. We move from one destiny point to another, and whenever or wherever challenges are presented, change is imminent as we seek to move higher. All transitions present a unique set of opportunities, all of which can work for our good, when we keep a dominative perspective. In chapter seven, we mentioned an account of that perspective.

This forced arrangement for me was like examples from many others. It was an awakening, and a gift in the form of an open door for me to focus on and start a multi-million dollar enterprise, that most importantly, positively affects millions of lives! No one desires forced and abrupt transitions in life, but remember the quote at the end of the previous chapter. When we remain confident, change becomes an opportunity. The closer that confidence is linked to the principles from God's Handbook for Success, the greater the outcomes.

"Remove the mental stones of excuses and perceived obstacles from your thinking or see them more as stepping stones and decide what will be and start catapulting to the next levels, where progress will not cease."

W.H. Dozier III, Founder, UTake Dominion

When something major has changed, that change will affect other things as well. I once heard former Verizon CEO, Lowell McAdam, say during a quarterly address to employees, "Change brings about change." Profoundly true and one of the systematic processes I have in place, is from time to time, I assess where I am, in relation to, where I think I should be. I go back and look at where my goals say that I should be at this point. We grow and have the opportunity to grow stronger by assessing, refocusing, and committing to each goal one by one; changing the trajectory, which changes the course, the direction, and the destination is imperative as we consistently assess and reassess our status.

However, you deal with procrastination or change, employ, or build a system to put in place the focus points that give you constant assessment, evaluation, and enable course correction. This will be a momentous factor in helping you to stay motivated and working towards completion of the milestones for the outcomes you desire. Having an assessment tool in place allows you to be consciously aware if you are dominating or not, whether you are achieving your goals or not.

This assessment approach allows you to have a sense that you are not being distracted by anything that is unnecessary; not to say that you do not make time for healthy distractions so that you can decompress, but it is a matter of balance. The constant things in life may define you best. For example, having a connection with God or studying success principles from His Handbook will produce an effect. Constant overeating and the excess consumption of alcoholic beverages have its effects also. Anything done constantly or consistently, especially at an unyielding measure, will produce an outcome that will define your life. Be careful where you put your time and energy. It may be lawful but not expedient.

The system that we put in place may also include dealing with insecurities that hold us back from being our best. Sometimes we need professional help in overcoming crippling situations that may have occurred in our youth. Making this a part of the system allows us to grow unfettered; if we do not address the deep-seated problems, then we do not address the very things that are causing us to fall short or fail without a hint of learning from the experience. It is much like a professional athlete seeking a coach to help with the mechanics of getting better. Making progress in the small details may make the difference in winning a championship versus just being good at what you do.

According to his Wikipedia page, my last NFL Special Teams Coach, Frank Gansz, was once hailed as "the best Special Teams Coach ever" by former coaching great, Dick Vermeil. Coach Gansz would often say to his players, "small wins, focus on achieving the small wins guys and eventually we will end with great victories." There was a reason why he was touted as the best Special Teams coach ever. He found a way to get his players to focus only on the smallest of details to produce prolific special teams' results.

"If outcomes and results truly matter to you, then assess your habits, adapt where needed, and finally acknowledge that managing small details is the vital part of the equation to achieve."

W.H. Dozier III, Founder, UTake Dominion

The main point is that you have a system that is running unconsciously for most people. I am suggesting that when we spend the time by examining the results and habits of our lives and look at where they have propelled us, there is a certain predictive element that sheds light on where we are heading. Purposefully change your direction by making deliberate habitual changes, and the course of your life will change. It will not be easy, but then again, living with the unnecessary failures in life as you grow older will not be either.

Today is your last day to decide and act to begin to dominate your life. What if that was a true statement? To a certain degree, this is true. Whether tomorrow is promised or not, today should be considered as your last day. We touched on this in previous chapters, but let me explain in greater detail. Today when you look at the day, date, and year on a calendar, it is the last time you will have access to this day, date, and year. At midnight, it becomes yesterday never to be physically visited again, so we owe it to ourselves to maximize the here and now. Daily focus will produce daily habits and those habits become a dominant force in our lives.

So, in reality, by choosing our focus and habits directly or indirectly, by default, we succeed, wallow in mediocrity, or altogether fail. Again, this happens by default. It's a fair assumption that you are not interested in wasting time since you are still reading this book. You must connect a sense of urgency with the results that you are getting. There is obviously a time when we cannot turn back the clock and physically or mentally do something we could have done when we were younger. That is true at any age.

Here is a simple and effective approach. Daily, marry activity to outcomes without seeing or acknowledging a separation between them. Begin to eliminate what you do that has no purpose or is not in line with your desired outcomes. There is a time to relax and to do things for enjoyment but, of course after the work is done. I tell my son all the time that it is okay to play hard but only after you have worked hard. Too much work could lead to a life with a displacement of overall purpose while too much relaxation leads to an impoverished mind or lifestyle. Discovering and implementing in a balanced way is the key.

To be able to hone in on the outcomes that you are getting, and have the greatest influence on them, you must become a master of the concept of seedtime and harvest. In other words, you must become a master of consequences based on accumulated actions. Remember, you reap what you sow. In plain terms, you do not sow apple seed to grow corn, yet people every day look at themselves and wonder how they are where they are and how is it that their dreams are no closer today than they were 15 years ago. It is because we have not mastered the laws of seedtime and harvest; taking the right action and doing the right things consistently to get the results that are desired or what matters most.

The part of that concept we do not like to talk about is the concept of delayed gratification. There is always a pause between what you do and the results you get. I do not mean acts like putting your hand on the stove; I mean larger outcomes such as eating right or wisely investing your money. The harvest does not come overnight; you must be wise enough to trust the process, and keep consistent habits even when the results do not show up immediately. You must learn to do the right thing and delay your gratification or the natural impatience of wanting everything now.

You know what you do will come back to you, but consciously we sometimes associate this with when we do something wrong. We do not always associate it with the condition of our lives just merely events for the good or bad but not affecting the everyday total condition of our lives. If you had to honestly look in the mirror at yourself physically, financially, etc., you would have to say, "I did this to myself." Whether you are experiencing success or not in some areas, apply that logic to all areas. Would you ask yourself, what was I thinking when I decided to create this life or experience? You must master the consequences so that the daily grind is where you live and not a place to avoid. It is the habitual things you do that have the greatest impact on you personally, relationally, and professionally. You must connect the dots between where you are and where you want to be, realizing that you must be responsible for making it happen. The difference is always made in the thinking and followed by the doing. This is certainly true for your business as well.

"Growth is the great separator between those who succeed and those who do not. When I see a person beginning to separate themselves from the pack, it's almost always due to personal growth."

John C. Maxwell, Author, Professional Speaker, & Pastor

I was blessed with having two very motivated parents that instilled and poured confidence and a "can do" spirit in us. Think about this, as a child you had an idea of what you wanted to be. Your thought process may have been immature, but it was pure. A lot of children who are encouraged to dream to believe the best, based at least in part on happiness and having their basic needs fulfilled. Children who dream to believe that they can. That is the power of the imagination, and when they believe they cannot, that is the power of the environment. I have yet to hear a child say they want to grow up and be a felon or be in prison. Today the majority is in a place where we never expected which is strange knowing that we are the ones making the decisions, even if we allow others to make decisions for us or by proxy it is still our life, and no one else can be responsible for it.

One day while driving with my mother and passing a large hotel I asked her if she thought if I could manage a hotel one day; it was a large hotel. She replied with an unhesitant "Yes, of course, you can do anything you want." That was the type of response we always heard from our parents, and this dialog, as well as, many other impactful discussions with my parents enforced and reinforced unwavering confidence in me. Unwavering was the key. I knew that I could achieve anything.

Growing up in the resort city of Virginia Beach, I spent many days at the beach with friends. We would hang out at the parking lot owned by Uncle Kyrus & Family which was managed by his nephew and my very good friend Panikos, aka the Greek. As teenagers, Greek and I would often discuss entrepreneurial ventures, and how we would make our mark on the world. Years later, I went to college to major in Tourism.

Although I never actually managed a large hotel; however, thanks to some clever negotiating from my good friend and attorney, Rich Puleo, I did manage to own one. Along with other investors, I had the privilege of becoming part owner of a small boutique hotel with a 5-star restaurant in Northern Virginia. Developing real estate ventures were part of a Puleo family tradition, and I leaned on Rich's expertise from my first investment in Minnesota over 30 years ago. He has had plenty of incredible deals over a longer time span, owning office buildings, hotels, apartment complexes, strip malls, restaurants, etc. The largest deal he was involved in was a converted hotel that was recently purchased for just under $295 million. Unfortunately, Rich was bought out early and missed the full part of that uptick but managed to collect a healthy return on his investment. The boutique hotel in Northern VA was one of best ROIs he has delivered at over five times the original investment, but of course, not all investments are equal. Obstacles come, and obstacles go, and Rich sees it this way.

"I grew up as a wrestler, and I was taught if you can't go over, you go under...so obstacles were made for overcoming; we succeed in life by overcoming them. There's always a solution where there's a problem and setting goals and striving for them is almost as important as reaching them!"

Rich Puleo, Attorney, Real Estate Investor

You must become solution oriented with an introspective approach and pragmatism. Your life is being formed by the mundane of everyday habitual thoughts, prejudices, decisions, and actions that you take. Any negative-habitual act becomes a series of blockades to self-development; until you become aware of them, evaluate, change what is necessary, and then align your habits with the outcomes you want, the road ahead is doubtful.

Change and new achievements start in the thinking, and that requires thinking differently so that your actions are different. Learning to think differently requires hardcore discipline and exposure to new ideas, as well as, tons of constant information to change the programming in your mind to something else. If you are not where you want to be, then it is your habitual thinking that you are not conscious of that is robbing you of your future. Remember part of the quote from the second chapter;

"...it's a simple equation, desire plus hard-work and a host of other actionable habits, produce a worthy result; if you are not satisfied with where you are or what you have attained in life, change your habits within the equation."

W.H. Dozier III, Founder, UTake Dominion

I use the analogy of your subconscious mind being like a huge file cabinet. If the information in it allows you to draw from a limited number of files that control your conclusions, as well as, your actions, then you must change the files that your mind accesses to make new decisions and have new experiences. Permanent change requires new connections in the brain to be created. Ideally, education and personal development cause your brain to be re-wired for success. That cannot happen until new massive amounts of information are introduced, and old paradigms are challenged.

Become solution oriented, because if you become aware that you are off course, being emotional about it changes nothing. Learn to use emotions for motivation. You need to engage the feelings that come with the emotions you experience with failures, as well as, successes. This will allow you to overcome the fear of initiating necessary actions to learn, grow, and progress. Being solution driven uses emotion but also logic to see where you went wrong in the strategy or implementation, and it makes necessary changes. Solutions always require new questions to be asked and information to be accessed. Change requires a different thought process which is patterns of arranged information. If you ask the same questions with no new information, you only are accessing the old frame of reference. You may be able to make incremental changes, but fundamental life-altering changes require thinking at a different level. Solution oriented people also use emotions differently. They use them for fuel to change and not just be connected to the experience.

You must seek new information in the form of facts, studies, and examples; learning from others so that you can use their examples as what to do and what not to do. The question of how I can do that better or why they do it that way must be asked for new answers to start developing.

Once you move into patterns of awareness based on sowing for the harvest you want and providing solutions to problems, then you must learn to manage your life in detail and small chunks. You must learn to compartmentalize life better than you have in the past. When you spend time with your significant other or children, you must be able to bracket work, leave it in the box, and be present for them and even yourself both mentally and physically. If you bleed over from one thing to another, it robs everyone, including you. When you are talking to someone and allow a phone call to interrupt your conversation, it affects those relationships because you are telling them that the call is more important.

When you are working out and taking calls on your cell phone, you are telling yourself that working out is not the priority. In a few years, if you were dealing with major surgery or a serious illness, and could turn back time; you might deal with your workouts and diet as if you were training for the Olympics. You are training for the life you want every day. When people look at their lives, they must be honest and say this is the life I wanted, and I got it. If you truly want a new or better life, then a change in process and management is required. Remember, we can change the equation!

If ever you are shocked by the outcomes, go back and see if you were conscious that the things you were doing were causing this outcome. If not, then you were sowing apples and got corn instead; in a lot of cases you were sowing weeds and thinking apple trees were coming. Here is a financial example that I have used many times. When some people are behind in their bills, their first thought is to borrow money. We think this way because being broke is a temporary condition that once the bills are paid and if there are no other problems, they can move forward until the next crisis; surviving on living paycheck to paycheck. When you act on borrowing money to pay normal living expenses, then you pass from broke and move closer to bankruptcy. You cannot borrow your way out of broke; you must assess, cut short-term and long-term expenses, create more long-term income, and invest the difference.

A good number of individuals want to live like the wealthy but have limited or displaced insight regarding how that wealth was attained. That line of thinking, along with low self-confidence, sets the stage for consistent disruptive outcomes. For example, some envy the assets of the others, when instead they could become inspired by those same assets. That inspiration would instead cause one to work both hard and smart, take a calculated risk, make necessary sacrifices, and invest all the time and energy it takes to move forward to an expected end, the right end. Remember the movie, "The Pursuit of Happiness," a true-life story about Chris Gardner's struggle and life-changing professional endeavors. Well, his character, played by Will Smith, had an interaction with the man that drove the red Ferrari; he did not ask himself why him and not me out of envy, he asked the man "What do you do and how do you do it?" He asked a "how to" question and became inspired to start blazing a similar path and journey of the success of his own. He asked an inspiring question that today equates to an estimated $60 million answer regarding his net worth.

So, sowing good seed toward acquiring, purchasing, and owning assets and not bad seed toward personal liabilities is part of a solid strategy to build wealth. Earning money and purchasing large amounts of consumer goods for status and many other emotional fulfillments is one method of how poverty can creep in and choke material wealth. The more you invest in self-development tools and act on it, the better off you will be, moving thru to and beyond the next levels. The more you invest in an exclusive entertainment lifestyle, unless you are an entertainer by trade, the worse off you are going to be. So, invest with the good vibrant seed that produces the lifestyle of substance that you truly want. In short, make investing in tangible and intangible assets the highest priority. Remember our identified purpose is our true currency and accompanies significance in our lives.

Investing behaviorally with clear vision and honesty helps to paint a real picture of our lives, but we are often not honest enough about the word bankrupt. Dishonesty about the facts continues the same behavior until the inevitable crisis appears and forces change or brings destruction. If you were someone that knew and accepted the fact that you are beyond break even, broke, or that you are bankrupt, you would have the opportunity to change. The cure is hard-work, budgeting, and consistently managing your money and the financial goals you want to achieve. Then you would have changed and also, changed the fate of future outcomes.

This is one reason why you need professionals or mentors, as well as, massive educational processes in your life. Some do not know that they are sowing toxic weeds; as crazy as it seems; they do not realize the toxic daily habits and decisions are destroying their potential. Others realize their daily decisions are creating the life they want. In this respect, it is not just knowledge but its training, preparation, implementation, and assured execution. The question is what you are preparing yourself to do versus what you have been conditioned to do.

If you are not training to win, to dominate, or to reach your goals, then this needs to change. We must be conditioned to go the distance. You are not equipped out of the box to win but just merely to exist. Let us unpack this a little. As a human being, you are born with the base desire for pleasure, the avoidance of pain, and to have certain needs fulfilled. This gives you certainty. When they are not fulfilled or done so sporadically, then you are uncertain and must figure out how to get what it is that you want. But what if you are in training and the training is not assisting in your growth? It is imperative to learn from this compromised situation sooner than later. The question is how you would know or discover that your failings are due to something that you lack such as information or guidance? One solution is to be surrounded by seasoned mentors and advisors. From this, you gain consistent counsel, positive learning reinforcements, find safety and security, while others who did not use such resources, may not.

At about the same time, when you start experiencing life with a certain level of maturity, you begin to make evaluations based on what you think the meaning of things are in the form of pleasure, pain, or whether it is harmful or beneficial. Sometimes the pain of training for sports is evaluated as necessary and even desired if you want to win. I might convince someone to push me to my limits if I believe the payoff is winning, endorsements, and/or other types of payoffs. So, I am evaluating the cost of the short-term pain against long-term success. The opposite is true if I say that I do not want to go through that much pain now and believe that I can still be a champion without paying that price or worse yet, being okay with just being on the team.

There are many though who will not push themselves anywhere near their limits because they feel that the pain can be avoided, and they still can perform at their highest level; some are even convinced they can win without sacrifice. Look at the guys with long-term success in any sport or business and their life will tell a different and more accurate story. You must be clear about what you want and begin to condition your life for this journey of success. We are talking about aiming and hitting the bullseye, not just the board.

Having clarity of vision and people assigned to you as advisors put you in a solid position to aim and hit the target. When we have mixed thoughts and emotions about something, we hesitate and procrastinate because we say we want to do it, but we are not sure it is worth the payoff or the pain that it will bring. That is where the conversation begins, and we can either talk our way into or out of doing something daily. Simple procrastination becomes later justification and later just plain old effortless failure. We can deceive ourselves into thinking that it is something else or someone else that is to blame, but deep down we know the buck stops here for our lives and nowhere else.

Once you genuinely make up your mind to do something that is inconsistent with what you already convinced yourself is the path, then all hell is going to break loose because your mind will want the certainty of what you know and scream bloody murder to stay captive in Egypt. The place of my captivity is also the place I learned to be comfortable. I say learned, but it also could be said conditioned. You look at others and ask, "How could they allow themselves to underachieve or live that way?" Understand, they have allowed themselves to fall in that condition, and so, in most cases, they can learn and be conditioned at a higher level of living and success, but not without a price to pay; this involves going through pain and uncertainty. People learn to adapt to their environment and are slaves to their thoughts and beliefs. Unfortunately, it is the adopted thoughts and opinions of others that often dictate the philosophy of our life.

Every day we have an opportunity for more discoveries and to train ourselves to think in a certain way. You do this by learning to focus on momentous things that propel you toward further development while rejecting frivolous things no matter the argument or justification.

Gambling high is the same as a drug high because it brings such a sudden release of endorphins until they wear off and you must do it again to experience the high. If you think about the long-term exhilaration of being wealthy, to the extent that you can travel anywhere, drive anything, and create change for yourself and others, then the short-term sacrifice would be worth it rather than the lifetime of living in poverty.

Learning to take dominion or being dominant is honing in on understanding the art of controlled consequences. That is, you act by what you want or what you think you want at all times. It is taking control and demanding more of yourself and those around you to live consistently because if they do not, you must be willing to leave some people behind in your life to embrace others going in the same direction. It is time to choose either chickens or eagles. If you run with chickens, just remember to some you are just food, and sooner or later you are going to be boiled, baked, grilled, or fried.

As we talked about seed as an earlier principle, the seed produces like a seed. Responsibility is the lens that you must see the world through. Until you look through that lens, then you cannot see the breadcrumbs of the clues that lead from where you are to where you desire to go. The lens of responsibility is in part a mirror that reveals your flaws, as well as, where you need to change. Thinking of this in biblical terms, you must see the plank in your own eye, before you can see and assist with the splinter in someone else's. The only business you should be managing is your own. That metaphor is true in business as it is in our personal lives. Mind your business is something we always say but do not always apply. Mind means to mine your business; focus on your own goals and get everything possible out of the development of it as you can.

We have discussed a lot about actions, talent, skills, or seed sown but let us talk about where or what you sow the seed into. I want to discuss this with you for a minute because this is important. Seed or more precisely, the most vibrant seed in a real sense is a metaphor for spermatozoa (stay with me). Think about God sowing his seed in the earth means that he has sown a piece of himself in it and thus in us. This is a powerful thought, especially when we decide to receive that concept that seed sown in fertile ground promotes growth and produces a mighty harvest.

When you think about building a business or a career within a corporation, you are sowing a part of yourself that is replicating you in your endeavors and personal relationships in your life. Sow yourself in that business and endeavors and let part of it be an organic expression of you and discover the masterpiece that could be there because of you sowing your gifts and talents! It is not just a job; it is an opportunity for you to replicate not just what, but who you are sowing there. How are you influencing your life and your business?

To take responsibility for one's life means to understand that you are sowing your substance, your knowledge, dreams, finances, talent, emotions, etc., into the ground that may or may not be able to produce the harvest that you are seeking. So here is the thought. You have to realize that you are sowing yourself and your resources which replicates you in good soil that produces and multiplies you (provide equity, produce and multiply like assets); or you are sowing yourself and your resources into businesses, jobs, partnerships, and relationships which are not or will not pay dividends (build zero equity). The latter scenario can never produce a reasonable amount of assets or profit. One of the base principles of nature is multiplication.

Your life is multiplying either to the good or the bad, healthy, or unhealthy, and sometimes canceling effects stifle the progress, but the principle of multiplying seed sown is what I am trying to get across. Sometimes we take two steps forward and three steps back. We must be more consistent in our thoughts and actions, our choices, and decisions!

So, let us go a little further and then I will wrap this up. When you are sowing seed, you are sowing a part of you (self or resources) into something outside of yourself to replicate and produce more than what you have put into it. If you are in a job or involved in an entrepreneurial endeavor that underpays you for your efforts, then by principle you must either seek or create the opportunity that pays you more for your efforts on a long-term basis. That is not just the law of reaping but the law of profit. The Lord requires profit on the investment of Himself in you and what he has given you regarding those TAGS.

The next time you think about your vocation, think about this. Where am I in my job? Where is my expression in it, to produce in it, and receive back as much as I put in or more to the point that I am profiting from it? Remember you are investing your life in your vocation, what is it paying you back? The focus should be to profit, not just in money, but life satisfaction. Do I want to sow my life into this job or business and if I do, what is the return on investment? What are my life's passion, talent, acquired skills and energy worth? How am I creating value for my company and myself? The first realization of taking responsibility is knowing that you are sowing you, and your life's energy, and the second is realizing where you are sowing seed in the good ground it will eventually produce a profit on your investment. If you continually sow and are not receiving more than you have sown, then there is an imbalance with the seed or the ground, but a change is in order. Maybe the cheese has moved on, and it is time to set out for a modified strategy or on a new venture altogether.

The next principle is where you want to sow the seed that is consistent with getting what you want. I firmly believe that you cannot always control the outcome, but you can control the effort and always influence the outcome. In your personal life, you mitigate risk the same way you do in business, your research, and you ask questions; sooner or later you must decide with the data you have. Continue to refine your decision-making process including adding mentors with the experience to help you.

My good friend, Jerry Horstmann, who recently passed away, was a retired TV Director, Producer, and an amazing visionary. I can say without hesitation, his ability to see beyond was awe-inspiring and quite contagious. He trained his kids to spell success with four letters: RISK. Think about that for a moment; this is what he taught them as youngsters. If you want to be successful throughout life, you are going to have to take the risk along the way. This was just one of the seeds that he would sow into his children. Today his kids are now adults thriving in business as entrepreneurs and life.

Karl, the oldest sibling of the three, is a Film Director and Producer operating as the Founder and CEO of Triple Horse Studios where he has produced motion pictures, television series, title sequences and hundreds of television commercials. His son Ken is a creative Film and Television Director, Writer and Partner at Spyplane Films; both sons worked at Turner Broadcasting before launching out on their own. Jerry's youngest, Kim, is also very successful as a self-employed Freelance Casting and Craft Service Provider. Jerry witnessed over and over again the seed that he sowed in his children, and he saw that it was good!

The action of sowing must be then consistent with what you want, in a place that can produce what you want, and then sow in season and as often as possible. There is always a time to buy and a time to sell to reap maximum profit and build equity. Depending on the philosophy that works for you that is how you have determined to live but make sure you have a philosophy that works for you. How do you know? Look at the consequences. I once heard someone say that if you wanted one woman to spend your life with why you would date and accommodate 50. Male or female, you will never find the one giving your life's energy and resources to the 50.

Now I know you feel you may have to "kick a few tires" or date various people. It's not what we teach our kids, so I am not getting into that discussion, but you know some do not fit what you want beyond a conquest of the fulfillment of physical desires.

Remember that sowing seed has consequences; ask yourself if it is worth it before you do it. In this case for men and women, chastity makes more sense or at least limiting yourself on purpose to find and give your resources to the right one and build the life with the one you want. To give your resources away randomly without the hope of profit can drain your time and emotional account and simply does not makes any sense.

Let us briefly discuss time management again and its role since we are discussing that it's *Time to Dominate*. Time is obviously a very important commodity. Arguably, the investment or allocation of time could be the answer to most problems and acts as part of the solution to every challenge or at least the management of that time. Managing time is the key to opening many doors in our lives, but those of us that unlock those doors and decide to dominate or master time, is truly set apart.

We seemingly have plenty of it to accomplish what we want, and at times it seems we do not have enough to get anything done. Time is a great way to look at the theory of relativity; meaning that we all experience it differently based on how we use and experience the time we have. If we are focused and moving at the relative speed of our success, then time moves in sync with our accomplishments; we have enough time. If we randomly invest our time in an unfocused way, time seems to be in short supply and out of sync with what we need to get done.

When we seemingly are unfocused, moving out of sync with time or captured in an over-extended stay of daydreaming, we ask ourselves, where has the time gone? When you are out of balance or out of sync with what you desire or spend too many unbeneficial moments pondering and contemplating, time becomes less manageable; you may never open the door to dominate or master time. Remember there are only 1,440 minutes in a day; if we are sidetracked, we can never have enough time.

Time management is like everything else; it must be used and measured based on outcomes that are achieved by it, then dominating or mastering time is all the more relevant. To say that time is working for or against you is simply experiential unless you can say that you have achieved within that period what you set out to do.

Some of the best time management programs available are tied to achievement or results, not just activity. Activity is good, but alone it is not a good measurement because you can be busy doing something that does not produce the kind of results which are meaningful. Driving activity with meaningful results determines the separation between those who are dominating or mastering time and those who are dominated by it and not properly managing time.

The difference is not in the doing or not doing but in the outcome. Have a vision/mission statement for your personal and professional life drafted. When you do, you will have a roadmap with greater clarity to work with and the outcomes of what you want to become based on the larger picture. That outcome must be broken down into measurable outcomes or milestones. The milestones can be articulated into smaller activities that are time sensitive that can help you determine whether you are on track to accomplish your larger big picture goals. Those goals then should be broken down into daily activities that allow you to focus your activities relevant to time and resources that eventually should accomplish the vision and mission. It is exciting to know you are only decisions away from accomplishing things that may have eluded you in the past!

I have seen more than one program that takes small increments of time and asks you to program them based on every 15 minutes or 30 minutes of the day. I am personally not that tight with my schedule, but I know that it works for some. The key for me is to understand the relevance of tying time to activities so that in whatever increment you choose to program your time, it is done with relevant and meaningful activity in mind. The larger picture is accomplishing what you set out to do again and again with all time and activity moving toward accomplishing larger milestones and outcomes. Remember, there are only 1,440 minutes today to make the best of it. Going back at the end of the day and determining what was accomplished on your to-do list, and evaluating how you did based on what you got done is a good habitual practice. Not that everything was checked off but that you accomplished meaningful activity relative to your larger goals. I have seen very few who attack a daily to-do list like "The Marine."

That is the philosophy but here is the practical application. Break your goals down into a daily activity list or things to do list, but start now. Review at the end of each day and see how your activities for that day help you accomplish your larger goals. Once you are in the habit of making things to do lists for each day, now plan from the time you wake up to the end of the day, break each activity down based on the time in which you should accomplish it. I would suggest 30 and 60-minute increments depending on what type of work you do. This is an awareness tool primarily, so you understand how you use your time and how to use it more effectively. Once you have the tool, then using it to your advantage becomes critical, so the time that is relative is working to your advantage.

"But time is yet another of God's creations, and as such, it has a life of its own. So, during those first moments of the day, which are yours and yours alone, you can circumvent these boundaries and concentrate fully on spiritual matters. And this gives you the opportunity to plan the time management of the entire day."

"When you waste a moment, you have killed it in a sense, squandering an irreplaceable opportunity. But when you use the moment properly, filling it with purpose and productivity, it lives on forever."

Menachem Mendel Schneerson, Orthodox Jewish Rabbi

A compelling vision implemented and executed leads to a compelling story to be told. It's one that has the reach to inspire many to do likewise, which is further perpetuated from the original planting of the seed in fertile soil. Planting and cultivating that seed allows it to take root and continue its growth toward maturity. I imagine the only thing God can love more than seeing His creation fulfill their purpose, is the person who is fulfilling it!

Dominant Factors

1. **Realize that seedtime and harvest or sowing and reaping are the easiest ways to understand the study and application of consequences**; you sow consistently what you want to reap, and sowing is an investment that will or will not pay dividends, but all investments have a return.

2. **Train from the perspective that your God-given purpose is the currency that matters most.**

3. **Understand that seed produces like seed because the likeness is in the seed**; if you want your circumstances to change, sow the appropriate seed to reap the harvest you desire.

4. Understand that the **Law of Profit requires we be cognizant of the TAGS we were given and the ROI the Creator desires** from His investment.

5. Find good ground; **where or with whom you sow your seed is important because the harvest is tied to the quality of the ground** and if sown into bad ground or ground that is not properly prepared to receive the seed and produce, then a part of you that is invested is wasted.

6. Take note that **when the harvest is produced and looks good on the outside, remember the experience of it has to do with either the richness or the toxicity in the ground** that it is sown. Make sure you dig into opportunities to understand the experience precisely.

7. Know when it is time to **respell success with RISK**.

Heirs of Domination

One central theme that kept coming to the forefront in past business acumen or branding was our alliance with God. As a believer in Christ, I believe in the development of the whole person: mind, body, and spirit. The opportunity to become a believer is without a hint of arrogance; I say that with not only joy, but with great humility because of the sacrifice that was made for me. Something that I could do nothing to earn.

I believe without an alliance with God domination is a temporary state. On the other hand, perpetual success is achieved by living a rich spiritual life that is aimed beyond the temporal. So, I'm convinced that without God, it is impossible to dominate in every area of life but that every set back can be overcome with Him. I am not naive enough to think that in this life we are not going to have problems or that we will escape the expiration of this body. In life, we will directly or indirectly deal with tragedies. The difference is that with an alliance with God we never walk alone.

If I were going to start this conversation, it would be with the fact that man was created. I do not presume to believe that everyone who is reading this is going to believe that. Whether you see a common origin or design in all life is up to you, but I believe that life has a consistent design and purpose. There is an infinite intelligence in which we are all a part, who desired us into being and seeks a connection with us that we might have a fulfilled life, as well as, know our purpose.

Is it that simple? No, because I do not know anyone who has a relationship with God who has not failed and who is not at some point struggling with failure in one area or another? Our purpose is one of those things, like character, that is revealed and evolves over our time on earth and in the struggle.

This is not about giving a voice to the debate of the origins of man, of course, you are entitled to believe what you think gives you the greatest sense of purpose and meaning for your life. I have experienced God in real ways beyond religion and believe that He created man in His image and likeness though most of the time we do not resemble Him at all in our actions and thoughts.

The creation of man is tied to purpose. According to God's Handbook for Success, from the book of Genesis when God breathed life into man, until the book of Matthew, we see God saying that He is the One that has sown good seed in the earth. He calls His seed the children of the kingdom or translated children of dominion. God is still sowing today; it's not just about us being placed here on earth with a purpose, but for influence, authority, and dominion. It's acquiring knowledge and being reminded as I learn from His handbook which describes a loving God who created me. He also placed me here, gave me talents, and continues to provide for me along the way. Understanding His dedication to walk with me and guide me for a purpose, gives me significance and a greater sense of myself in this world, than without that understanding.

An understanding that reveals He knows me and desires that I seek to know Him also.

Some are not conscious that they have decided to be their god with their own set of values and a belief, only relying on what feels good to shape their behavior and values. Therefore, there are going to be long held debates about such things as death and tragedies or when bad things happen to good people. While I cannot explain them all, I can seek the One who has the answers, as well as, the knowledge and revelation I need to continue to live by faith. When you were created to influence and have authority, it is much easier to accept that understanding, when you know it is connected to your purpose.

I believe we are the sons and daughters who were created for dominion. Dominion is achieved first through submission to God; He who has all dominion and power over all things! Submission does not mean that we are slaves in the sense that we have no voice; it means that we are in the right position with God, knowing that the Creator does not always create something from nothing but merely changes matter. God is the essence of all creation and holds all matter in place. We exist in Him. We obviously did not create God; however, my dominion is in Him. As I learn to walk and commune with Him, I move deeper into my purpose for which I was created and stewardship of the life He has purposed for me to live.

So, my opportunity for domination and perpetuated success are because of His domination over what He created. My authority then comes from God, and not to His exclusion. He has an exciting life planned for you, but within that, there are decisions that must be made that control the direction and trajectory of your life. These are decisions that no one can make for you because you were created as an individual with free will and consciousness. It's safe to say, I have only begun to unpeel the layers of what it means to walk in dominion with God. The journey with Him is real, and I invite you to become aware of the opportunity to know and understand God as the Heir of Dominion. This is an opportunity that positions you to live and fulfill a life of purpose, significance, and hope for you, your family and your circle of influence. Our ultimate goal is a life that leaves a legacy here on earth and one that perpetuates throughout eternity.

"Deciding to dominate is not just about succeeding in life to its fullest; it also includes the perpetual kind of success that leaves a legacy here on earth while preparing and storing up rewards in the place we call heaven...In other words, I want everything good this life has to offer and then when it's time to collect the rewards and TRUE RICHES, give me the full dose and the eternal portions."

W.H. Dozier III, Founder, UTake Dominion

The Final Decision

I have enjoyed the journey of writing, consulting, researching, and interviewing for this book and sharing with you what I believe are the few secret strategies of attracting perpetuated success along this journey in life and learning to dominate. I know that it is an alarmingly descriptive and yet a misunderstood word because initially, it was unnerving for me as well. Although in my professional athletic career I did not accomplish all that I set out to do, the life lessons that I learned are still working for me today in business as they did in the sports industry.

I feel the same spirit of competitiveness that I did as a child, as a college athlete, and in the pros that I do now pursuing business endeavors and as a professional speaker. Many skills are transferable from one career and endeavor to another. What you must have is the tireless nature, that drive to find out your true limits and not the limits set by you or another. Remember you compete with yourself; you are the CEO of your brand, life, and purpose; you decide how you will invest and apply your TAGS within the endeavors, on your incredible journey.

You can do anything that you were designed to do. You say how do I always know what that is? You will not. You must do a lot of soul-searching, contemplation, and plain old hard-work to discover your limits on an ongoing basis. Sometimes your desires are connected to childhood dreams, and some are revealed along the way in new relationships and opportunities that stretch our perceptions in new ways. Know who you truly are and what your value is; with everything you have, be relentless and become more, create more value, and set no limits on yourself. Failure is a part of the learning process, and if you tell me you have no failures, then I am telling you, you have severely limited your life and its potential. Above all, remember you were created with significance in mind. George Washington Carver's life and dedication provide us an example of what is possible when we depend on the wisdom of the Creator combined with our gifts and hard-work. If the Creator revealed the secrets and uses of just a peanut to a man, how much more would He reveal the purpose and bless the greatest part of His creation? That is, the one you see in the mirror!

Deciding to dominate is establishing ourselves in the intended positioning the Lord originally proposed and purposed for us. Creating perpetual success is our prerogative and our destined purpose in this life to reap the benefits in all of eternity. Investing in the now is good and certainly profitable but investing in the never-ending tomorrows is the time of the greatest of profits. Thank you for taking time out of your life's schedule to read this book; if you have not done so already, put the book down and Decide to Dominate!

For more information and resources to help you live your dreams and become a dominant force in life and business go to www.djdozier.com or decidetodominate.com.